Ruth L. Crawford
Williamsburg, Va. 1982

WILLIAMSBURG

EYEWITNESS TO HISTORY

SERIES

WILLIAMSBURG EYEWITNESS TO HISTORY SERIES

*The Journal and Letters of Philip Vickers Fithian*
*The Journal of Major George Washington*
*The Journal of John Harrower*
*The Journal of John Fontaine*

# THE JOURNAL OF JOHN FONTAINE

John Fontaine

# The
# Journal of
# JOHN
# FONTAINE

## An Irish Huguenot Son
## in Spain and Virginia
## 1710-1719

EDITED, WITH AN INTRODUCTION, BY
## Edward Porter Alexander

THE
COLONIAL WILLIAMSBURG FOUNDATION
*Williamsburg, Virginia*

*Distributed by* The University Press of Virginia
*Charlottesville, Virginia*

Library of Congress Catalogue Card Number 74-165362
Colonial Williamsburg ISBN 0-910412-96-0
The University Press of Virginia ISBN 0-8139-0382-3


PRINTED IN THE UNITED STATES OF AMERICA

# Contents

# Illustrations and Maps

## Illustrations and Maps

# Preface

DR. DIXON RYAN FOX, an inspiring teacher of early American social history at Columbia University, used to urge his graduate students to immerse themselves in travel accounts in order to understand the life of another era. I was one of those students, and through the years I have secured much information and a keen sense of realism from scores of such accounts. Thus I have been more than willing to undergo the pleasant labor of following John Fontaine about and trying to provide useful annotation for his Journal. I hope that my efforts will repay in some measure what I have taken from these rich historical assets and perchance build up a credit to be drawn against in future work.

My debts to others are heavy, and the footnotes give specific credit to about half a hundred persons. A dozen Fontaine descendants shared their knowledge with me, but two have been most important—Kathleen Busfield of London who has encouraged me constantly and run down many clues for me, and Anne Fontaine Maury (Mrs. William G.) Hirschfeld of Delray Beach, Florida, who allowed Colonial Williamsburg to acquire the manuscript copy of the Journal made in 1840 by Ann Maury and permitted me to reproduce the drawings of Thomas Worlidge as illustrations for this volume.

Almost every member of the Research Department of Colonial Williamsburg has assisted me and especially Dr. Edward M. Riley, director, and George H. Reese, sometime assistant director, who corresponded in my behalf with many British sources. My long-time friend, the late William J. Van Schreeven of Richmond, gave me perceptive advice on Virginia matters. On the Spotswood expedition to the Blue Ridge, Edward F. Heite, formerly archaeological historian, Virginia Historic Landmarks Commission, was ever valuable and resourceful.

More than a score of libraries and manuscript depositories patiently have answered my queries, in person or by mail. Chief among them are the Earl Gregg Swem Library, College of William and Mary (William C. Pollard, librarian); Virginia State Library (Randolph W. Church, librarian); Alderman Library, University of Virginia; Virginia Historical Society; Library of Congress; New York Public Library; Historical Society of Pennsylvania; Delaware Public Archives; Maryland Hall of Records; New Jersey State Library; Guildhall Library, London; British Museum; Public Record Office; Principal Probate Registry; National Library of Wales; National Library of Ireland; Trinity College Library, University of Dublin; North Devon Athenaeum, Barnstaple; the public libraries of Bideford, Exeter, Dublin, and Cork; the county archives of Carmarthenshire; and the county and city archives of Exeter.

Making the book has been facilitated by the skills of the Publications Department of Colonial Williamsburg—Joseph N. Rountree, director; Richard J. Stinely, assistant director and designer; and Thomas K. Ford, editor. My secretary, Mrs. Frances D. Griffin, typed numerous versions of the manuscript, and Mrs. Gay M. Curtin, formerly of the Research Department, did much service in helping construct the maps that Mr. Stinely drew. My wife, Alice B. Alexander, was a good companion while retracing Fontaine's footsteps, though sometimes during the library research she referred to herself wryly as "John Fontaine's widow."

E. P. A.

# INTRODUCTION


## JOHN FONTAINE AND HIS JOURNAL

# John Fontaine and His Journal

JOHN FONTAINE, aged fifteen, knelt behind the homemade rampart—a mattress atop a large basket used for carrying peat—and fired his musket. He was aiming at the French privateersmen trying with iron bars to enlarge a breach in the stone wall of his father's house. While he reloaded the flintlock, one of his brothers fired, and then another. Their enemies succeeded in rolling a grenade beneath the basket, and its explosion sent the boys scurrying in fright to the next room. But when they saw their father, who had suffered a broken collarbone and badly torn right hand when his overcharged blunderbuss burst, arise grimly and start for the breach, his pistol in his left hand, they returned to their post without a word and resumed firing.

The year was 1708, with England and France engaged in the War of the Spanish Succession. The place was Bear Haven on Bantry Bay along the desolate coast of southern Ireland. James Fontaine, John's Huguenot father, had bought a farm there in 1699, settling thirteen destitute French refugees on it and establishing a fishing business. He had become a justice of the peace and fearlessly prosecuted Irish robbers and smugglers who were in league with French privateers. Naturally, he was not beloved by his Irish Catholic neighbors. On June 1, 1704, a French privateer with eighty men aboard had attacked his fortified home. Fontaine with the help of his family (John was then only eleven) and seven Huguenot and Scottish neighbors had beaten off a landing party of twenty, killing three and wounding seven. The victory brought Fontaine praise from the English authorities who gave him £50, five cannon, five hundred cannonballs, four barrels of powder, two kegs of musket balls, and an abundance of match. He built a small sod fort next to his house. Queen Anne in 1705 granted him a pension of five shillings per day (more than £91 annually) for his courageous conduct. But his fame also reached the

French corsair base at Saint Malo, and several of the captains there vowed revenge.

At daybreak on October 8, 1708, a column of eighty men, landed near Bear Haven by a French privateer, marched on Fontaine's house. A frightened servant fetching home the cows gave the alarm. None of the English officers supposed to keep an eye on the house was near, and Fontaine began its defense assisted only by his wife, five sons ranging in age from twenty-two to eleven, and four servants with no military experience. The invaders fired the outbuildings and haystacks, and suffocating, blinding smoke soon filled the house so that it was difficult for the defenders to see their enemies who used long poles to pry off slates on the roof and apply burning straw to the rafters. Three times fires started and three times the besieged family put them out.

The fight lasted about ten hours, and the defenders wounded several privateersmen; but after Fontaine, the father, was injured, the breach in the wall grew steadily larger. The besiegers kept offering "good terms," and finally Fontaine and his family were forced to accept them. The Frenchmen took Fontaine aboard ship and held him for £100 ransom. His resourceful wife, as persuasive in negotiation as she had been brave in battle, raised £30, and the enemy released her wounded husband, holding his son Peter (aged seventeen) as surety for the remaining £70. The privateer took Peter to Saint Malo but eventually returned him without further payment when the English put their French prisoners at Kinsale and Plymouth in irons until he should be freed.[1]

These two encounters remained vivid in the family memory for long, and the four Fontaine children who settled in Virginia sometimes gathered with their families on June 1 in a solemn religious ceremony of thanksgiving to commemorate their remarkable and, in their opinion, providential deliverance from the French privateersmen.[2]

## THE FONTAINE FAMILY

John Fontaine belonged to an energetic, courageous, and close-knit family. His father, Jacques or James, born in 1658 at Jenouillé in Saintonge, was the son of another Jacques, the Huguenot minister of the United Churches of Vaux and Royan. The family had been zealous Huguenots since about 1535. James was a cripple, and the family story ran that when his nurse's daughter dropped him as a baby, the frightened

Jacques (James) Fontaine and his wife Anne Elizabeth Boursiquot
Fontaine

mother concealed the injury until it was too late to remedy. His family destined James for the ministry, and though for a time he rebelled against some of the dull pastors who taught him while wielding the rod freely, he eventually attained the degree Master of Arts with honor at age twenty-two. He then studied theology with his brother-in-law Peter Forestier at Saint Mesme in Angoumois.[3]

In the 1680s the Huguenots began to experience increasingly sharp persecution from the French government. Their churches were torn down, their services disrupted, and members of the congregation and ministers thrown into prison unless they recanted and turned Catholic. James Fontaine preached in the woods, argued stubbornly in court, and once when in prison prayed softly to encourage a large crowd of Huguenot prisoners to resist. In a meeting of ministers and elders at Coses in 1685, he advocated abandoning passive resistance, taking up arms, and leaving the issue to the Lord of Hosts, but the meeting refused to heed this belligerent advice. The persecution became ever more bitter, and in October the government revoked the Edict of Nantes that had promised toleration to Huguenots.[4]

James Fontaine thereupon resolved to leave France and to take with him his fiancée, Anne Elizabeth Boursiquot, her sister Elizabeth, and his niece and god-daughter, Janette Forestier. He secretly booked passage at Marennes with an English captain, who picked up Fontaine's party and several other Huguenot refugees from a small boat at sea after they had outwitted a French frigate intercepting would-be emigrants. Fontaine and his companions landed at Appledore in north Devonshire on December 1, 1685. They went on to Barnstaple where they were kindly received. James stayed with a Mr. Downe and Anne Elizabeth with the Fraine family.[5]

Mr. Downe, who owned property near Minehead worth £10,000, had an unmarried sister of about thirty-three possessed of an estate estimated at £3000. She found Fontaine most attractive and finally persuaded her somewhat embarrassed brother to suggest a switch to James; it would be more sensible for the sister to wed James and for her brother to take Anne Elizabeth as his wife. When Fontaine told his fiancée of this offer, she burst into tears, released him from his promise to marry her, but said she never would wed Mr. Downe. Fontaine was also moved to tears, and Anne Elizabeth and he decided to wait no longer; they were married at the parish church in Barnstaple, February 6, 1686. Though Miss Downe did not conceal her displeasure, her brother generously gave the young couple a fine wedding feast, to which he invited the other French refugees of the town.[6]

James Fontaine was enterprising, hardworking, and versatile. During the next few years he lived at Barnstaple, Bridgewater, and Taunton. He did not join the Church of England because he preferred the simpler Huguenot ritual and he somewhat distrusted bishop rule and the former Anglican connection with Romanism. He received holy orders from the Protestant Synod (Presbyterian) assembled at Taunton, June 10, 1688, but did not serve a church.[7] He was an inveterate trader and sent several cargoes to France, though he lost heavily on some of them. He taught school at Bridgewater and Taunton, attracting students from as far away as Plymouth. He ran a shop at both places, with especial success at Taunton, but his greatest achievement was a textile manufactory he began there in 1690. He invented a cheap way of making calimanco cloth that enabled him to accumulate £1000 in three years.[8]

Yet during this time Fontaine was often uncomfortable. Once his competitors took him to court for not having served an apprenticeship as a weaver. Another time his neighbors accused him of being a Jesuit in disguise. When he heard that there were many Huguenots in Ireland, he went to Dublin to investigate. Late in 1694 Fontaine moved his family to Cork where he served without pay as pastor of a Huguenot congregation and set up a woolen manufacture. For a time all went well, but in 1698 a schism developed in the church, and Fontaine resigned, though he continued to preach occasionally to a Presbyterian congregation. In 1699 Parliament prohibited the export of woolen goods from Ireland, and Fontaine's broadcloth business was ruined. He then decided to move to Bear Haven.[9]

Meanwhile, James and Anne Elizabeth Fontaine's family was increasing: it included James (born at Barnstaple, 1687), Aaron (Barnstaple, 1688), Mary Ann (Taunton, 1690), and Peter (Taunton, 1691). The fourth son and fifth child John was born at Taunton in 1693 and thus was six years old when the Fontaines left Cork for Bear Haven. He was followed in the family by Moses (Taunton, 1694), Francis (Cork, 1697), and Elizabeth (Bear Haven, 1701). All the children lived to maturity except Aaron who died from tuberculosis at Cork in 1699 after he and his brother James had returned from a stay of two years with relatives in Holland.[10]

At Bear Haven, James Fontaine set up his fishing business. His men would catch the fish in Bantry Bay and off Dursey Island, salt them at his farm, and then ship them to Spain and southern Europe. To secure the necessary equipment and funds to carry out these ambitious plans, he entered into partnership with his cousin John Arnaud and three other London merchants. Meanwhile, he preached occasionally in the area, and Bishop Dive Downes of the Church of Ireland reported that most of the Protestants went out of curiosity to hear him at an ale-house in Skibbareen one Sunday afternoon in May 1700. That year the fishing was poor, but in 1701 Fontaine cured more than two hundred thousand herring. His partners, however, failed to send him the ship intended to carry the fish to Spain, and the delay ended in financial disaster. The French privateers completed his downfall; the 1708 raiders ruined his house and took off three boatloads of booty.[11]

When General Ingoldsby, commander of the English forces in Ireland, paid Fontaine £100 for his losses and the county of Cork added another £800, he decided to move again. He bought a run-down stone house on St. Stephen's Green in Dublin and fixed it up as a combined home and grammar school. His prospectus promised to take day students and to board "Gentlemen's sons," teaching them "the French, Latin and Greek Tongue; also History, Geography and . . . Mathematics, and especially Piety" for £20 a year and two guineas entrance. He also called in masters to provide instruction in writing, common arithmetic, drawing, dancing, and fencing.[12] His academy enabled James Fontaine to give his own children, both boys and girls, "an education inferior in no respect to that bestowed upon the first nobles of the land." His sons Peter, Moses, and Francis eventually were graduated from Trinity College, Dublin University.[13]

The school was so successful that in 1716 Fontaine apparently declined an invitation to become the first professor of philosophy and mathematics at the College of William and Mary in Virginia. This offer came about because of the friendship of John Fontaine and Lieutenant Governor Alexander Spotswood. The annual salary would have been £80 plus twenty shillings per student. In 1721 Anne Elizabeth Fontaine, James's wife, died; that September he closed his academy.[14]

During the remaining seven years of his life James Fontaine could look back with satisfaction on the way Anne Elizabeth and he had raised their family. The four children in Virginia and the three in England had been given a comfortable material start. More important, they had been taught piety and love of God; again and again they had seen their father refuse to compromise with his conscience. Each child also had received a sound education, no mean resource in that illiterate age. Both parents had set admirable examples, and the children could not reproach them for lack of courage, industry, or willingness to take risks and try new things.

## ADVENTURE IN SPAIN AND AT SEA

The skirmishes with the French privateers had not discouraged John Fontaine. As he reluctantly studied Greek and Latin with his father at St. Stephen's Green, he dreamed of becoming a soldier. Clever at drawing, he delighted in sketching military fortifications; he was strongly built, too, and learned to wield a sword effectively. In 1710 Lord Wharton, the lord lieutenant of Ireland, was ordered to send all Irish regiments to Spain for service in the war. Though James Fontaine could not afford to buy John a commission, on the advice of General Ingoldsby he took his son to see the lord lieutenant. Lord Wharton was impressed by some specimens of John's military sketches and by his sturdy appearance but still hoped to sell all his commissions.

The story had a happy ending. On the very eve of the regiments' departure, General Ingoldsby found that some of the officers' posts were still unfilled. He went to the lord lieutenant and obtained an ensign's commission for John, for which his father paid only the fees of office, though the necessary equipment cost an additional £75. The seventeen-year-old John thus joined a regiment of foot commanded by Lord Slane, who was reputed to be a cruel, avaricious man, a drunkard and a debauchee.[15]

John apparently saw no serious fighting in his three years of service. He contracted malaria on arrival in Spain and was in bed for six weeks at Tarragona; the soldier then was much more likely to perish from disease, in quarrels with his companions, or at sea than on the battlefield. Fontaine's descriptions of the countryside of southern Spain are clear, and as a good Huguenot he examined with interest and some disapproval the Catholic church and its ceremonies. When his regiment abandoned Barcelona in November 1712, he recorded the righteous anger of the common people there who called the English traitors and threw stones at them; the soldiers had great difficulty in getting aboard their transports.

John visited his uncle Peter Fontaine and his cousin John Arnaud in

London on his way home. He was back in Dublin in July, studied navigation for ten months with Mr. Hepburn, the mathematician, and in November 1714 prepared to make a voyage to America, where he hoped to buy land for his family. With characteristic Fontaine enterprise he took four indentured servants with him, for in Virginia such servants sold well, and he also could claim fifty acres of land for each person imported including himself. He had aboard a cargo of linens, frieze cloth, shoes, ironwork, stationery, Bibles, and prayer books when he sailed from Cork, December 10, 1714, on the "Dove" of Bideford, Captain William Shapley. The one-hundred-ton, square-stern vessel carried four guns, was Virginia built though registered and owned in Bideford, and shuttled back and forth between the Potomac and Bideford carrying tobacco one way and mixed cargoes of textiles, ironmongery, and miscellaneous manufactures the other.

The journey was an unlucky one. John was seasick at the start and later quarreled with the seamen over the beating of one Thiboult, possibly his servant. Fontaine struck one of the sailors, and they held him over the side of the ship, threatening to let him drop, while the captain locked up his sword and pistols. The ship was west of the Azores on December 29 when a terrible storm tore away her masts, sails, and rigging, and she came within a hairsbreadth of capsizing. Both master and crew then agreed to turn back for England, and Fontaine, probably the only man aboard who could write save the captain, drew up a protest against the ship, to which the men agreed. The "Dove" finally reached Devonshire and limped over the bar of Bideford on January 23, 1715. Fontaine's Journal for the previous week contains many pages of fervent prayers.

Fontaine spent more than one month in Bideford and Barnstaple while the ship was being repaired. Thomas Smith, the owner, asked the sailors to continue the voyage, foregoing their wages for the past three months, and they were forced to agree to these hard terms. Fontaine visited several of his father's Huguenot friends and cultivated Presbyterian pastors and the merchants trading with Virginia. He also found time to frolick with young ladies, on two occasions buying them oranges; once he thought the money ill spent, but the other time he was well treated.

Fontaine's account underlines the close commercial connections Bideford and Barnstaple enjoyed with Virginia, Maryland, and to a lesser degree New England. The merchants also were concerned in the Newfoundland fishery, the building of ships, the Irish wool trade, the manufacture and export of North Devon pottery, the processing of woolen goods—almost every house in Barnstaple contained a loom—and miscellaneous coastal and European commerce. Public-spirited projects, such as the opening of Bridgeland Street by the Bideford Bridge Trust and the building of a merchant's exchange, Queen Anne's Walk, at Barnstaple, give the impression that the merchants were unusually able and far-sighted.[16]

The second journey of the "Dove" was relatively uneventful. She left on February 28 and nearly three months later, on May 26, sighted the Virginia capes. During the long voyage, Fontaine carefully put down Captain Shapley's description of how the Devonshire men fished for cod in Newfoundland. He also recorded in detail the use of the forestaff in taking an observation of the North Star and calculating the latitude. He had given a similar description of shooting the sun on the other voyage. The "Dove" went up Chesapeake Bay to the Potomac River, where Fontaine hired a shallop and with his servants and goods sailed down the Bay and up York River and Queen's Creek to Williamsburg.

## LAND HUNTING IN VIRGINIA

John Fontaine remained in Virginia for four years except for a journey of some six weeks to New York. He made three important trips of exploration in the province. The first was a jaunt in November 1715 to Germanna on the Virginia frontier west of the present Fredericksburg. Fontaine's companion on the trip was probably John Clayton, son of the attorney general of the province and later to become a well-known botanist.

On the journey Fontaine rode in a canoe, saw a muskrat and its nest, and met his first Indians. The two young men stayed several days with Robert Beverley, the historian, on his plantation "Beverley Park" at the headwaters of the Mattaponi. Beverley's self-sufficiency impressed Fontaine—"no curtains and instead of cane chairs he hath stools of wood, and lives upon the product of his land." Likewise, Beverley's winemaking venture was worthy of remark, though Fontaine from his observations in Spain thought "he hath not the right method for it, nor his vineyard is not rightfully managed." Fontaine did not buy a plantation from Beverley; one tract the historian offered him was to be leased for 999 years, not sold in fee, and another Fontaine considered too dear.

The two young men visited Germanna where Governor Spotswood had settled nine German families in nine houses in a line, each with its small sheds for hogs and hens. They were within a palisaded pentagonal fort with a blockhouse of the same shape in the center. The Germans ostensibly were protecting the frontier from Indians, but they were skilled ironworkers, and Spotswood intended to use them to mine and smelt iron—quietly so as not to arouse the prejudices against colonial manufacturing of the Board of Trade. The Germans had their Reformed minister with them and used the blockhouse for daily prayers and two sermons on Sundays. They were most devout and melodiously sang psalms in their native tongue.

Fontaine's entire expense for eighteen days and 292 miles of travel and ferriage for himself and horse was only £3 10s., the 10 shillings being a gift to the German minister. The remainder included ferriages, a meal at an ordinary, and probably gratuities to servants. As Robert Beverley remarked in 1705, "A stranger has no more to do, but to inquire upon the Road, where any Gentleman or good House-keeper Lives, and there he may depend upon being received, with Hospitality."[17] This treatment was occasioned not only by a generous spirit but by the intense loneliness of living in the woods on isolated plantations as well as by the cheap and plentiful food and numerous domestic servants.

Fontaine's second Virginia tour was made in April 1716 with Governor Spotswood to Fort Christanna on the south side of the Meherrin River near the North Carolina border. The trip covered nearly 200 miles and lasted ten days. The governor agreed to grant Fontaine a patent of 3000 acres, which he laid out, probably with the help of Captain Robert Hicks, an Indian trader and commander of the rangers at the fort. For some reason, Fontaine seems to have allowed the patent to lapse and never to have acquired the land.

Fontaine's account of this journey is especially important because of the full description of the Indians at Christanna. They were remnants of several Siouan-speaking tribes—the Saponi, Occaneechi, Stenkenocks, Meipontski, and Tutelo. Fontaine included a vocabulary of "Saponey" words, and since Miss Maury left it out of her edition of the Journal, it has never before been published. Of the forty-six words, phrases, and sentences, thirty-eight can be assigned to a definite language group—eighteen Siouan, fourteen Algonquian, four found in both languages, and two used in both Algonquian and Iroquoian. Though the sample is too small to be definitive, it seems to prove that the Christanna Indians were chiefly Siouan. Yet the number of Algonquian and the couple of possible Iroquoian words may well mean that this vocabulary is the first example yet discovered of the trade language described by Robert Beverley, the historian, in 1705 as

> a sort of general Language, like what *Lahontan* calls *Algonkine,* which is understood by the Chief men of many Nations, as *Latin* is in most parts of *Europe,* and *Lingua Franca* quite thro the *Levant.*
>
> The general Language here us'd, is said to be that of the *Occaneeches,* tho they have been but a small Nation . . . but in what this Language may differ from that of the *Algonkines* I am not able to determin.

One may speculate as to how Fontaine secured the list. He may, of course, have talked with one or several Indians and spelled out the words phonetically as best he could. This would be a laborious process, however, and the list was entered in the Journal on the second day of his week-long stay. He well could have obtained the words from Charles Griffin, teacher of the Indian school at Christanna. The Reverend Hugh Jones accompanied Spotswood on a visit to the fort a year later in April 1717, and he attributed most of what he learned about the Indians to Mr. Griffin.[18]

The pictures of Indian life given by Fontaine are most colorful—the solemnly conducted negotiations of Governor Spotswood and the twelve old men who governed the Indians; the young warriors looking like so many furies in their war paint and distinctive hairdress; the wild, shy, and half-naked young women; and the boys shooting arrows at the eye of an ax or shrieking hideously in a war dance. Fontaine has many observant comments on the habitations and everyday life of the Indians.

## THE SPOTSWOOD EXPEDITION

The best known of Fontaine's Virginia journeys was the one he made in August and September 1716 with Governor Spotswood over the Blue Ridge to the Shenandoah Valley. This expedition included at least four surveyors and some of the canniest land speculators in all the province, together with several rangers and Indian guides. Its primary purpose was to explore the western Virginia frontier, thus encouraging settlement and hopefully enabling the land men to turn handsome profits. Governor Spotswood also intended to steal a march on the French; he hoped to establish a fort at the pass so as to secure for Virginia the trade with the Indians beyond the mountains and perhaps to build another fort on Lake Erie, which he thought—incorrectly—was only three or four days' march away. In addition to these serious aims, the expedition was also a pleasant social occasion—a camping jaunt for congenial gentlemen.

Before the travelers left the rendezvous at Germanna, they had their horses shod. This act, noteworthy because in Tidewater there were few stones and horses often went without shoes, was to give the expedition a romantic name. Spotswood later is said to have bestowed upon some of the gentlemen small golden horseshoes with valuable stones representing the heads of nails. These souvenirs, according to Hugh Jones in 1724, had on one side a Latin motto, *Sic juvat transcendere montes* (How delightful it is to cross mountains!), and "The Tramontane Order" was inscribed on the other. In 1845 Dr. William Alexander Caruthers of Lexington, Virginia, brought out a historical novel, eventually called *The Knights of the Golden Horseshoe*. Although it wildly distorted the historical facts, it made the expedition widely known.[19]

Fontaine's Journal contains the only contemporary detailed description of the journey. Spotswood's travel accounts show that sixty-three men, seventy-four horses, and several dogs went along. Fontaine mentions the surnames of ten gentlemen in addition to the governor and himself. They can be identified as Robert Beverley, Jr., the historian; Robert Brooke, surveyor from Essex County; Captain Jeremiah Clowder of King and Queen County; Colonel George Mason of Stafford County; Colonel William Robertson of Williamsburg, clerk of the Council and General Assembly; probably Christopher Robinson of Middlesex County; Augustine Smith, surveyor, of Essex County; Captain Christopher Smith, surveyor, of New Kent County; James Taylor, Jr., surveyor, of King and Queen County; and William Todd, also of King and Queen. All of these gentlemen, except Mason and possibly Christopher Smith, soon afterwards took up land grants within the Rapidan drainage area. The careful naming of the nightly camps for these men and Fontaine's descriptions of their departures for their homes after the return to Germanna make it rather unlikely that there were other men of prominence on the trip.[20] If each of the twelve gentlemen brought along an average of two servants or "boys"—probably Negro slaves—they and fourteen rangers and four

Indians would account for fifty-four of the sixty-three men on the expedition.

The route taken by the expedition is a matter of lively controversy. In 1877 Philip Slaughter with the aid of local surveyors and historians made an analysis and map of the journey that had the explorers push up the Rapidan and Thornton rivers to a point east of Stanardsville and then circle north crossing the Conway River, going south along the foot of the Blue Ridge, recrossing the Thornton, camping southwest of Stanardsville, and passing through Swift Run Gap to the Shenandoah River between Port Republic and Elkton.[21] William Wallace Scott, an able historian of Orange County and state law librarian, carefully examined this route and in 1923 accepted Slaughter's general course but took out the northern circle and had the travelers go up Blue Run to Swift Run and reach the Shenandoah near Elkton.[22] Charles E. Kemper, who wrote about the route between 1924 and 1929, finally decided that the mountain crossing took place "either at Swift Run or Milam's Gap—most probably the latter."[23] In 1951 Randolph W. Church, the Virginia state librarian, published a carefully drawn map of the expedition based on both study of the documentation and inspection of the sites. It supported the traditional route as outlined by Scott but had the travelers descend from Swift Run Gap by Elk and Dry runs to reach the Shenandoah just south of the municipality of Shenandoah.[24]

The controversy was heightened considerably in 1965 when Delma R. Carpenter, professor emeritus of mathematics at Roanoke College, cogently presented an entirely new hypothesis. According to him, when the travelers reached the fork of the Rapidan and Robinson (Robertson) rivers near the present village of Rapidan, instead of following the Rapidan to the southwest, they turned northwest along the Robinson, continued to follow it to Quaker Run, then crossed southwest to the head of the Rapidan, went through Milam's Gap near Big Meadows, and descended Tanner's Ridge to strike the Shenandoah at Alma.[25] Charles E. Hatch, Jr. in 1968 reviewed the entire controversy and accepted Carpenter's route.[26]

The nub of the argument is whether the expedition crossed at the head springs of the Rivanna River or of the Rapidan. At Swift Run Gap the eastern branch of Swift Run rises and flows into the Rivanna which empties into the James. Since the course of the James farther west was not yet fully known, it was a natural mistake for the explorers to consider

Swift Run as a source of the James. At Milam's Gap, about fourteen miles northeast of Swift Run Gap, is Mill Prong, a spring and headwater of the Rapidan River in the Rappahannock drainage system.[27]

In order to try to decide between the two routes, one must begin with the Journal itself. Fontaine clearly states at four different times that they ascended the source of the James River.[28] He was traveling with the most knowledgeable land men of that day in Virginia, and when they told him it was the James (that is, the Rivanna) they should have known what they were talking about. Thus Fontaine's own words would seem to uphold the traditional Swift Run Gap crossing.

Other documentary evidence is positive for neither route. The act establishing Spotsylvania County in 1720 defined its southern boundary as ascending the North Anna River as far as convenient, and thence, by a line run over the high mountains to the river on the northwest side (that is, the South Fork of the Shenandoah) so as to "include the Northern Passage through the said Mountains within the said County."[29] The line just does include Swift Run Gap, but since Milam's is only fourteen miles farther northeast, the quotation could be interpreted as referring to either gap. Governor Spotswood explained to the Board of Trade on January 16, 1721, that "Spotsylvania is bounded according to my observations when I view'd the Northern Pass over the Great Mountains at the head of Rappahannock River, there being little more of it known than what I discovered."[30] The expedition, of course, was at the approximate heads of both the James (Rivanna) and Rappahannock (Rapidan) systems, but the governor says "Rappahannock" and not "James." Robert Beverley, Jr., in the preface of the second edition of his *History* (1722) states that he was with Spotswood at the head springs of both the York and Rappahannock rivers, "and their Fountains are in the highest Ridge of Mountains."[31] Beverley was commenting upon a mistaken statement of John Oldmixon that the two rivers issued out of low marshes, and he was not considering the James. He was in error himself about the York, some headwaters of which (the North Anna and South Anna branches of the Pamunkey) rise in the Southwest Mountains, not the Blue Ridge.

Another bit of evidence that would seem to support the Swift Run Gap route is William Mayo's manuscript map of 1737. It was based on actual surveys of the area between the Rappahannock and Potomac in dispute between Lord Fairfax and the colony of Virginia. The map shows a short stretch of county road crossing the Rapidan near Blue Run in the general direction of Swift Run Gap and thus suggests that the route was in common use by that time.[32] Bishop Madison's map of 1807 has a similar road running all the way from Fredericksburg through Swift Run Gap.[33] Thus the Swift Run Gap route apparently was known by 1737, and no such road was shown for Milam's on either map.

So much for the documentation. What can actual exploration of the route contribute to a solution of the controversy? First of all, Fontaine does give daily distances traveled by the expedition. His estimates sometimes are difficult to interpret, because the group did not go in a straight line and often kept back from the river banks with their heavy growth of trees and other vegetation, marshy swamps, and steep declivities. Fontaine calculated the outgoing trip at seventy-four miles and the one coming back at seventy-two miles. The camps and their accompanying landmarks for the Swift Run Gap route as determined by Church are in accord with Fontaine's daily distances and total seventy-four miles each way, but Carpenter's Milam's Gap route is only about sixty miles for one way and does not match closely the daily distances.[34]

Traveling over the alternate routes today enables one to visualize Fontaine's descriptions and to recapture the general feeling of the trip but not to pinpoint exactly the places he mentions. The expedition left behind too few artifacts to give much hope of recovering them through archaeology. Conceivably, traces could remain of the Hospital Camp, which was in use for four and one-half days, though searching for them would be seeking the traditional needle in the haystack. Nor could one hope to find the bottle with the paper taking possession of the land for King George I that Spotswood buried near the Shenandoah or the numerous bottles containing beverages used to toast the King and others. The river has flooded and changed course too frequently in more than 250 years.[35]

Still, there is one area that offers a good chance for positive identification, and that is the summit of the range with its two springs. Fontaine wrote that as the travelers ascended the eastern slope they

> came to the very head spring of James River where it runs no bigger than a man's arm, from under a large stone. . . . This is the very top of the Appalachian Mountains. About a musket shot from this spring there is another which rises and runs down on the other side. It goes westward.[36]

[ 17 ]

Scott was certain that he had identified these springs at Swift Run Gap. In 1923 he wrote:

> Before the turnpike was built the road through the gap ran by this spring [the eastern one], and a shortcut bridle path leads by it now. I myself have drunk of it and of the one "A musket shot beyond" many, many times.

The latter spring Scott placed near the pyramidal monument erected to the expedition in 1921 by the Colonial Dames of Virginia and still in place.[37]

The building of the Skyline Drive about 1936-1937 and the improvement of U.S. Route 33 changed much of the topography of the region. But two National Park Service maps made just before the changes enable one to identify approximately the two springs and then to confirm their general location by actual visit. The western one rises in a swampy area south and across Route 33 from the pyramidal marker. The eastern one is more difficult to locate. The 1937 topographical map shows the former turnpike mentioned by Scott lying north and next to the present Route 33, and Scott placed Fontaine's spring to the north of the old road. Two springs are found today housed in concrete cubes on either side of Route 33 about six hundred feet southeast of the western one, and they discharge down the eastern side of the mountain. Another spring lies to the northeast considerably above the rather deep cut that contains Route 33. This series of springs is in the general position described by Fontaine, and the distance between them and the western one is within one-half mile, the approximate range of an eighteenth-century musket.[38] Thus, even today with all the changes, Fontaine's description rings true at Swift Run Gap.

At Milam's Gap, springs cannot be found that match Fontaine's description as closely. Carpenter thinks that Lewis Spring on the edge of Big Meadows is the western spring, but it lies considerably down the western slope and would have been difficult for the travelers to encounter. The spring southeast of it would apparently feed into the Mill Prong of the Rapidan, but though swampy, water-producing conditions are found in that area it is more than one mile from Lewis Spring. There is not the clear, identifiable placement of springs and passage through the gap as found at Swift Run.[39] The advocates of Milam's Gap have not succeeded thus far in overthrowing the traditional route.

None of the small golden horseshoes described by Hugh Jones in 1724 is known to be extant, though several persons in the nineteenth century said that they had seen them. There are skeptics today who wonder whether the little horseshoes ever existed. In 1722, however, Governor Spotswood traveled to Albany in New York to negotiate a treaty with the Five Nations. At the Indian council, he urged the Iroquois to pay special attention to their presiding chief, "*gave him a golden horse shoe* which he wore at his Breast & bid the Interpreter tell him there was an inscription . . . which signified that it would help to pass over the mountains." Any of the Iroquois coming to Virginia should bring this horseshoe with them. This account makes it clear that Spotswood had at least one golden horseshoe, and the inscription on it sounds like Hugh Jones's description of the motto.[40] Perhaps some day an authentic original golden horseshoe will appear.

It was probably after his return from this expedition that Fontaine purchased a plantation in King William County on the north side of the Pamunkey River in the area of Jacks's and Nectawance (today Harrison's) creeks. Fontaine may have bought the plantation, which was eventually divided between his brother James and brother-in-law Matthew Maury, from Captain Richard Littlepage, who lived across the Pamunkey in New Kent County and had large land holdings there and in King William. More information on Fontaine's land is not available because fires have destroyed the King William county land records for the period.[41]

## JOURNEY TO NEW YORK

About one month after returning from the Blue Ridge, John Fontaine left his land papers with Major John Holloway, the Williamsburg lawyer, and rode off to Hampton. There Michael Kearny and he arranged to take passage on a sloop bound for New York. When they reached Sandy Hook, the fog was so thick that the sloop had to remain at anchor. Finally, on October 25, 1716, the two travelers were set ashore on Staten Island, walked four miles to the ferry, and crossed to Long Island. After spending the night at Hendricks's Tavern, they hired horses and rode to Brooklyn, where they took the ferry to New York.

Obviously armed with good letters of introduction, Fontaine at once went to see Andrew Freneau, an enterprising Huguenot merchant. Thereafter he attended social meetings of the French and Irish clubs in various taverns and met some of the chief men of New York province—Governor Robert Hunter, Lieutenant Governor Richard Ingoldsby, Chief Justice Lewis Morris, Mayor Dr. John Johnstone, Postmaster General John Hamilton, Collector and Receiver General Thomas Byerly, Surveyor General of the Customs Maurice Birchfield, and Colonel Stephen DeLancey, Huguenot immigrant from Caen and perhaps the wealthiest merchant in New York.

Fontaine and Kearny twice crossed Harlem River to visit Chief Justice Morris at his manor of Morrisania. Kearny apparently had been married to Morris's daughter Sarah since 1715. The young couple afterwards moved to Perth Amboy, where by 1719 Morris, serving as president of the Council of New Jersey, had had his son-in-law appointed treasurer of the province, secretary, surrogate, clerk of the Assembly, and clerk of the Court of Common Pleas.

Fontaine was impressed by the prosperous condition of the Huguenot exiles in New York and by the economic freedom and religious tolerance they enjoyed. He thought the French the most numerous element in the city, though actually the Dutch outnumbered them. Fontaine attended the beautiful French Church (L'Eglise du St. Esprit). His relations with Freneau were most cordial, and the New York merchant afterwards sent a vessel laden with merchandise to Virginia consigned to Fontaine, who sold the contents.

After spending two weeks in the city, Fontaine and Kearny retraced their path over Long Island and Staten Island and went on to Perth Amboy, New Jersey. From there they rode to Burlington and then to Philadelphia, where, unfortunately for the historian, they spent less than a day. They next made their way to Delaware, visited Kearny's brother Philip at his tannery near Dover, and set out through the area then claimed by Maryland but today Delaware.

On November 21, 1716, they stopped for dinner in the early afternoon at Sutton's Tavern (in the present-day Redden state forest in Sussex County, Delaware). About eight rogues were drinking there, and when Kearny went outside, they knocked him down and broke his sword with blows of their heavy stakes. Fontaine drew his sword and wielded it so fiercely and skillfully that the travelers managed to mount their horses. After riding six miles they stopped at dark in a poor man's house; the rogues caught up with them at about ten o'clock, determined to steal the horses. Fontaine and Kearny drove them off and slipped away at two in the morning so as to avoid further trouble. Fontaine remarked that strangers were customarily robbed in that heavily timbered, sparsely inhabited country.

The travelers continued down the Eastern Shore to Accomack County, Virginia, where they stayed with the affable James Kempe, second husband of Naomi Anderson Makemie, widow of Francis Makemie, the Presbyterian clergyman. With difficulty Fontaine and Kearney got across the Chesapeake into the Rappahannock River and then went overland to Yorktown. A mile south of the village they separated, Kearny returning to Hampton and Fontaine riding to Williamsburg. The journey had cost him £24. He was glad that he had decided to purchase a plantation in Virginia, because he heard that the New York climate was cold and forbidding during a long winter.

By the summer of 1719 Fontaine had finished his work in Virginia as advance man for his family. He had helped find his brother the Reverend Peter a church at Weyanoke in Charles City County, and when Westover Parish was formed in 1720, Peter became the minister at Westover Church.[42] Brother James had brought over his family in a brig with a stock of goods and had sent the ship back to Bristol with cargo; he was settled on part of the plantation John had bought in King William County.[43] Brother-in-law Matthew Maury had come to Virginia on a trading voyage, arranged to take part of the King William County plantation, and returned to Ireland for his wife and baby son.[44] Still another brother, the Reverend Francis, was to bring his family to Virginia in 1721. He became the minister of Yorkhampton Parish and also served as professor of oriental languages (Hebrew) at the College of William and Mary for twenty years beginning in 1729.[45]

John Fontaine sold two ship cargoes consigned to him, one by his friend Andrew Freneau of New York, and in June 1719 set sail in the second ship out of James River for England. He was in London for several months selling the cargo and planning another voyage, which fell through, and in late November he set out for Dublin. At Holyhead on the western coast of Wales he sentimentally climbed to the top of a hill from which he could glimpse the Ireland he had left five years earlier.

## WATCHMAKING, MARRIAGE, SILK WEAVING

John Fontaine remained at his father's house on St. Stephen's Green in Dublin for nearly a year but in December 1720 went to London with his brother Francis, who had received a master's degree from Trinity College

Mary Magdalen Sabatier (Mrs. John) Fontaine

Moses Fontaine, with engraving tools

and was ready to take the king's bounty and seek a parish in Virginia. John for a year or so studied watch- and clockmaking with his cousin Peter Forestier at St. Giles in the Fields in London. Peter was known for his excellent repeating watches. By 1722 John was in business for himself and soon entered partnership with his brother Moses, who had studied engraving. They made clocks and watches at "The Dial" in Middle Moorfields.[46]

Anne Boursiquot Fontaine, John's mother, died toward the end of January 1721, and his father closed his academy but continued living in Dublin, looked after by the youngest child Elizabeth until his death in 1728. In that year John was married to Mary Magdalen, the daughter of John Sabatier, a well-known and well-to-do silk weaver of Spitalfields, and in 1729 Elizabeth Fontaine wed Daniel Torin from Wandsworth, a watch- and clockmaker who recently had completed his apprenticeship to David Lesturgeon in London.[47]

Some time after John's marriage, he decided to become a silk weaver. By 1742 he was living in a brick house on Artillery Street and was listed in a fire insurance policy as "Citizen and Weaver." John Sabatier's will of 1745 described Fontaine as "Silk Weaver of the Old Artillery Ground in the Liberty of the Tower." By 1742 Daniel Torin had replaced him as Moses Fontaine's partner at "The Dial." John Fontaine's son John was apprenticed to John Howell, the London watchmaker, in 1748 and by 1761 was working with his uncle Torin in Middle Moorfields.[48]

Most of John and Mary Magdalen Fontaine's children were christened at the French Church in Threadneedle Street—Ann (1729), James (1731), John (1733), a second John (1734), David (1739), Mary (1741), William (1742), but not the twins Daniel and Moses. Of these, the first John, Mary, and the twins died young.

## COUNTRY GENTLEMAN

By 1748 Fontaine and his family had moved to south Wales and were living at Llanllwch, a mile or so west of Carmarthen, the seat of Carmarthen County. John apparently had given up both watchmaking and silk weaving and was listed simply as "Gentleman." The death of John Sabatier in 1745 had left John and Mary Fontaine well off. Sabatier's will bequeathed a trust fund of £100 in government or parliamentary funds to his granddaughter and goddaughter Ann and another trust fund of £600 for the education of the other Fontaine children. The latter amount counted as part of a full half of the residuary estate, the other half going to Mary's brother John, another important Spitalfields silk weaver. John Fontaine apparently decided soon afterwards to embrace the life of a gentleman farmer and to purchase the Llanllwch farm. Many Englishmen about that time were moving to Wales where agricultural land was comparatively cheap.

In November 1752 Fontaine expanded his holdings by purchasing a small neat farmhouse called Cwm [Twin] Castle (still standing today) about four miles west of Carmarthen in the parish of Newchurch. He had been angered when Parliament in 1750 forced the Bank of England to cut the interest rate on government annuities from four percent to three percent, and he decided his money would do better invested in Welsh farms.[49] Not only did John and Mary Fontaine and their children live at Cwm Castle, but also Moses Fontaine and Elizabeth Torin. The adults made a rather complex series of agreements about their financial arrangements and just where they were to live in the manor house. Daniel Torin continued to reside in Middle Moorfields and later at Hoxton; John and Mary, Moses, and Elizabeth all showed the highest regard for him. Both Moses and Elizabeth were considered in delicate health, or as their American nephew, the younger Peter Fontaine, put it, were "the greatest invalids, and of most crazy constitutions."[50]

John Fontaine held a respected rank in the parish of Newchurch and county of Carmarthen. County politics were heated in 1754. John Vaughan of Golden Grove, largest landowner of the shire and a staunch Tory, had served the county in Parliament since 1745 but relinquished his seat in the hope that his son Richard would be returned. George Rice of Dynever, a clever young Whig, opposed the Vaughans, and rumors, untrue but damaging, circulated that they were Jacobites and Catholic sympathizers. On April 25, 1754, Rice won the election decisively, 785 votes to 390, and among his Newchurch supporters was "John Fountain, Gent." The political strife in the municipality of Carmarthen continued so warm that troops were called to suppress bloody rioting. George Rice retained his seat and became increasingly powerful until his death in 1779. He secured a new royal charter for the County of the Borough of Carmarthen in 1764 that give the municipality county powers within its boundaries. The Common Council under the charter admitted thirty-three new burgesses of the county borough on October 15, 1764, and the list included not only

Richard Vaughan and George Rice but also John Fontaine, freeholder, of Cwm Castle.[51]

The Welsh and Virginia branches of the Fontaine family corresponded regularly. John and Moses Fontaine and Elizabeth Torin represented the Welsh side, and sometimes the letters from America went through Daniel Torin who read them before sending them to Cwm Castle. Mary Ann Maury and then her son, the Reverend James Maury (who in 1763 succeeded as plaintiff in the Parson's Cause, only to have Patrick Henry persuade the jury to award him damages of one penny), and the Reverend Peter Fontaine and then his son Peter were the American correspondents. The four Virginia families kept in close contact and even looked after each other's children occasionally, though James dropped out of the circle after the death of his first wife about 1735 when he moved to far off Northumberland County on the Potomac and remarried. The other members of the family also disliked Francis's second wife, née Susanna Brush, whom he married about 1737, and thought she dominated her husband and treated cruelly his first wife's children.[52] The correspondence was frequently sentimental; thus, the younger Peter Fontaine, surveyor and planter at Rock Castle, Hanover County, Virginia, wrote his uncle Moses in 1765:

> When your annual letter arrives, it yields me much more substantial pleasure than is felt at the feastings on the return of a birthday. . . . I am persuaded there is a kind of instinct in souls; for though I never saw with my bodily eyes either you or my dear uncle John, yet I am better acquainted with nobody. . . . I seem quite intimate with you both.[53]

The two sides of the family took a deep interest in education. The Reverend Peter Fontaine wrote from Westover Church that he approved John's "disposal of your boys to good trades. Labor was ordained by our good Creator to quell the impetuosity of our passions, lest they should run into riot if left unsubdued and unemployed." The Reverend James Maury compared the way he was educating his family with the methods Moses Fontaine used with his nephews and recommended the careful definition of words as an excellent teaching device. Maury was an admired teacher of Thomas Jefferson.[54]

In 1752 Ann Fontaine, John's only daughter, was married at Carmarthen to James Fontaine, her first cousin, who had been born in Virginia and was living in Spitalfields, then or later following the cutler's trade. She died in childbirth in 1753, though her son John lived. The Reverend Peter Fontaine sent his brother John his sincere sympathy but added:

> had you taken me into your counsel when you were deliberating about marrying my deceased niece to so near a relation, I should have opposed it, and advised you rather to a stranger for her, as I did in the case of my own daughter being married to James Maury, all friends here being very intent upon the match.[55]

Another family misfortune is not commented upon in the correspondence, though it may have been mentioned in some of the letters that are missing. John Fontaine's son John, who was apprenticed to the London clockmaker John Howell, received his freedom from the guild in 1759 at age twenty-five. Before that date or later he had an illegitimate son, Joseph, by Mary Bradneck. In 1762 he was serving against the French on a sloop of war commanded by Captain Clarke. Both John's uncle Moses and his father provided in their wills for Joseph Fontaine, alias Thompson.[56]

The two branches of the family took similar sensible approaches to assure the future well-being of their younger members. Whether in Wales or Virginia, they tried to leave each child enough land (and in Virginia, slaves) to give him a comfortable start. Peter Fontaine, Jr., in 1754 explained to his uncle John:

> My father has by his last wife, my mother-in-law [stepmother], five children, three boys and two girls, the oldest about twelve years old. He has made use of my opportunities as a surveyor to procure lands for them in Halifax County . . . five tracts . . . amounting to about six thousand acres, which he designs, with near . . . twenty slaves, to divide amongst them at his death.[57]

The Fontaine family experience shows how rapidly the Huguenot element was assimilated into the British background, whether in Wales or Virginia. Of the seven children of James and Anne Boursiquot Fontaine, Moses was unmarried, but the other six all took marriage partners of Huguenot descent. When the three brothers in Virginia lost their first wives, they remarried, but none of the second wives had a Huguenot name. In the next generation, of the children's twenty spouses who can be identified, only three have Huguenot names.[58]

Not often did the two groups of correspondents differ in their opinions. Once, however, John and Moses Fontaine asked the Reverend Peter two pointed questions—whether colonial breaches of Indian treaties had caused the red men to join the French in warring upon the frontiers and whether "enslaving our fellow creatures was a practice agreeable to Christianity." Peter replied to his brother Moses, March 30, 1757, that the colonists had not broken their treaties, but he argued that they ought to have intermarried with the Indians so as to have obtained their lands while converting them to Christianity. He held the home authorities responsible for frowning on such unions and even threatening to hang John Rolfe for marrying Pocahontas. How much better it would have been to have had Indian children as white at birth as Portuguese or Spaniards rather than that the colonists pollute or smut their blood by copulating with Negroes and producing swarms of mulatto bastards.

As for slavery, Peter pointed out that the Negroes enslaved others of their race and sold them to the African Company. The Virginia Assembly repeatedly had laid an import tax of from £10 to £20 per head on slaves but it was disallowed by the home government that always favored the African Company. The economic facts of life in Virginia, Peter thought, required slave labor as long as "that stinking, and, in itself, useless weed, tobacco" continued the staple crop.

> It is a hard task to do our duty towards them [the slaves] as we ought, for we run the hazard of temporal ruin if they are not compelled to work hard on the one hand—and on the other, that of not being able to render a good account of our stewardship in the other and better world, if we oppress and tyrannize over them.[59]

Peter's will of 1757 bequeathed nineteen slaves to his wife and children, and he added this note: "As I have made no mention of Primus and Sabina in my will I desire my Executors will maintain them and treat them with humanity especially old Sabina who hath been a very good Servt."[60]

James Maury on December 31, 1765, wrote John Fontaine a long, strong letter criticizing the Stamp Act. In his opinion Parliament had no right to tax the colonies without their consent. Magna Charta and the colonial charters gave them all the rights of Englishmen. Worse yet was the provision that the trials under the Stamp Act should be decided by the Admiralty Courts. All the colonies had joined in opposing this act, for which "some may brand us with the odious name of rebels, and others may applaud us for that generous love of liberty which we inherit from our glorious forefathers."[61] But neither John Fontaine nor his brothers or sisters lived to see colonial resentments develop into the American Revolution.

John Fontaine's last known letter to James Maury of January 2, 1764, congratulates him on the victory in the war against the French and especially for "the great deliverance from . . . popery and idolatry." John goes on in a practical vein:

> I received the Timothy grass you were so kind as to send me. I sowed some in my garden, and it grew well. I tried in the field, and the grass killed it. It would grow well in well cultivated lands if well weeded, and I think would produce a great crop; but I am too old and too feeble to undertake anything, and I am often confined with the gout.[62]

John's four boys were grown now. James (1731–1801), the eldest, became a pewterer and married Lucretia Lemoine. He inherited Cwm Castle but moved to Hoxton in the London area.[63] John (1734–), the former watch- and clockmaker, did not marry.[64] David (1739–ca.1800), a tinsmith, and his wife, Mary M. Plowman, left several children.[65] John's youngest son William (1742–) became a farmer, lived near Carmarthen, and was married to Margaret Howell, who bore him five children.[66]

John's life had run its course. At seventy-four he was the last living child of James and Anne Boursiquot Fontaine. His brother Moses had died in 1766 and his sister Elizabeth in about 1764. His sister Mary Ann Maury and brothers James, Peter, and Francis were all long since dead in Virginia. At last it was probably his old enemy the gout that overcame him, and he was buried on November 26, 1767, in the Newchurch churchyard. His widow, Mary Sabatier Fontaine, did not join him there until 1781.

All in all John Fontaine had lived a long and successful life, had his share of adventure, and seen much of the world for one of his time. He had gained the respect of many men and had known much of the joy of life. He had prospered financially and left his widow, four sons, and two grandsons well endowed with fine Welsh farms. He also had seen that his sons were well educated, though he did not send them to a university. Each had a dependable trade to help support him. Perhaps best of all, each

Cwm-Castell, near Newchurch, Carmarthenshire, Wales
John Fontaine purchased this seventeenth-century house in 1753 and spent
the remainder of his life there. The house still stands today.

had been brought up in the Huguenot and then Anglican faiths with a sufficient supply of piety. John's parents would have approved the way he carried out their teachings and his responsible attitude when one of his sons got into trouble. Courageous, enterprising, and versatile, John Fontaine had attained the station of a modest country gentleman relatively early and passed the last twenty years of his life in a comfortable rural retirement. And the Journal that he had kept of his travels had guaranteed him at least one kind of immortality.

## THE JOURNAL

When Fontaine set off with his regiment for Spain in 1710, he began to keep a journal. He continued it until his return from the war, resumed writing to cover his passage to Virginia, and then recorded each journey he made in the New World. He ended the Journal when he returned to Dublin in 1719. Unfortunately for the historian, he kept little record between trips, and thus we know almost nothing of his daily activity in Williamsburg or on his plantation in King William County.

In 1722 John's father, James, at age sixty-four decided to write his Autobiography for the use of his children. As a widower, he then was living in Dublin with his daughter Elizabeth. He began his account (it was in French) on March 26, 1722, intending to send it to his four children in Virginia but offering to let John and Moses see it in London so that they could make their own copy. They protested that they would rather have the original in their father's handwriting so that he decided to make a word for word transcription which he completed on June 2.

In the Autobiography, James Fontaine said that he would let John tell his own story of his adventures, an obvious reference to John's Journal.[67] The black pencil drawing of John made by Thomas Worlidge about 1735 and used as the frontispiece of this volume shows him with his right hand resting on a book that must certainly be the Journal.

Ann Maury (1803–1876), the daughter of James Maury, United States consul to Liverpool, was the great-granddaughter of Mary Ann (John's sister) and Matthew Maury. She was unmarried, energetic, and much interested in family and Huguenot history. In 1838 she had J. S. Taylor in New York publish an incomplete and rather poor translation of James Fontaine's Autobiography entitled *A Tale of the Huguenots*. Fifteen years later, in 1853, she brought out a second book with G. P. Putnam that contained a full and excellent translation of the Autobiography, a version of John Fontaine's Journal, and a generous portion of correspondence between the Virginia and Welsh branches of the Fontaine family. This volume, entitled *Memoirs of a Huguenot Family*, was reprinted by Putnam in 1872 and 1907 and more recently (1967) by the Genealogical Publishing Company of Baltimore. James Fontaine's Autobiography was republished in London, 1876, and two French editions appeared: one after Miss Maury's 1838 version (Toulouse, 1877) and the other after the 1853 edition (Toulouse, 1889).[68]

John Fontaine's Journal as published obviously had been shortened and was almost entirely without the annotation it deserved as an important source of Virginia history. In 1957 the editor determined to try to find the original and to annotate it carefully for the "Eyewitness to History Series" published by Colonial Williamsburg.

Miss Maury in a footnote to her 1853 publication said she had obtained the Journal from two descendants and kinswomen who lived near London. They were the Misses Frances Elizabeth and Sophia Fontaine of Bexley, great-granddaughters of John Fontaine.[69] The editor wrote to Putnam's but they did not know the whereabouts of the original Journal. Nor did the Virginia Colonial Records Project, then surveying Virginia manuscript materials in British depositories under the direction of George H. Reese. The editor had read *Intimate Virginiana; a Century of Maury Travels by Land and by Sea* (Richmond, 1941) compiled by Anne Fontaine Maury (now Mrs. William G. Hirschfeld of Delray Beach, Florida), but, though she had many family papers, she knew nothing of the Journal. The Huguenot Society of London published a note on the search in its *Proceedings* and introduced the editor to Miss Kathleen Busfield of London, a Fontaine descendant who was knowledgeable and willing to help.[70] Finally, at the Alderman Library at the University of Virginia the editor found a promising lead in the James Fontaine Minor Papers. The late Mr. Minor had written about 1930:

> I have learned that Mrs. Anne Fontaine Maury Adams [now Mrs. Hirschfeld] has a m.s. copy of the Journal from the papers of her Great Aunt Miss Ann Maury, which I have seen. It is longer than as it was published, a good deal being left out in publication.[71]

Mrs. Hirschfeld then went through her voluminous papers and in the fall of 1966 found the notebook that contained the copy Miss Maury had made of the Journal; the ten-year search had achieved its first success. Mrs. Hirschfeld generously allowed Colonial Williamsburg to acquire the bound notebook of 198 manuscript pages 7¾ × 6¼ inches that contains the Journal and twenty-four items of family correspondence. Miss Maury's handwriting is as legible as any typewriter, and in the Journal she said she began the copy at Duke Street, Liverpool, October 8, 1840, and finished it at Ham Common, Surrey, on November 13. No wonder that her brother Matthew in 1840 teased her about "her scribbling disorder" and cautioned her against writing too "hard for 5 days, even if you *are* copying 'Fontaine letters.' "[72]

The manuscript Journal contains five important sections that Miss Maury omitted or greatly shortened in the published version. They cover:

Fontaine's military service in Spain, August 31, 1710–July 7, 1713 (summarized in two pages by Miss Maury);

Unsuccessful voyage for Virginia, December 7, 1714–January 22, 1714/15 (considerably shortened);

Respite in Bideford and Barnstaple, January 23–February 26, 1714/15 (omitted almost entirely);

Successful journey to Virginia, February 28, 1714/15–May 25, 1715 (summarized in one and one-half pages); and

Vocabulary of words used by Indians at Fort Christanna, April 15, 1716 (omitted entirely).

Thus far the original Journal has not come to light, though Miss Busfield has traced its existence to as recently as 1915.[73] If it is found one of these days, it probably will not add greatly to what Miss Maury's 1840 copy tells us, though in a few cases it may correct spellings of names and add a few other details. The internal evidence of the copy shows that Fontaine made daily entries during his trips, though he occasionally may have written them several days later, and it is conceivable that he made a finished copy of the whole Journal after his return to Dublin. He made a few serious mistakes, but on the whole his account agrees well with other sources. The historian could wish, of course, that Fontaine wrote more introspectively and with more humor. Still, the Journal is a most important and useful first-hand account—a matter-of-fact and yet very human document of considerable general interest and especially valuable for the light it throws on early Virginia history.

## Introduction

The editor has followed Miss Maury's copy of the Journal almost verbatim. He has added chapter headings for the convenience of the reader. All the dates in the Journal follow the Julian calendar and are Old Style, eleven days behind our modern Gregorian calendar, not adopted in Great Britain until 1753. In the Old Style, the new year began on March 25, and dates from January 1 to March 24 were written to show both old and new years; for example, George Washington's birthday was February 11, 1731/32. All dates have been treated uniformly, as have compass directions, degrees, and minutes. Abbreviations have been extended and capitals have been used to begin sentences.

# JOURNAL OF JOHN FONTAINE

# JOURNAL OF JOHN FONTAINE

Copied from the journal of John Fontaine who was born at Taunton in Somersetshire on April 28, 1693. He was brother to Mary Anne Fontaine, my great grandmother, who married Matthew Maury. Copied by Ann Maury, December 1840.

## I. Military Service in Spain

Commission signed August 31, 1710.[1]

*September 16, 1710.* General Ingoldsby[2] gave me a commission of ensign in my Lord Shawe's[3] Regiment of Foot in the company of Captain Connier,[4] the regiment now being at Cork.

*November 10, 1710.* General Ingoldsby gave me a letter of introduction to my Colonel and I had orders to go to the Regiment.

*November 20, 1710.* Set out from Dublin in the stage coach and November 22 came to Kilkenny where the next day I hired a horse for Cork where I arrived on November 26.

*November 27, 1710.* I wayghted on my Colonel and gave him the General's letter upon which he made me several fair promises.

*November 28, 1710.* I was presented to the regiment by Captain Philips[5] and November 29 I treated all the officers of the Regiment. I had my lodgings at the Barracks. We have coal and candle allowed us here. I stayed until such time as we got orders for to embark our men on board the transports which were at Cove.[6] Before the latter end of January we were all embarked and on February 1, 1710/11 we set sail, wind fair and it continued so that we kept on our way till February 7. About ten of the clock at night the wind came contrary and blew very hard so that we were all obliged to put away before it. There was a very great sea and about twelve of the clock at night our foresail was blown away and we shipped a sea by the stern which broke all the cabin windows, by which we received abundance of water in the steerage, and the long boat on the booms was filled, and the waist of the ship and the meat [mast?] of the ship mortally bruised, but God be praised we received no other damage.

*February 8, 1710/11.* The fleet was scattered, but the commodore made us a signal to sail and make for England and on February 11, 1710/11 we got into Plymouth, and February 13, we had an account of the loss of one of our transports which foundered in the storm with 3 companies of men and Colonel Chester.[7] We remained here to March 25, 1711, and during our stay here several of our men made their escape.

*March 26, 1711.* Set out from Plymouth but the wind being contrary we put into Torbay where we came to an anchor.

*March 29, 1711.* We set sail, wind fair, met with no accident and April 20 we came to the [blank—Cabo Raso or Bay de Cascais?] and April 22 came up the Tagus before Lisbon where we cast anchor and we diverted ourselves ashore and I went to Belle Isle[8] and to see several of their churches.

*May 11, 1711.* Gibraltar. We set sail from thence about 7 of the clock in the morning and had a fair easy wind with the help of which and the current which runs always in very strong—we got through the Straits' mouth before night. We had a great deal of calm weather. Our men were very sickly and we threw several overboard, as also some of our officers, and we took several sharks of a great bigness and see several large fishes. We kept the Spanish shore, and tho' the weather was hot yet we see the snow upon the tops of the Pyrenean hills.

*May 31, 1711.* We came to an anchor before Barcelona[9] where I went on shore but being taken with a violent head ache I was obliged to go on board again. The place where large ships must anchor here is very open and deserves hardly the name of a bay. The mole is very good for small ships.

*June 2, 1711.* I had a violent fever; June 3 we hoist our anchors and went for Terragona[10] where we arrived June 5 at 12 of the clock in the day where I immediately disembarked, (my fever continued very violently) and arrived at the town by 6 of the clock where they gave me an old house without glass or bedding in it. My fever continued for 6 weeks, and whilst I was sick I was robbed of all my linen and was obliged to cut off my hair.[11]

*July 17, 1711.* By the help of two of my acquaintance I was able to go a little abroad and my sickness left me. I was obliged to buy two wigs. We have duty but twice in the week and have not as yet been exposed to any enemy. Our officers and soldiers die very fast and several are murdered by the Spaniards which they revenge by murdering them again. There may be good laws in this country but 'tis certain they do not put any in execution, but what is to be admired amongst those bigotted people is that tho' they do not [an error in copying?] punish murderers yet they will protect them from being punished if they will fly to their churches for protection which the inhabitants make a continual practice of; for if any man is murdered it is commonly by a church, because they can immediately run to them, and after they are there it is sacrilege to offer to lay hands on them. They will not only protect them from the law and the party offended, but also maintain them and give them a friar's habit, the better to hide the villainy of the murderer, and passports from convent to convent, until such time as they convey them where they desire to be, and money to bear their charges. This I know to be true by one of our serjeants who having stabbed another of his companions in a duel, flew to them and they protected him and conveyed him to Lisbon and gave him money to pay his passage in the packet boat to England where I have seen him and had it from his own mouth. This place is very hot in the summer and very moderate in the winter. They make abundance of wine, oil, wheat, barley and indian corn. There are many great plains which are watered by several pretty rivers. Seville oranges and small limes grow here as also abundance of pomegranates and all sorts of garden stuff and a great many delicate fruits. They have no good beef; there is very good mutton but small, as also goats which is the chief meat they have; there is a good many quail, some partridge and hares which are very large. In the season they have abundance of pilchards and other small fish which they take with nets, for they catch but little fish with their lines. There are several good villages about this place but are not half inhabited and the people very beggarly and live miserably. The country seems to be very fruitful but there are not people to cultivate the lands; and all along the sea shore, which is the best, places are not settled, because the Moors very often make descents and carry away with them all they can meet, as also all the people they can which they make slaves of.

*October 1711.* Terragona. There are several very good buildings of free stone now extant. All their rooms are vaulted and laid with fine tiles as also the sides of some of their rooms and cabinets which makes them very cool in the summer. Most of the houses have large free stone cisterns. There is but one spring in the town to furnish it with water which is by their cathedral church which they say hath been one of the first churches in Spain. It is very large and supported by a great number of marble pillars, the glasses adorned with extraordinary paintings. It is the finest building in all Catalonia.[12] There is also several fine convents of several orders of friars, and two large nunneries there. There is a large bay before this place but not safe in bad weather. There is a small mole under the shelter of which small Tartans may lay safe tho' no security for ships.

*November 1711.* Terragona. We were commanded to go to Tortosa[13] to assault it and take it by storm, but the project being discovered by the enemy we did not proceed.

From this time to September 1712 we remained in the garrison and had no engagement with any enemy and in September 1712, we were, by orders of the Duke of Argyle,[14] incorporated into another regiment and the officers dismissed from any duty.[15] About the beginning of October following we left Terragona and went to Barcelona.

Barcelona is a large place fortified all round and most of the works faced with brick. The works towards the sea or mole are faced with large stone and defend all within the mole. This town lies upon a plain place. There is a small river which runs through part of the town. Within the fortification there are several void places which are very fine gardens. There are several convents and nunneries here, as also near the gate which goes upon the mole. There is the King's palace which is four square, built

with free stone, with iron balconies on two sides and three large gates to
go in at below.[16] There is a gallery from the Palace which is covered and
hath a communication to the cathedral church[17] and they of the Royal
Family go in their pew without being seen by the people that are in the
church. When the King or Queen[18] comes in then the service begins
which consists chiefly in a few Latin words, a great many antic motions
performed by the priests and a great deal of good music such as the
trumpet, hautboy, organs, big and small violins and bass viols, and vocal
music, which make a most agreeable concert, and I have observed that
every lesson or part of the service that is performed, the priest goes to the
King or Queen and opens the book for them, and lays it before them, then
he comes before the altar and performs the service. The King never went
by this gallery but when he had a mind to go incognito without any train.
The great altar of this church is built in the middle of the body of the
church and all round enclosed with iron rails. All the Roman churches in
general the windows being painted are very dark, so that there is wax
torches and lamps constantly burning in them day and night.

*October 1712.* Barcelona. This place is commanded by Fort Mountfoy[19]
which is situated upon the top of a height or hill, the side whereof toward
the sea is steep and made almost inaccessible, towards the land is well
fortified and defends all the places between it and the town which is a
small mile. The fortification is a small square with two whole and two half
bastions, but not of the common bigness of bastions in a regular
fortification. Part of one of the curtains is casemated or vaulted and in the
bottom and sides of the inside it is all laid with cut free stone and made
staunch in form of a cistern and the top of the rampart is all laid with free
stone and very even with a small border of stone all round it about a foot
high for to gather the rain water that falls and then by pipes it falls into
the large cistern which I make mention of under it in the vault of the
curtain. By this means they are always provided with water. This Citadel is
well fortified but would require a great number of men to defend it well.
The natives are in general pale yellow and very slender. They are active;
the poorer sort of people that are obliged to work abroad both men and
women are very swarthy and tawny, of a Moorish colour, and live very
miserably. Their chief food is bread which they have very plenty and
onions, garlic, oil and pilchards and other small fish. They drink abundance
of picket[20] and wine and have all sorts of fruit in plenty. The richer sort of

[ 41 ]

people live but very indifferently and are very pale, but the ladies that keep themselves from the sun are in general very handsome and fair, all black straight hair, they dress very genteelly, and in the streets are always vailed and seldom dare look out of a window, when it is open, but are continually at their windows which have lattices to them and small squares about an inch every way, so that you cannot see them perfectly through those lattices,—so that to have a fair view of them you must go to their churches and gaze on them whilst they are at their devotion.

*November 1712.* Barcelona. The first we embarked on board the transports for the Island of Minorca, but we were ordered on shore again and we disembarked and remained here for three weeks until such time as we eat all our provisions. The latter end of November we had orders to embark again, accordingly we did, and as we were leaving the town, the poor Spaniards seeing they were left in the lurch, they called us all the traitors and all the most vile names they could invent, and the common people threw stones at us, saying we had betrayed them into the hands of King Philip.[21] With a great deal of difficulty we got on board, and November 28 we set sail, and December 1 we all arrived at Port Mahon, that is, within a league of it, but the wind changed and blew so strong that the ship I was in, and two more, were blown off the Island and were drove in the Gulf of Lyons. We had very bad weather and were almost starved on board, and there was continual quarrels about the provision. We see several water spouts, one of which passed over our ship, which we were afraid would fall upon us. I have seen them spouts as they call them forming themselves which is after this manner. First you see in your horizon or rather in the clouds which seem to be elevated above the horizon a small black cloud which forms itself, and in the form of a serpent lengthens itself downwards towards the sea, then you see the sea water rising in little streams out of the sea till it meets with this black cloud; you see all those rays of water which joined the black cloud form itself in a body or column, and looks like a large pillar, very black, supported as if it was by the sea, and supporting the cloud, and while it sticks to the sea and cloud it grows bigger continually, until such time as this column or body of water quits the sea. It is transported in the air by the wind and goes with the wind for some way, then it falls into the water again with a great clash, never being transported very far before it falls; but it oftener happens that it holds fast to the sea, and brings down part of the cloud with it, which also makes a great noise with its fall. The mariners affirmed to me that if one of those columns of water should fall upon a ship it would stove her to pieces and that if a ship should happen to be in the place where the cloud is gathering the water would sink her. We were seven days before we could come into Port Mahon[22] again which was on December 8, 1712.

*December 9, 1712.* Minorca. We came up this harbour which is one of the finest and most secure harbours in the world. The coming in is very narrow, on both sides prodigious high rocks, but the channel clear from rocks, and very deep. There is a good fort at the entrance and a very good battery of guns which command the entrance of the place; about three miles up is the town where we landed, which is a small place walled in. The houses are but indifferent, but one church of any note. This island is distant from Majorca about seven leagues, and high ground. The chief product of this island is wine, very little wheat or other grain, few cattle. But the inhabitants being Spaniards they have all sorts of garden stuffs in abundance. Some fish—there are several fine springs of water upon the harbour side.

*January 1712/13.* Minorca. January 1 we embarked[23] and January 3 we set sail with a fair wind. January 8 we had a violent storm of rain, wind and thunder which lasted about six hours, but God be praised we received no damage. January 12, we came out of the straights' mouth and sprung our fore mast in the step. January 13 at night we were by bad weather separated from the fleet and from our convoy the Charles galley. January 17 being in the bay of Biscay, a great sea, we lost one of our men off the round top, who fell into the sea. January 22 we came in sight of the Land's-end of England and instead of going in St. George's Channel we came by mistake into the Irish Channel and before we made land we came amongst the Bishop and his clerks,[24] but, God be praised, got clear. January 24 we arrived at an anchor in Milford Haven.[25]

*January 25, 1712/13.* We dined with the Mayor[26] at Haverford west, and took all our things out of the ship, we remained in Wales about 10 days to February 4.

*February 5, 1712/13.* Embarked on board of a small ketch for Bristol.

February 7 arrived at Bristol, and February 9 we went in the stage coach for London. The first night we lodged at Bath, the second at Marlborough town, and the third at London.

*February 12, 1712/13.* London. Went to the sign of the Black Horse on the Mall where I lodged, and was there until February 24 before I could find out any of my relations, and am very short of cash. February 26 I received a letter from my father and found my Uncle Fontaine at the Pest House[27] from thence I went to Mr. Arnaud's[28] at Islington where I remained to June 18, 1713. June 20 hired a horse and came with Mr. Gout,[29] in five days to Chester. From Chester I went to Park Gate,[30] where we remained six days. July 2 we left Park Gate, forded Chester river and went to Holy Head.[31] The first night we lodged at Holywell in North Wales. The next morning we went to see the spring which they call Holy Well. It is very large, and within two hundred yards of it, it turns a mill and before it goes to sea, it turns two others. It is extraordinary good water and they say hath cured several people by bathing in it, of rheumatic and other pains. The next day we went to Conway where we crossed the ferry. This is a good harbor for small ships, there is a large Castle which commands the town and the harbor. It is built upon a rock and was a very strong hold in former times. The town is also all walled in. There is but few good buildings in this place. The next morning we set out and about three of the clock we came to Holy Head. The roads are very bad. July 5 we embarked on board the packet boat and had the wind contrary all the way, but July 7 we arrived to Dublin. I disembarked and took a rings end car[32] and came home to my father's[33] where I met them all well.

*Dublin, Ireland.* Here I remained, learned the art of navigation from Mr. Hayborn,[34] until the last of March 1714. Then I left Dublin and went down to my brother James[35] where I remained for about three months and came up to Dublin again in June 1714, where I remained to November 9 following, and designing for Virginia[36] with four servants, I took my passage on board a sloop for Cork with my servants, where I arrived safe November 13, 1714, but not finding a ship there, I landed my goods and servants and there remained to December 7. From Cork I went to Yoghall where I did my business with Mr. Downs[37] and November 26 came to Cork again where I bought linens and frieze cloth and shoes.

*December 3, 1714.* Cork. A ship from Biddeford arrived in the Harbor. I agreed with the master Captain Shapley for my four servants and my self for which I paid him £25.

# II. Narrow Escape from Death

*December 7, 1714.* We embarked and December 10 the wind proving fair we set sail for the Virginias with God's blessing. The wind continued fair from December 10 to 17 and blew fresh from December 17 to 28, 1714, the winds variable from N W to N hard gales.

*December 11, 1714 from Cork Cove.*
A Journal of our intended voyage by God's assistance in the Dove of Biddeford Captain John Shapley Commander from the Old Head of Kinsale in the Lat [51°36′N] Lon [8°32′W].[38]

*December 11, 1714.* At sea. The wind being at N E in the morning we set sail the weather something stormy. At 12 we came up with the head of Kinsale. The one with the other we sailed 6 knots an hour and continued so all that night. About five of the clock the wind changed from the N E to N E again. Our course for the first 16 hours was S W. We run at the 49°51′ and sailed S W course 50 leagues. I was sick. A rough sea.

*December 12, 1714.* At sea. Wind N by E. Fresh gale, we sailed 6 knots per hour. About four of the clock the wind came N blew very hard. I was somewhat sick. A rough sea.

*December 13, 1714.* At sea. The winds from N E to N by W and back to N E again. Our course for the first 16 hours was S W. We run at the rate of 10 knots per watch, by our observation we were in the Lat of 47°4′ and reckon ourselves to be from the old Head of Kinsale course S W 120 leagues.[39]

*December 14, 1714.* At sea. Wind at N E. A brisk gale, our course

W S W. No good observation, but by our reckoning we are in the Lat. 46°39'. Sailed by our log 54 leagues. Seen nothing remarkable only some reak bats.[40] The weather somewhat warmer than on the coast of Ireland.

*December 15, 1714.* At sea. Wind at N E. Our course steered W S W. No observation, the day being hazy. Winds not very hard; this day sailed 50 leagues. Not very well at sea yet.

*December 16, 1714.* At sea. Wind at N E, not very hard. The sea some what assuaged. Our course is W by S. We sailed at the rate of 5 and 6 knots per hour. We had no right observation, but we reckon ourselves to be in the Lat. of 44°33', but not very certain for it was cloudy and no shade. We see many sea hogs.[41] The method of taking an observation at sea. You see first as high as you can the latitude you think yourselves in, then you fix your veins, then you look for the horizon. You must observe that if the shade of the sun comes to the upper part of the slit of the horizon vein and that the sun at his full height, and that you see your horizon through the slit of the horizon vein, then you are assured of a good observation. You must begin to look before the sun is at his full height that you may look whilst it is moving higher, and you must continue till you find it declining, and when you find the sun declining then you must leave off observing. Then take of the degrees of the quadrant and look in your table and you will find the sun's declination to be, which you must subtract from your Latitude by observation and the remainder will be the latitude of the place you are in. Now as the sun is going from us we subtract, but when it comes to us you must add. If the sun dont shine out so that you can take an observation, if you have a mind to know when it will be twelve o clock, set the sun with the compass, and when the sun bears due south, then 'tis twelve of the clock. You must always allow for the variation of the compass which you may find by the north star, or an observation of the sun with an azimuth compass. You may also find it by your tables of the variations which give it for every latitude.[42]

*December 17, 1714.* At sea. Wind at N E by E, very calm and our sails spread. Had a good observation and found that we were in the latitude [blank]. We were becalmed made little way and see a great many sea hogs; found the weather much warmer than in Ireland and the days lengthened.

[ 47 ]

*December 18, 1714.* No wind at all. We drove about 10 miles. We see a gannet and a mur.[43] By our observation we found ourselves to be in the latitude of 43°44'. This day is Sunday.

*December 19, 1714.* At sea. Had a good observation and found ourselves in the latitude 43°37' and our course was W something N. By about 12 at night we broke our fore mast shrouds, and the wind blew something hard and changed to S by W.

*December 20, 1714.* At sea. The wind at S W, very stormy and not being able to bear sail we lowered our fore sail and put a reef in our main sail and so lay under our mizen driving to the N E, all the night long the weather thick and in the morning we had rain which assuaged somewhat the winds but the greatness of the sea made us to continue under our mizen sail. We shipped some water and see thousands of sea hogs. We lay to the Westward of the Island of Azores where commonly there is bad weather. Distant N 100 leagues but as far to the westward.

*December 21, 1714.* At sea. The wind at W by S, somewhat stormy.

*December 22, 1714.* Wind at E by N, a very pleasant breeze, and we loosed all our sails and made our course W by S. I have a dispute with the men for beating Thiboult.[44] I struck one of them and they took me out of the ship to throw me overboard but brought me in again, in which time the master locked up my sword and pistols, so I was forced to be easy. No observation.

*December 23, 1714.* At sea. Wind at S by W, something hard and showery. We had a good observation and found ourselves to be in the latitude 43°20'. Our course was W N W and because of the variation of the compass we reckon that we made our course good. We run at the rate of 5 knots per hour. We sail under our courses. The weather temperate and warm.

*December 24, 1714.* Wind at S by W. Stormy. Made our course W by N and W N W at the rate of 5 knots per hour. We took our reef in our main sail and shipped some water. The sea run high.

*December 25, 1714.* At sea. Christmas. Wind W by N, very stormy and rainy—not able to carry any sail so we lay by under our mizen. A mighty sea. We remained so all day and night and made but an ordinary Christmas. Peas as hard as shot for breakfast. Two fowls killed by the bad weather for dinner, and stirabout for supper. In good health God be praised.

*December 26, 1714.* Sunday. Wind at W by N. At 5 in the morning not quite so stormy, but a great sea and much rain. We set our main sail and fore sail and steered S by E at the rate of 3 knots per hour. Provisions scant, all our fowls dead.

*December 27, 1714.* Winds from N W to W by S, very varying and rainy, cloudy, dismal and stormy, the sea great and raging, we not able to carry any sail.

*December 28, 1714.* The wind at S W very stormy, we endeavoured to scud before the wind, but the ship would not steer, so we were forced to bring to under our mizen, driving at the mercy of the sea. The sea was extraordinary great and the weather cloudy. At the rising of the moon a star rose close after and followed the moon, which the sailors said was a great sign of a tempest and upon the like occasions that it commonly happens.

*December 29, 1714.* Going to Virginia in the Dove. The wind rose and blew very hard in the morning and increased continually until it blew a mere tempest. About 10 of the clock at night the wind blew to such a degree that we were obliged to take in our mizen and lye under our bare poles, but about two hours and a half after the wind blew so terribly in the rigging that it clapped one side of the ship under water to that degree that the sea water from the steerage door came in in such abundance that had it continued long it would have filled the ship. The sailors was for cutting away the main mast, but two went up and cut away the main top mast, then the ship righted. The main topmast fell overboard but all the ropes not being cut, the sea drove the mast with such violence against the side of the ship that we were afraid it would stave her through, but at last we got clear of it, and cut all the ropes which held it, and were in hopes that we should receive no further damage, but it was God's pleasure that half an hour after one, the wind blowing most dreadfully and the night dark as possible it could be, the wind drove the water out of the sea, and the foam and water was mixed together 7 feet above the deck, so that the air seemed to be all on fire. The sea was also a continual flame and foamed upon our deck ready to tear us to pieces. One wave came on board which tore away our bowsprit close to the foot of the foremast and the shock was so terrible that we thought the ship must stove in pieces. What a terrible cry the people gave expecting to go down every minute, but as God would have it, it broke nothing but the bowsprit, but the ropes holding the bowsprit, it was every sea striking violently against the ship's head. Two of our best sailors went up the foremast to cut away the fore topmast and the ropes that held the bowsprit. In the meantime we shipped another sea which carried away the foremast close by the board, and one of the men that was in the round top with it in the sea, the other his body was bruised between the mast and the side of the ship, but not unto death God be praised. He that fell in the sea, a rope had him by the leg, so that he fell in the sea but got no further hurt than that the rope hurt his leg. He got in safe but had drunk so much salt water, and worked himself so that he was not able to stir. By that time those two men were well in the steerage another comes in that had almost cut off his left hand as he was cutting the ropes of the masts to let them go clear. Those three men were disabled and the best men we had. And what can a man imagine more terrible than to see the head of the ship all under water, and the sea foaming amongst us upon deck, and the men that remained almost disheartened, and those poor men that were disabled grieving that they could not help themselves and encouraging the rest to disengage the ship from the foremast and bowsprit which was a thumping the ship to that degree that we expected every minute the masts would come through. We were surrounded with nothing but death and horror within and without and it would make the most brave to submit himself, and what could we think to see so many misfortunes one after the other but that it was God's pleasure that at last we should perish and be destroyed for our wickedness but when we called upon God for relief he helped us, and at last we got quit of our foremast and bowsprit without any damage to the sides of the ship.

Now the Lord doth shew us that it was not by the arm of flesh we are preserved from the raging and terrible sea, but by his Almighty hand and powerful stretched out arm. O Lord we see that it is in the All one we must trust, and have all hopes of relief from thee and thou sheweth us as our lives this day are witness of, that it is not in vain to humble oneself before thee and call upon our God and Saviour in the time of our distress. Let us therefore perform as far as we can on our side what we have promised unto thee O God, in our great distress. Thou hast granted unto us our lives, so let us according to our good resolutions be strengthened by thy Grace to employ the remaining part to thy honor and praise, never forgetting how sweet thy help is in distress, when no other can help. O Lord, it is not only on this occasion that thou hast been pleased to preserve my life to me in imminent dangers, but several times, therefore let me never forget thy blessings upon me, and be thankful to thee to the uttermost of my power, until the latter end of my days. Help me O Lord to perform thy commandments. Amen.

*December 30, 1714.* We lay under our mizen all the day like a log of wood, and suffered much by the greatness of the winds and sea, being almost always under water, but seeing that through his infinite mercy God had preserved us until now, we comforted ourselves, relying upon his mercy. The wind was at N W, very showery and full of hail.

*December 31, 1714.* We lay a hull with our mizen sail out. We shipped several seas, and were almost continually under water. The wind, God be praised is somewhat fallen, as also the sea; but not being in a capacity of proceeding on the voyage to Virginia for want of masts and sails. We were then 400 leagues to the westward of Cape Clear in Ireland. About twelve of the clock we all consulted what was best and most proper, to continue on to Virginia or to return to Europe. But all the sailors with one consent gave their voice to set sail for England, or some part of Europe lest by continuing on the voyage to Virginia either for want of provisions or rigging we should perish. The wind being at W and by N we set our main sail and mizen sail before for a stay sail, and steered our course for England W by S, but made little way. We were by our reckoning in the Latitude 42°20′ and were farther westward than the island of Flores which is the western Island of the Azores. We are setting our ship in as good order as we can, she is miserably shattered. We hope God will continue the wind fair for Europe, but what may we not expect from so merciful a God. Thou hast already saved us from such imminent dangers that we must be without any knowledge or faith not to trust quietly upon thy mercy for the future, for thou art O Lord Almighty, not like to us feeble men that propose to ourselves and endeavour at several things, but fall short of the performance, which makes us admire thy strength and our own weakness and infirmities. O Lord if thou wilt that we be saved out of this danger we shall be saved. Do thou more especially preserve us from sinning against thee. If this be thy pleasure who will contradict thy power, or who is able to withstand. Will the sea devour when thou commandest the contrary? Will Satan rise against us when thou defendest us? No, O Lord, the sea is quiet and falls at thy command; Satan is destroyed and obedient at thy word; therefore strengthen we beseech thee our faith, and by thy help we shall trample upon him, and all his devices shall fail, and prove to our advantage rather than hurt us. Thou canst O Lord draw comfort out of the greatest appearance of afflictions. As thy chastisements are great do thou also give us strength to bear them, and to look upon them as a chastisement coming from thee O God who has a love for us, and a desire that we may make use of them for our salvation, and give us strength to behold those dangers, submitting all to thy will, and not at all regretting this feeble life of ours, and the leaving this wicked world. Life we must lay down, and the world we must leave. Life is only a burthen to our souls if we can persuade ourselves that thou wilt receive us into mercy. O Lord, give us strength that at all times we may do the things that are right before thee and have a firm faith in our Saviour, that through his merits with our weak endeavours, we may be made partakers of the heavenly kingdom, for nothing can conquer so effectually the fears of death and make us happy even in dying as the firm hopes of another world. Therefore, O Lord, we desire that through thy grace, thou wilt so fill us with the heavenly hope, that we seeing thy glory, even in the extremity of our sufferings, we may rejoice, which the consideration of the foolishness and insignificancy of what we leave here, and the manifold miseries we escape, by leaving the world betimes, that those considerations may encourage us instead of afflicting us. Let us run to thee with joy and thanksgiving and begin to praise thee even here before we are transported into heaven. O Lord, we thank thee for thy preserving us to this day, because we thought on thy statutes and employed ourselves in the meditation of the commandments, which were before us at all times, but ease, prosperity and health were the reasons that we did not think on thee, which we humbly beg forgiveness for, through the merits of our Saviour Jesus Christ. We thank thee for that thou hast been pleased for to delay thy just judgments upon us until now, and hath given us time to examine what we have done, as also to see the folly of laying our hearts to the things of this world, which are all as frail as him that possesses them which is feeble man, who is gone in a moment. What comfort could all the riches of this world afford us in distress, none at all, but rather grief, but God is strong when we are in distress, and able to preserve us when in prosperity from the dangers of it. O Lord let us feel that real satisfaction within us that thy servants feel, that have made peace with their God. Let us have a quiet conscience, which is the great seal of thy peace with us. O Lord forgive us, for nothing can terrify but sin and then with content and Christian joy, we will embrace any death thou art pleased to appoint for us, and leave the frivolous world with its shew of content to enjoy the sight of my God forever, where I shall praise thee to all eternity and enjoy the fullness of content. As we see and can't but admire thy most miraculous works both by sea and land, and are persuaded that according to thy word and will, all things will come to pass; so we trust in thee O Lord for the resurrection of our bodies and souls, which through the merits of our Saviour will rise to everlasting happiness. O Lord thou knowest what is most requisite for us, which according to thy wisdom, thou wilt grant to us. Amen.

*January 1, 1714/15.* At sea. The wind at S W by S something calmer, but the sea ran very high. We lay by under our main sail, but rolled miserably for want of masts and sails. We received many very dangerous seas that night, which we thought would founder us, but God was pleased to preserve us from all those threatening dangers. We made of our mizen sail a sprit sail to make the ship steer, we also took down our mizen top mast and fastened our main mast as well as we could with our running tackle, and are preparing sails, and contriving some posture to put the ship in, waiting for fine weather, when God will be pleased to send it. We are almost wasted by the violent motion of the ship being without masts, but we still trust in thee O God that thou wilt not suffer Satan to prevail against us, and wait patiently for our deliverance from thy Almighty hands. Stretch forth thy hand to us O Lord and bear us up in this our distress lest we sink and fall under the weight of our sins. Suffer us not to repine against thee in our trouble, but let us confess that we do merit to be afflicted, but who is able by his own sufferings to make satisfaction for the sins he hath committed, who can stand before thy Justice seat and by his own sufferings be justified. No mortal man, but thou hast O Lord supplied our infirmities by giving for us thy only Son our Lord Jesus Christ. To his merits we fly and through him we hope for salvation. Do thou pardon us O Lord, and accept of these our feeble and imperfect prayers, and if thou seeth it proper to take us to thyself do thou also cleanse us that we may be worthy of appearing before thee. O Lord, thou knowest our hearts and that it is not the loss of this life that afflicts us, tho' it is the desire of all flesh to live if it was thy pleasure, but because we have sinned against thee and hope for the future we should take better heed to our actions. O Lord we desire life upon no other account than that we may glorify thee, for the performance of which we beg thy Holy Spirit; without which our inclinations and the world will lead us away daily. Thou knowest O Lord the temptations that we are the most inclined to, do thou give us strength to resist them boldly, when we are attacked by them, and also avoid all occasions of meeting with them, as knowing well our own weakness. We all know that we are in affliction and that we have a feeble view of thy anger against us. We all with our conscience confess that we have offended against thy laws, and that it is our wickedness that hath brought the just judgments of God upon us at this time, but all those thoughts come now before our eyes because we see death as if it were playing before us, waiting for the sentence of our Almighty God to destroy us. Nothing makes this sight so terrible as our sins, and it is our weakness and ignorance that makes us think of death more now than when we are at our own homes and in our accounted places of security, but if we rightly consider thy Almighty power and our weakness, we should think ourselves safer here than if we were at home in prosperity, for it is one of the devil's greatest cunning to put in our hearts that we are in a safe place, that we have long to live, and that a final repentance will be sufficient for our salvation, and to represent to us the distance that is between us and the judgment seat. All these notions which are the fruits of plenty and riches are the most dangerous temptations in the world, therefore O Lord guard us from them, by giving us a heart to consider our weakness, and by seeing that there is no time prefixed in this world for to live, and that our life is but as a phantom or blast of wind that passeth away, and that death is always waiting upon us; and give us the grace that we may always think death as near as we do think it now, and every day that we live we ought to look upon it as a miracle considering the many enemies life hath. It is most certain, we should not be guilty of many of the sins we daily commit, if we laid always before our eyes our frailty, the small distance between eternity and us, and thy just judgments, if we thought as we ought to do that we have but one day or one hour or perhaps but one moment to live, before we must appear before the judge of Heaven and Earth. I am persuaded that the most wicked amongst us would not employ that small time in sinning, and to make himself miserable to all eternity. Give us grace, O Lord, that while we live, we may live unto thee, and have death always before our eyes, which most certainly will not cheat us, but come and rid us out of this troublesome life, and if we are prepared for it when death calls, then shall we have our recompence for all our past watchfulness. Therefore let us cast off this world so far as it may be prejudicial to our everlasting inheritance, and seek after thy laws, expecting mercy through the merits of our Blessed Saviour and Redeemer. Amen.

*January 2, 1714/15.* Coming to England. Wind being S by W, a fresh gale. By our observation we found ourselves to be in the Latitude 43°0′ and that by our reckoning we were 338 leagues to the westward of the old head of Kinsale. All the mariners came to the master and told him that if they proceeded on the voyage to Virginia that they were sured to perish by the way, and told him that they would not proceed, but would return to Europe, but the master would not consent to it, without they would protest against the ship that she was not able to go to Virginia. I writ the protest, they signed it, and we set our sails and our course N N E. The wind being fair and blowing fresh, we went at the rate of 4 knots per hour. About 2 of the clock in the morning we shipped two seas, that we thought would have foundered the ship, but God be praised it did us no great damage. All our men are recovering of their wounds and bruises. I am, God be praised, in health. By the log we have made this last 24 hours 40 leagues of our way homewards.

*January 3, 1714/15.* Wind hard at S W a great swell. We steered our course N E and this 24 hours we made 58 miles. No observation. We shipped several seas but not dangerous; the weather looks as if it would clear up. We see some birds we call marling spikes, murs and rake bats. We esteem ourselves by our dead-reckoning to be in the latitude 45°30′.

*January 4, 1714/15.* Wind at S by W, tolerable. We steered our course E N E by N. This 24 hours we made 46 miles. No observations. We took out our mizen mast, and will put it in for a fore mast as soon as the weather will permit. We are always wet upon deck and the ship rolls most terribly. We reckon ourselves in the latitude of 46°0′.

*January 5, 1714/15.* Wind at S by W, blowing so hard that we could carry no sail and lay by. We got a spare main yard which we put up for a mizen mast. We roll enough to tear the ship to pieces. The weather dark and hazy, always wet upon deck as in the sea. No observation.

*January 6, 1714/15.* Wind at S by E, stormy. We lay under a skirt of our main sail, and so drove as the sea and wind carry us. The ship she rolls enough to distract one, and always shipping of water. We thank thee O Lord for all these afflictions, which thou art pleased to make us bear. Give us grace to amend our lives by those warnings for fear greater should come.

*January 7, 1714/15.* Wind at S by E, stormy, a great sea and we lying under a reefed main sail, we shipped several seas, one carried away our main tack and another came past in the steerage. We were forced to reef our main sail, not able to bear any, the wind so stormy. We had but an indifferent observation, and think ourselves to be in the latitude 49°30′ and reckon ourselves to the westward of the Lands End 258 leagues, but in a miserable condition for want of rigging.

*January 8, 1714/15.* Wind at S by E, tempestuous, a terrible sea. About 6 of the clock in the morning we were struck with a violent sea in the quarter and waist of the ship, that we were all assured to perish. We received several other seas, but not so terrible. No observation this day. O God be pleased to redeem us and sustain us, for we are all brought to nothing, and are terrified with thy judgments and are not able to withstand thee any longer. Turn thy face towards us and look down upon our afflictions, and take pity on us most miserable sinners.

*January 9, 1714/15.* Wind at S by W. No observation. Weather thick, wind abated. We lay under our main sail. The sea doth not break over us as it did, but there is still a great swell. No observation. We are in the latitude 50°0′ and west from the land's end 260 leagues.

*January 10, 1714/15.* The wind at S W by S, the weather fair and the sea somewhat assuaged. We have an observation and found ourselves to be in the latitude 51°21', and by our reckoning distant west from the Lands End 220 leagues.

*January 11, 1714/15.* The wind at S W by S, very hard and the sea runs high. We esteem ourselves to be in the latitude 51°50'. Cold.

*January 12, 1714/15.* The wind about 10 at night came from S to W by S, somewhat fair. We set our main sail and came our course E by S until about 9 of the clock in the morning. Then the wind blew so hard that we were able to carry no sail. It came to a storm. We shipped two seas, but received no damage. No observation, but reckon ourselves to be in the latitude 51°30'. West of the Land's End of England 200 leagues.

*January 13, 1714/15.* Wind at W N W abated and about 5 of the clock this morning we set our reef main sail. We sailed about 3 knots per hour and esteem ourselves to be in the latitude 51°10' and distant from the Land's End 175 leagues. About 12 of the clock in the night we shipped a sea that broke our waist board, and after another struck us in the stern, but did us no great damage. We are securing our bit of a fore mast. Hazy weather and cold.

*January 14, 1714/15.* Wind at W by S and almost calm. Our course steered S E. We made between two and three knots per hour. We had a good observation and found ourselves in the latitude 51°0' and distant from the Lands End of England 160 leagues. We made an end of rigging our mizen mast for a foremast, and got a spare topmast for a bowsprit. The weather clears up and the swell of the sea is something abated. Our ship is as well rigged as we can afford.

*January 15, 1714/15.* Wind at S by E, very hard, so that we can carry no sail and so continued for about 9 hours. Afterwards it cleared up and was more moderate, so we set our sails and steered our course W by N and went at the rate of three knots per hour, thick weather. No observation, but esteem ourselves to be in the latitude 51°0'.

*January 16, 1714/15.* The wind came about from S by E to N. After several heavy showers of rain, about three in the morning, we set sail, and made three knots and half per hour. The wind moderate, but the weather thick, so that we had no observation, but we esteem ourselves to be in the latitude 51°0′ and West from the Land's End 160 leagues. We see a wild duck which attempted several times to come on board, but at last fell into the sea by our side.

*January 17, 1714/15.* The wind at NW—a hard gale of wind, but still we carried our main sail and steered our course S E and went by our log at the rate of 5 knots per hour. We had no observation, but by our reckoning we esteem ourselves to be in the latitude 50°50′ and distant from the Lands End of England 120 leagues. By this day we may see that thy mercies are soon forgot, for now our miserable companions think that they are out of danger. They forget thy mercies to them and bemoan their losses, repining against thy providence for afflicting them; but O Lord give us grace to consider that notwithstanding the wind doth not at this time blow hard, nor the sea rage, yet we are still in thy hands, and that we have deserved many more afflictions than what we have suffered, making use of this time that thou doth out of thy goodness bestow upon us in humiliation and repentance. Let us not O Lord sin, lest we die in them and let us not be slothful in our repentance lest death overtake us unprovided, and Thou in thy justice should throw us into eternal suffering. But let us always mortify our ambitions and worldly designs by representing to ourselves the sufferings of those that neglect their salvation, and the reward promised by thy unfailing word to the penitent. Amen.

*January 18, 1714/15.* Wind at W by S. We steered our course S E by E, and went at the rate of 4 knots per hour, but not able to carry any sail, being under our poles. Weather hazy. No observation. We esteem ourselves to be in the latitude 50°30′ and westward from the Land's End 90 leagues.

*January 19, 1714/15.* Wind at W by S, a good gale, steered our course E by S. We had an observation and found ourselves to be in the latitude 50°24′ and westward from the Land's End of England 60 leagues. Continue O Lord thy favors to us. Let thy Almighty hand be with us to conduct us in a place of safety. Finish O Lord the work that thou hast begun to usward [archaic: "toward us"] keeping us in thy fear whilst we live, that we may employ our hearts and tongues to thy glory. Amen.

*January 20, 1714/15.* Wind at S by W and S W, blows very hard. We lay under our mainsail. About seven of the clock, the wind fell and we set our sails, and we reckon ourselves to be 53 leagues to the westward of the Lands End and in the latitude 50°40′.

*January 21, 1714/15.* Wind at W by S, a fair gale and about 6 in the afternoon hove the lead and found ground at 60 fathoms water. The first the lead brought up was fine sand, sounded again and found grey sand mixed with shells something reddish, sounded again and found small gravel stones mixed with reddish and blue stones, and about ten of the clock in the morning we see a brigantine on our starboard quarter that bore of us N N E. We made signals of distress to her, but she would not come to, so we did not speak to her. At eleven we met with a sloop belonging to Cork and spake with her, she told us that Scilly bore from us E 14 leagues, but at 12 we had an observation and found ourselves to be in the latitude 50°41′, and by our reckoning Scilly bears off us E by N. Northerly and run at the rate of 3½ knots per hour.

*January 22, 1714/15.* Wind S W and we run at the rate of 4 knots per hour. At 10 of the clock we see the Island of Lundy and at one it bore of us E Northerly. We were up with the south end of the island and at three the pilots came on board and at 12 at night we cast anchor in Clove Alley Road.

# III. Respite in North Devonshire

*January 23, 1714/15.* Clove Alley Road. Weighed anchor at Clove Alley and came over the Bar of Biddeford. Though the weather was calm, there was a great swell upon the bar. We came over at three quarter flood and in the shoalest place we found three fathoms water. I remained on board that night and unbaled all Mr. Binauld's[45] goods and distributed them amongst the sailors. I wrote to my father and Mr. Binauld that night, and sent the letter [to] the post by the master of the ship. I lay on board that night, not well, but God be praised, delivered from the dangers of the sea. We cast anchor before Appledore.[46] A handsome village.

*January 24, 1714/15.* In the morning I went ashore where I met with Mr. Smith's son. I immediately hired a horse and went to Biddeford[47] where I met with Mr. Smith[48] the owner of the ship and spake to him about the Bibles and paper and enquired what he designed to do about the ship, and he promised me he would make her ready as soon as possible and send her immediately for Virginia. I went and took up my lodgings at the post house, at the rate of seven shillings per week for my diet and all. I was much out of order so I went to bed immediately and slept heartily.

*January 25, 1714/15.* Biddeford, England. I writ to my father and my cousin Arnaud by the post of the disaster and that I should be forced to maintain my four servants until the ship was fitted out again. The people came from Appledore to me. I agreed for their diet and lodging at three shillings and sixpence per week at the same house where I lay. To my mind the people of this place are the most ungenteel nigardly and illbred that ever I see, most of the inhabitants being sailors. The chief trade of this place is to Newfoundland and Virginia.

## January 23 to February 1, 1714/15

*January 26, 1714/15.* I went to a gun smith in town and agreed with him for Morriset's[49] diet and six shillings per week. There is a very notable bridge over this river which is a quarter of a mile long, supported by 24 large arches.[50] The river abounds with salmon, mullet and all sorts of fish.

*January 27, 1714/15.* The ship came from Appledore to Biddeford quay, and I went to Mr. Smith's house in the night with Mr. Binauld's Bibles and paper which he gave me house room for, assuring me that if the officers knew of it they would seize them, and advised me to take out a cocket for them leaving this place.[51]

*January 28, 1714/15.* I was in company with some of the Virginia merchants and they gave me a great deal of encouragement. I dined and supped at home. My head is almost settled and I am much refreshed.

*January 29, 1714/15.* All possible speed is making for to order the ship, and the owner Mr. Smith had all the sailors at his house and asked them whether they would continue on the voyage to Virginia without expecting any wages for the three months which were past. The poor sailors consented to these hard terms.

*January 30, 1714/15.* Went to church to return God thanks for his mercies to me in delivering us out of so many imminent dangers. There is but one church in all Biddeford after the Church of England, and several meetings [that is, dissenting congregations].

*January 31, 1714/15.* Went to church, and we had a sermon on the Martyrdom of King Charles, but very bitter against the Presbyterians.[52] The ministers are very inveterate and one against the other here, but the presbyterians are the strongest side there being ten presbyterians for one churchman. In the afternoon I went to the Coffee House, where I met with two Presbyterian ministers.[53] We had a great deal of discourse, they offered me their services—so home.

*February 1, 1714/15.* Biddeford. I met with Dr. Mosey.[54] He dined with me and invited me to his house at Barnstable, but I could not go at that time, for my people were not quite settled and my goods not all landed.

[ 61 ]

*February 2, 1714/15.* I went to the town in which I see nothing worth taking notice of, only the market place which is made very convenient for the country people, and penthouses all round to cover the standings.

*February 3, 1714/15.* Being in company with the merchants and seeing they were getting all their ships ready for the Newfoundland trade, they told me that after being provided with hooks, lines, knives and salt which is but a very small charge, they must also provide three men for every boat they design to fish with, and all the provisions they carry is butter and pork, living for the most part of the time they are there upon fish, only Sundays they are allowed either beef or pork. They reckon it is time enough to arrive there by the last of April. As soon as they arrive they first unrig their ships, then the ship's crew set about building houses and stages for splitting the fish on. They always carry carpenters with them to build boats. The ship's crew are obliged to cut down the wood and draw it to the shore. There is no large timber there, the largest trees not exceeding one foot diameter. The knives for heading the cod are about 5 inches long in the blade, and with two edges in this form ⟨⟩ and the knives for splitting are about 8 inches long and but one edge, made after this form ⟨⟩. They have also drift nets for catching of bait. The chief bait is a small fish which they call Capeiulin [capelin]. Them that arrives first in the harbour take their choice place and are looked upon as Governor of the place for that season. They always call him My Lord. The Captains of the ships judge all matters. He that arrived first being President. The Inhabitants or planters being poor are no way regarded.[55]

*February 4, 1714/15.* I met with two French officers and was at the Coffee House. After went to one Mr. Davis[56] who is mayor of the town and I got a certificate from him with the seal of the town affixed to it which cost me half a crown. I drunk part of a pint of wine with him and left him. I writ to Mr. Arnaud, and sent the certificate enclosed in my letter to him desiring an answer from him.

*February 5, 1714/15.* I met with Dr. Mosey and he invited me to his house. I went with him. The road between Barnstable where he lives and Biddeford is very bad. They reckon it seven miles. About 3 in the afternoon I arrived at Barnstable where I was well received at his house, and after supper we drunk all our friends in Ireland and to bed.

*February 6, 1714/15.* I went with Dr. Mosey about five miles in the country to see one Dr. Barber,[57] an old friend of my fathers, where I was kindly received and well entertained. I gave a shilling to the maid. And about four of the clock we took our leaves of them and returned all along the road. I could not but admire the improvements and industry of the farmers. Every man had an orchard and cherry yard, which are both ornamental and profitable. They preserve their hedges after an extraordinary manner which furnishes them with hoops Lurgs [lugs, that is, boxes or baskets] and fireing, besides the shelter it is to their corn, hay and cattle against cold weather. Between five and six we arrived at Barnstable where we supped at the doctors and so went to bed.

*February 7, 1714/15.* Barnstable. I was at the electing of parliament men which was carried on in great order, without any dispute between the parties. They chose Squire Barlow and Squire Rouls.[58] There was a noble dinner and I was invited. I went there and got acquainted with the most of the gentlemen in town. After we had dined I retired with a clergyman of my new acquaintance. I went with him to his house where we supped and drank good wine. I took my leave of him and went to Dr. Mosey's where I lay.

*February 8, 1714/15.* About ten the Doctor and I mounted his horses and at 12 we came to Biddeford where I found all as I left it, only the board of my servants to pay. I waited on my merchant who told me he would despatch the ship.[59] I went to the doctor carried him to my lodgings, treated him with a dinner, and about five of the clock we mounted our horses, and arrived at his house about 7 where we supped and so to bed.

*February 9, 1714/15.* Remained at the doctors, where I laid out his garden for him, and contrived a summer house for him, which he was mightily taken with. We dined and supped here.

*February 10, 1714/15.* Went a visiting in town and was all day with the young ladies, where I passed the time very agreeably. I treated them with oranges. Money ill spent. Went to the doctors and to bed.

*February 11, 1714/15.* I went to visit Mr. Moonier[60] and after went to

Mr. Coulter[61] where I was well entertained and invited to come there when I would. If I send any tobacco here I design to consign it to Mr. Moonier. He having the name of a very honest man.

*February 12, 1714/15.* Barnstable. Doctor Mosey and I we went to Biddeford, where he got me acquainted with Mr. Buck,[62] Mr. Strange[63] and Mr. Pauly[64] the three chief merchants of Biddeford. They promised me letters of recommendation and gave me great encouragement to proceed on the voyage which God send may prosper. After I went with the doctor, where I treated him and about 5 we went out of town, and about 7 we came to the doctors where we supped and to bed.

*February 13, 1714/15.* Went to meeting and heard two presbyterian sermons. I returned to the doctors and to bed.

*February 14, 1714/15.* I went to see Mr. Pierd,[65] a dissenting Minister who was my fathers pupil, and I assured him my father was often talking about the kindness of the people of that place towards the French Protestants, and offered him my service. I went to see the town and it is most made up with old buildings, several of which are made with freestone. It is pleasantly situated upon a plain upon the side of a river that is navigable for small colliers who can come up as far as the Bridge which is very large.[66] This is one of the cleanest and neatest towns I ever was in. The chief part of the people are common spinners and weavers.[67] This is a place of no great trade because of the bar of sand that makes the coming in very dangerous for ships of any burthen. Biddeford and Appledore lying between this place and the sea impoverisheth it mightily. The country all about this place is very agreeable.

*February 15, 1714/15.* I went with Dr. Moss to Biddeford. I found all in good order, renewed my acquaintance with the merchants, and got acquainted with Mr. Berkeley[68] a presbyterian minister who promised me a letter of introduction for Boston. We dined in Biddeford and returned to Dr. Moseys house in Barnstable where we supped and to bed.

*February 16, 1714/15.* Barnstable. I went out a horseback with Dr. Moss into the country. We went to see several of my father's old acquaintance that entertained us very well. About 5 we came to the Doctor's house.

## February 12 to February 25, 1714/15

*February 17, 1714/15.* Being in want of money I went to Mr. Moonier's where I took up £5 and drew a bill upon Mr. Arnaud in London upon sight. The ship being almost ready, went down from the quay of Biddeford to Appledore, but the wind being out of the way I remained with the doctor.

[There is no entry for February 18, 1714/15.]

*February 19, 1714/15.* I went to visit the ladies and we diverted ourselves very agreeably. I was well treated. I treated them with oranges and so came to the doctors where we supped and to bed.

*February 20, 1714/15.* Dr. Mose and I took a walk all about the town to see all the good gardens there which are in abundance and very fine. I see abundance of Peach, Nectarine and apricot trees, which are very large, and they told me bear in abundance. There was several large vines and other fruit trees. We returned to the doctor's house where we dined and supped.

*February 21, 1714/15.* We rid out in the country about 6 miles where we were well treated by the farmers and drunk abundance of good cider and mead. They are well lodged and live extraordinary well. About 6 we returned and supped at the doctors.

*February 22, 1714/15.* Was invited to Mr. Jacob Moonier's, where I dined, and after dinner we drunk wine and passed the day away very aggreably with two young ladies and so retired to the doctors.

*February 23, 1714/15.* Dr. Mosse gave me a letter of recommendation to his wife's uncle who is a great merchant in Boston in New England, called Hugh Hutchinson[69] who is one of the chief men amongst the presbyterians in Boston. I took my leave of all my acquaintances in town and returned to the doctors where we supped and to bed.

*February 24, 1714/15.* I received a letter from Biddeford that the ship was in a readiness. I took my leave of the doctor and his wife and sisters and the doctor lent me his horse to Biddeford. I came to my lodgings at the post office about 5 of the clock, where I lay.

*February 25, 1714/15.* Accounting with my landlady, and paid of[f] my servants and my expenses. I bought several small provisions for my intended voyage and put myself in readiness to go on board.

*February 26, 1714/15.* Bought cooper's tools for More[70] and several other small goods. I hired a boat and sent all my people down to Appledore, where the ship is, to be ready to embarque.

*February 27, 1714/15.* I got my letters of recommendation from the ministers and merchants, took my leave of them and went down to Appledore to the ship.

# IV. Safe to Virginia and Williamsburg

*February 28, 1714/15.* In the road before Appledore. Wind fair we set sail for our intended voyage, by the grace of God, to Virginia. We passed over the bar of Biddeford. We take our departure from the island of Lundy in the latitude 51°18' for Cape Henry in the Virginias in the latitude of 37°6'—had the wind at S S E, almost calm. We met with a great current in the Channel. The Island of Lundy is in the longitude of 4°41'. The Capes of Virginia in the longitude 74°0'. Difference of Longitude 69°19', westing due 2850 miles, our true course W by S ½ W. This day being Monday.

*March 1, 1714/15.* At sea. Tuesday. Stormy weather. We steered our course W S W. The distance sailed for those last 24 hours was 51 miles. Southing we made 19 miles, westing 47 miles and we had no observation but reckon ourselves to be in the latitude 51°1'.

*March 2, 1714/15,* being Wednesday. We made our course good W by S, distance sailed 56 miles. Southing 11 miles westing 55 miles. Latitude by reckoning 50°40'. No observation. Weather stormy.

*March 3, 1714/15.* Thursday. We made our course good W by S ½ S 126 miles—southing 37 miles, westing 120 miles. No observation. Weather hazy. We reckon ourselves to be in latitude 50°3'.

*March 4, 1714/15.* Friday. In the morning we see a sail which came up with us steering the same course as we. It blows hard. We steered our course S W ½ Westerly. Distance sailed 56 miles—southing 43 miles—westing 35 miles. Latitude by our observation 49°23'.

*March 5, 1714/15.* Saturday. Wind N E—blew very hard. We lay by and drove due north about ten miles. Latitude by dead reckoning is 49°38′. We were still in sight of the ship that lay by with us. A very great sea.

*March 6, 1714/15.* Sunday. Wind N E. A good gale. We hoisted our sails and made our course good S W. Distance sailed 117 miles. We made southing 80 miles and westing 80 miles. We had an observation and found ourselves to be in the latitude of 48°18′.

*March 7, 1714/15.* Monday. Wind N E—not very hard. We made our course good S W by S 86 miles and made southing 12 miles westing 48 miles. We had no observation this day, but found ourselves by reckoning that we were in the latitude of 47°6′. We lost sight of the ship in company with us about eleven of the clock. She sails better than we do.

*March 8, 1714/15.* Tuesday. Wind came about S W by S, steered our course N W by W. Distance sailed 60 miles. We made 33 miles northing, and westing 50 miles. Latitude by reckoning 47°39′.

*March 9, 1714/15.* Wednesday. Wind contrary. We steered our course close haled [hauled] upon a wind, N W by W 55 miles. Southing 30 miles and westing 45 miles. Latitude by our reckoning in 48°9′.

*March 10, 1714/11.* Thursday. Wind continued foul, and we steered our course N W ¾ Westerly, made 48 miles. Northing 27 miles, westing 8 miles. No observation and we reckoned ourselves in latitude 48°20′.

*March 11, 1714/15.* Friday. Wind S S E fair. We steered our course N Westerly and made 48 miles. Northing one mile, westing 14 miles. We had no observation but reckon ourselves in the latitude 48°27′. The Master of the ship informed me that the boats which they build for fishing Cod in Newfoundland are built like the wherries at Dublin both ends sharp alike in this form ⬦. There are three men to every one of these boats and every ship fits out as many as they have men to send in those boats, and to save the fish catched, for the boatmen only take the fish and bring it ashore to the splitters, headers, throat cutters, salters and barrow men. When they have time, they save the tongues, sounds and fat. Of the fat they make oil, and the tongues and sounds they salt up in casks. The ships that first get into the harbour have the choice birth for their ships and for to build their stages, which is the place they split the Cod upon. The lower end of this platform or stage goes about ten feet in the water. It is supported by posts and planked upon the top, so that the boatmen can throw their fish out of the boat upon it. There is also a distance between the boards for the slime and guts to fall through into the water. This stage is about 35 foot long and 18 feet broad, at the upper end of which they build a small house to hold their salt in, and make a shed a little lower down to cover the fish from the rain whilst it lies in the salt. They have several tents made with their sails, that is upon the beach, they dry their fish on, to put the fish in at night. The chief provisions to be carried there is pork, flour, butter and a good quantity of brandy, without which there is no living there. The inhabitants not being able to raise any grain nor cattle, all they have is a few cows and goats which is the best thing they have. There are some horses. They have good gardens, which produce all sorts of things in the summer. We suppose that a ship keeps 6 boats a fishing, then he must have 3 men for every boat to go out a fishing, 3 throat cutters, 3 headers and 3 splitters, salters and barrow men 4—so you see how many men is requisite for to employ 6 boats fishing.

| | |
|---|---|
| Six boats, three men to a boat to fish only — | 18 men |
| Splitters for all the six boats | 3 men |
| Throat cutters for the six boats | 3 men |
| The headers for the six boats | 3 men |
| Salters and barrow men — | 4 men |
| In all to keep 6 boats a fishing you must have at least this number of men which is | 31 men |

The bait they have commonly to catch the Cod with is a small fish they call Capelin. There is abundance of lobster, shrimp and all sorts of good fish there. The masters of the ships when they arrive there, they agree together to judge of all things that shall happen in the time they remain there. The Captain that first comes into the harbour, he is President of the bench and called 'My Lord' for the time he stays there. The inhabitants of this place are very poor and miserable, therefore the masters of the ships take no notice of them but judge all matters amongst themselves.[71]

*March 12, 1714/15.* Saturday. Wind tolerable. Made our course S W ½ W 64 miles—and southing 40 miles—westing 45 miles. Had an observation and found ourselves to be in the latitude 47°47'.

*March 13, 1714/15.* Sunday. For this 24 hours we steered our course N N E and sailed 50 miles—northing we made 19 miles and easting 5 miles. We had an observation and found ourselves to be in the latitude 48°6′. Weather clear.

*March 14, 1714/15.* Monday. For this 24 hours we steered our course N W by W ¾ W and sailed 52 miles, northing ten miles—westing 22 miles. No observation, but reckon ourselves to be in the latitude 48°16′.

*March 15, 1714/15.* Tuesday. For these 24 hours we steered our course N W ¼ W and made 30 miles—northing 18 miles and westing 22 miles. Latitude by our reckoning 48°30′.

*March 16, 1714/15.* Wednesday. For these 24 hours we steered our course W S W and made 20 miles, southing 8 miles and westing 18 miles. The weather calm and clear. We had a good observation and found ourselves to be in the latitude 48°26′. Our ship in very good order.

*March 17, 1714/15.* Thursday. For this last 24 hours we steered our course S W by W and made 54 miles. Southing 31 miles and westing 44 miles. We had a good observation and found ourselves to be in the latitude 47°55′.

*March 18, 1714/15.* Friday. A fresh gale of wind and a smooth sea. We steered our course W S W ¼ Southerly and made 146 miles—southing 63 miles and westing 130 miles. Clear weather. We had a very good observation and find ourselves in the latitude 46°52′.

*March 19, 1714/15.* Saturday. The wind continues a good gale and fair. We steered our course for this 24 hours W by S ½ Southerly and made 117 miles—southing we made 32 miles westing 112. We have a good observation and find ourselves in the latitude 46°16′.

*March 20, 1714/15.* Sunday. Wind continues fair and for this 24 hours we steered our course W Southerly 113 miles—southing 12 miles westing 111 miles. Had a good observation and found ourselves to be in the latitude 46°4′.

*March 12, 1714/15.* Monday. Wind came about and the sea great. We steered our course W ¾ N and made 79 miles. Northing 11 miles westing 78 miles. Weather cloudy. No observation but reckon ourselves in the latitude of 46°15'.

*March 22, 1714/15.* Tuesday. Wind came about and blew a fresh gale and we steered our course S S W and made 138 miles—southing 2°8' and westing 58 miles. Latitude by reckoning 44°7'. No observation.

*March 23, 1714/15.* Wednesday. Wind at S E. We steered our course S by W and made 130 miles, southing 2°7' and westing 25 miles. We had an observation and found ourselves in the latitude 42°50'. We must correct our latitude by dead reckoning. About 12 o'clock we see some gulf weed and a turtle floating on the water.

*March 24, 1714/15.* Thursday. The wind moderate at E by S. We went at the rate of 2½ or 3 knots per hour. We made our course good W S W ¼ Westerly and sailed 70 miles. We made 23 miles southing and westing 66 miles. We have a good observation and find ourselves to be in the latitude of 41°42'. We reckon ourselves near the Island of Fayal [Faial in the Azores] and expect to see them. We see a small Blackbird about the bigness of a thrush which they call a Pettrell.

*March 25, 1715.* Friday. Wind at S and S W, almost calm till 10 of the clock in the morning it freshened up to N and N E—our course S W. We made 31 miles; southing 22 miles—westing 22 miles. No observation but reckon ourselves in the latitude 41°20'. We are 20 leagues to the westward of Faial and 410 leagues to the westward of Lundy Island.

*March 26, 1715.* Saturday. Wind at N W. We made our course good S W by S and made 66 miles, southing 55 miles—westing 36 miles and esteemed ourselves to be in the latitude 40°25'. We lay by 4 hours under our mainsail and wind blowing hard. We see a hazy ring about the sun which the sailors say is an infallible sign of bad or blowing weather and about 12 of the clock the wind came about westwardly against the sun, which they say is a sign of bad weather. So we have all the signs of bad weather, but I rely on Providence only.

*March 27, 1715.* Sunday. Wind stormy at W and W by N so that about 10 at night we brought to under our mainsail. We had a great sea. This 24 hours we made our course W by S ½ S—distance sailed 23 miles, southing 7 miles—westing 21 miles. Latitude by reckoning 40°18′—no observation.

*March 28, 1715.* Monday. Wind from W by N to W by S. It blew a fresh gale of wind. About 2 in the morning wind so strong that we lay under our mainsail two hours. After we lowered our mainsail and lay under our ballast mizen. We drove S by E ¼ Easterly 60 miles—Southing 55 miles Easting we made 26 miles. We had an observation and found ourselves to be in the latitude 39°18′. We shipped two seas but did not receive any damage.

*March 29, 1715.* Tuesday. Wind stormy from W to W by S. Lay under our ballast mizen and we drove S E by S ¼ Easterly 46 miles. To the south we made 38 miles, easting 28 miles. We had but an indifferent observation which shews we are in the latitude of 38°40′. We shipped several seas.

*March 30, 1715.* Wednesday. Wind somewhat abated being W Southerly we drove S E and made 48 miles—southerly 27 miles—easterly 27 miles. We had no observation but reckon ourselves to be in the latitude of 38°13′. We see a great deal of gulf weed.

*March 31, 1715.* Thursday. Wind very stormy at W S W, a very great sea. We lay under our mainsail and ballast mizen. We shipped several seas, but received no damage by them. We drove at the rate of 2 knots per hour E by N ½ N and made 20 miles—to the north we made 7 miles [and] to the eastward 19 miles. We had an observation but could not depend upon it. We reckon ourselves to be in the latitude of 38°20′. The weather is warm here and we find a sensible difference between this and Ireland. God be praised we are all in good health.

*April 1, 1715.* Friday. Wind at W by N Northerly. It blew very hard and we lay under our mainsail. About 5 of the clock at night the wind came to an excessive head so that it was as much as we all could do to lower and haul our mainsail. There came three squalls of wind that made the ship quiver like a leaf. We had no sail up. We drove away S S E distance of 20 miles, southing 8 miles, easting 18 miles. We had an observation and found ourselves to be in the latitude 38°12′.

## March 28 to April 9, 1715

*April 2, 1715.* Saturday. Wind from W by N to N W. Faired somewhat about 12 at night and we unreeved [unreefed] our mainsail and set it, as also our foresail. The wind abated, as also the sea. We made our course S E by S, 29 miles—southing 23 miles—easting 15 miles. Latitude by observation 37°49′.

*April 3, 1715.* Sunday. Wind at N W—a tolerable gale—the sea assuaged much. We steered our course S and made 84 miles, southing 1°25′. We had a good observation and are in the latitude 36°40′.

*April 4, 1715.* Monday. Wind at N W by N, almost calm, weather warm. Our course we made W ½ Southerly 11 miles, southing 1 mile—westing 9 miles. We had an observation and found ourselves in the latitude of 36°24′. We see a great log of wood pass by with barnacles about it.

*April 5, 1715.* Tuesday. Almost calm. What wind there was it came from the east. We steered our course west and made 12 miles, westing 12 miles. We are in the latitude 36°24′.

*April 6, 1715.* Wednesday. Wind came to blow a good gale at W S W and we steered our course W Southerly and made 83 miles. Southing 14 miles westing 82 miles. We had a good observation and found ourselves in the latitude 36°10′.

*April 7, 1715.* Thursday. Wind S W by S, a good easy gale of wind. We made our course good N W ¼ Westerly 100 miles, northing 1°6′, westing 75 miles. Latitude by observation 37°16′. We see a large tortoise floating upon the water with a piece of wood before him, on which they say he feeds.

*April 8, 1715.* Friday. Wind at W by N, a good gale of wind and showery. We steered our course N W 1/3 Westerly 72 miles. Northing 45 miles westing 55 miles. Latitude by dead reckoning 38°1′.

*April 9, 1715.* Saturday. A good fresh gale. We steered our course N W ¼ N—made 60 miles—northing 46 miles—westing 38 miles. We carried our courses. Gale hard and a chopping sea. We had no observation but by our reckoning we esteem ourselves to be in the latitude 38°47′.

*April 10, 1715.* Sunday. Wind at W. We steered our course S and made 60 miles—southing 60 miles. We had a good observation and we find ourselves to be in the latitude 37°47'.

*April 11, 1715.* Monday. Wind at West, very little. We made our course S 34 miles—southing 34 miles. We had a good observation and found ourselves to be in the latitude of 37°13'. At two in the afternoon we see two ships which bore of us W by N and coming stem for stem with us. When within a league of us one of them fired a gun, and when within a mile another fired, both under Turkish colours. They made us bring to, then they hoisted out their boats, and came on board of us, and would have bought any thing from us, but the master was afraid to trade with them. We found that they were Spaniards come from the river De la plata. They were laden with plate, furs and skins. They had been three years out of Cales [Cadiz?] in Spain and were now bound home. We told them the first news of the peace, which rejoiced them. They were very civil and paid well for what little things they had of us. Each gallionn was about five hundred tons and had forty guns a piece mounted, and full of men. Their reckoning and ours agreed very well together. They left us.

*April 12, 1715.* Wind at S by W—a fresh gale. We made our course good W by S Southerly and sailed 95 miles, southing 20 miles and westing 92 miles. By observation in the latitude 36°53'.

*April 13, 1715.* Wednesday. Wind S W by S. We made our course W by N ¼ Northerly. Northerly 10 miles, westerly 41 miles. By observation we are in the latitude 37°3'.

*April 14, 1715.* Thursday. Wind at S W by S, a good gale. We made our course N W ½ Westerly 87 miles. Northing 50 miles westing 63 miles. By observation found ourselves in the latitude 37°53'.

*April 15, 1715.* Friday. Wind S by W, a fresh gale. We steered our course W by S 108 miles, southing 20 miles, westing 105 miles. No observation, but reckon ourselves to be in the latitude 37°33'. The weather showery and it thundered and lightened the most part of the night.

*April 16, 1715.* Saturday. Wind at S by W. We steered our course westerly by N ½ Northerly 70 miles. Northing 20 miles, westing 66 miles. No observation. We reckon ourselves to be in the latitude 37°53'. We saw a sail which bore of us S W, and steered her course E. We could not speak with her. We suppose she is going for England. We see a large tortoise asleep.

*April 17, 1715.* Sunday. We steered our course N by W ½ Westerly and made 44 miles. Northerly 43 miles, westerly 13 miles. We had a good observation and found ourselves in the latitude 38°36'. Moderate weather.

*April 18, 1715.* Monday. Wind at N W by W, a fresh gale. We steered our course S W by S and made 90 miles, southing 16 miles westing 15 miles. Latitude by observation 37°20'. Every body was put upon allowance of a bottle water for 24 hours and a biscuit. The servants and people suffered. This saved the salt beef.

*April 19, 1715.* Tuesday. Wind at S by W. We steered our course W 32 miles. We had an observation and found ourselves to be in the latitude 37°20'.

*April 20, 1715.* Wednesday. Wind at S W by S. A fresh gale. We made our course W Northerly 39 miles. Northerly 2 miles, westerly 38 miles. Had an observation and are in the latitude 37°22'. We see flying fish.

*April 21, 1715.* Thursday. Close hulled [hauled] upon a wind. We made our course W S W and sailed 33 miles. Southing 13 miles—westing 30. By observation in the latitude 37°9'. We see a large ship bear of us N by W.

*April 22, 1715.* Friday. Wind at N by W. We steered our course N W by W 82 miles. Northing 48 miles. Westing 69 miles. Latitude observation 37°33'.

*April 23, 1715.* Saturday. Wind S W. We steered our course W Northerly 76 miles, northing 13 miles, westing 75 miles. Had a good observation and found we were in the latitude 38°6'. Stiff gale of wind.

*April 24, 1715.* Sunday. Wind at S W by W. Steered our course W N W ½ Northerly 57 miles, northing 24 miles, westing 52 miles. Latitude by observation 38°30'.

*April 25, 1715*. Monday. Wind at N W by N. We hoisted our sails and steered our course S S W 85 miles, southerly 72 miles, westerly 32 miles. By observation latitude 37°10′.

*April 26, 1715*. Tuesday. We steered our course N W by W ½ W. Made 54 miles northing 27 miles, westing 46. Latitude 37°37′.

*April 27, 1715*. Wednesday. We made our course W Northerly 61 miles. Northerly 2 miles and westerly 61 miles. Latitude by observation is 37°39′.

*April 28, 1715*. Thursday. We steered our course W by N Westerly, a swinging gale. We made 115 miles, northerly 26 miles, westerly 110 miles. By our observation we are in the latitude 38°5′.

*April 29, 1715*. Friday. Wind at S W by S. We steered our course W N W and made 93 miles, northerly 35 miles, westerly 86 miles. By observation 39°6′. We have a brisk gale of wind.

*April 30, 1715*. Saturday. Wind at N W. We steered our course S S W 59 miles, southing 54 miles, westing 23 miles. Latitude 38°30′. We had a great gust of wind and lightning, with rain. Had like to overset the ship. Sprung the maintop mast and laid the ship down in the water, and I see upon the fore and main topmast heads a small light fixed there like unto a small star. It continued there about 7 minutes. The sailors call this light a peazance[72] and they say tis a spirit, but it never appears only in the night and in rainy weather, so I believe it is some slimy thing or other that casts that light. About 10 of the clock in the morning we got a dolphin about 3½ feet long. It is a very dry fish and requires a great deal of sauce.

*May 1, 1715*. Sunday. Wind at N E, a good fresh gale. We sailed our course S W and made 150 miles, southing 106 miles, westing 106 miles. We had a good observation and find latitude 37°35′.

*May 2, 1715*. Monday. We steered our course W S W ¼ Westerly made 64 miles—southerly 27 miles, westerly 57 miles. Latitude 37°8′ by reckoning.

*May 3, 1715*. Tuesday. For this last 24 hours it was calm, no wind stirring but by our observation by the sun we find that we have been carried by the current[73] to the northward about 20 miles. So that we are now in the latitude of 37°28'. Weather warm and sultry.

*May 4, 1715.* Wednesday. Wind at E N E, steered our course S W made 67 miles, southing 47 miles, westing 47 miles. Latitude 36°41'. We see some dolphins and bonitos which is a fish larger than a Cod, and jumps out of the water like a salmon. We see some flying fish, which are about 6 inches long, and have leather wings like unto a bat, and fly when pursued sometimes  hundred yards and will dip themselves in the water and take their flight again, but can fly no longer than their wings or fins are wet.

*May 5, 1715.* Thursday. Wind from N W to N W by N, very little wind and sometimes calm. We steered our course S W and made by our reckoning 19 miles, southing 13 miles, westing 13 miles. We had a good observation and found ourselves in the latitude 37°17'. By our observation we find that there is a great current that hales [hauls] us insensibly away to the northward. For this last 24 hours it hath halled [hauled] us away about 23 miles.

*May 6, 1715.* Friday. We steered our course W by N, 60 miles, northing 12 miles, westing 53 miles. We had a good observation and find ourselves in the latitude 37°59' by what we find the current sets N E by N. It hath carried us to the northward this 24 hours 30 minutes.

*May 7, 1715.* Saturday. Wind at N W by W, a fine gale. We steered our course S W by S and made 68 miles, southing 33 miles and westing 56 miles. We had a good observation and found ourselves in the latitude 37°28'.

*May 8, 1715.* Sunday. Wind at N E. We steered our course S W by S ¼ Southerly and made 39 miles, southing 23 miles—westing 31 9/10. Latitude by our reckoning 37°5'. Weather hazy.

*May 9, 1715.* Monday. Wind W by N, a good gale. We made our course S ¾ Westerly made 74 miles, southing 13 miles westing 10 miles. By our observation we are in the latitude 36°19'. Good weather.

*May 10, 1715.* Tuesday. Wind at N W. Course steered S ¾ Westerly 58 miles northing 57 miles, westing 8 miles. No observation. We reckon ourselves in the latitude 35°22′. The use of the fore staff to take an observation by the north star. There are three veins that belong to this staff, which are made use of according to the distance you are from the pole. There is one vein called the vein of 90 degrees, which is never made use of but when you are near the pole. The vein of 60 degrees is also made use of in a north latitude and the vein of 30 which we made use of. There is but one vein made use of in a place. The degrees of latitude are marked upon the fore staff, so when you have a mind to observe you must take your vein and put it on your fore staff as near as you can guess to the latitude of the place you are in. When your vein is so settled you must place the end of your fore staff to the corner of your eye, so that by moving your eye you may be able to see the north star upon a line even with the upper edge of your vein and the horison even with the lower edge of your vein. When you can bring the vein to that place of the staff, that by putting your eye to the end of your staff you can see the star in a line from your eye and the upper end of the vein and that in the same time without stirring your head you can from your eye and the lower end of the vein see the horizon then your observation is right. Then when you have so found it, you must find the star's declination and work this observation after the same manner as an observation by the sun.[74]

*May 11, 1715.* Wednesday. Wind at N N W. It blew very hard. We lay by most of the time and drove to the S 48 miles. Had a good observation and found ourselves in the latitude 34°33′.

*May 12, 1715.* Thursday. Wind at N by W, a hard gale. Course S W ¼ Westerly 45 miles, southing 26 miles, westing 36 miles. Latitude by observation is 33°50′.

*May 13, 1715.* Friday. We have the wind at W N W, a fresh gale. We steered our course N and made 84 miles. We had an observation and we find ourselves to be in the latitude 35°14′. A great swell.

*May 14, 1715.* Saturday. We had a good gale of wind and steered our course N by W ½ W, made 27 miles, northing 25 miles westing 7 miles. We had a good observation and found ourselves in the latitude 35°40′. We see a great bank of gulf weed passing by us.

## May 11 to May 21, 1715

*May 15, 1715*. Sunday. Wind at S W by S, blew fresh. We steered our course N W by W 82 miles, northing 45½ miles, westing 58 miles. Latitude by observation 36° 19'. Warm weather and clear.

*May 16, 1715*. Monday. Wind variable and squally from S W to N by W. A great sea. Course made good was W by N ¼ Northerly 51 miles, northing 12 miles, westing 49¾ miles. Latitude 36° 31' by observation.

*May 17, 1715*. Tuesday. We steered our course W by S and made 45 miles, southing made 8¾ miles, westing 44 miles. Latitude by observation 36° 31'. About four in the afternoon we see two ships, one bore down upon us and we spake to her, she is called the Speedwell Gally of Bristol bound home from Jamaica, but would not take in any letters. The other ship steered on the same course and we suppose her to be bound for Virginia.

*May 18, 1715*. Wednesday. Weather calm till about four in the morning then it came up fresh to S W by S and we steered our course W N W 30 miles, northing 11 miles, westing 27 miles. Latitude by reckoning 36° 42'.

*May 19, 1715*. Thursday. Wind fresh at S W. We steered our course N W by W ½ Westerly 77 miles, northing 48 miles, westing 59 miles. Latitude by reckoning 37° 30'.

*May 20, 1715*. Friday. Wind at E N E. Made our course W N W 51 miles, northing 19 miles, westing 49 miles. Latitude 36° 23' by observation. We had a great fog all night and at 6 in the morning we were surprised by a gust of wind, thunder and lightening accompanied with a heavy rain. We had like to have received damage but God was pleased to preserve us as at other times. We find by this observation that the current sets S E at a great rate.

*May 21, 1715*. Saturday. We steered our course W ½ Northerly 50 miles. Northerly 5 miles, westerly 49 miles. We had no observation, but find ourselves in the latitude 36° 28'. About seven in the morning we see a ship on our larboard bow, and are in company with her. She steers the same course. We have taken a large shark with eleven young ones in the belly, each one above a foot long and all loose. They say that those young sharks goes out of the mother to feed and returns again into her mouth. We see several dolphins but got none.

*May 22, 1715.* Sunday. We steered our course W N W 27 miles, northerly 10 miles, westerly 24 miles. Had a good observation and found ourselves in the latitude 36°25'. We got a dolphin that was four feet five inches long and one foot broad by the head. We have a smooth sea and fair weather, but hot.

*May 23, 1715.* Monday. We steered our course W by N 63 miles, northerly 12 miles, westerly 61 miles. Had a good observation and find ourselves in the latitude 37°7'. About 12 at night we had a great gust of rain and thunder and find by our observation that there is a great current here which carries us away to the northward.

*May 24, 1715.* Tuesday. Wind at N E. We steered our course west 98 miles. We had a good observation and found we were in the latitude 37°5'.

*May 25, 1715.* Wednesday. We made our course W by S 60 miles, southing 11 miles, westing 58 miles. Latitude by observation 36°42'. At 12 we hove the lead and found 15 fathoms water and the sand was reddish with small stones. As soon as we came in soundings, the water changed his colour, and we see no more carvills nor gulf weed, but we meet with rock weed, a bird they call a penguin and gulls which they take to be undeniable marks of land.

*May 26, 1715.* Thursday. About 9 of the clock in the morning we see the land and this 24 hours made 20 miles—westing. About 12 we were up with Cape Henry.[75] We took an observation and found ourselves to be in the latitude 37°6'. I see a ship bound for London and sent a word by them to my father that I was well.

*May 27, 1715.* Friday. Chesapeake Bay, Virginia. We continued, wind being fair and before night we passed over the horse shoe, and by 2 in the morning we came by the Wolf-trap,[76] and about 10, we entered the mouth of Potomac River, which is made by Virginia on the west side, and Maryland on the east side. Those are the finest rivers that ever I was in, and all the borders of the rivers covered with noble trees. The planters that have been on board inform me that there is not much tobacco in the country this year. I have not been ashore as yet.

*May 28, 1715.* Saturday. Potomac River, Virginia. In the morning about 10 of the clock I landed in Virginia and walked about four miles to the collector one Mr. McCartney[77] to land my things, which cost me an English crown.[78] I enquired if my men would do well there, but I found no encouragement. A guinea passes for 26 shillings and all foreign coins go by weight. An ounce of silver passes for 6/3; and four pennyweight gold for 20 shillings.

*May 29, 1715.* Sunday. About 8 of the clock we came ashore and went to church[79] which is about 4 miles from the place we landed. The day was very hot and roads very dusty. We got to church, but came a little late. We had part of the sermon. The people seemed to me very pale and yellow. After the minister had made an end every one of the men pulled out their pipes and smoked a pipe of tobacco. I informed myself further about my own business, but found that Williamsburg was the only place for my design. I was invited to dinner by one Mrs. Hughes.[80] She lent me a horse and the master of the ship another and we went to her house where we dined, after which we went on board. I am resolved to hire a sloop and go to Williamsburg.

*May 30, 1715.* Monday. In the morning I went to one Captain Eskridge[81] and bargained with him for a shallop to go to Williamsburg. I am to give him £5 for the hire of her and to maintain my people. I went with the sloop on board and loaded my goods on her and made all things ready for this second voyage. I lay on board the ship where we had several planters that got drunk that night.

*May 31, 1715.* Tuesday. Virginia. This morning Captain Eskridge came on board our ship and I agreed to pay him his £5 in goods at 50 pr. cent. I gave him

| | | | |
|---|---|---|---|
| One piece of Linen containing 20 yards which came to | £3 | 6 | 8 |
| Eight pair shoes at 4/ a pair ..................... | 1 | 12 | 0 |
| One pair gloves I gave him ...................... | 0 | 1 | 4 |
| | £5 | 0 | 0 |

and so we left the ship and went that day as far as a place called Cone,[82] and here we remained the night. We had a gust but it did no damage.

*June 1, 1715.* Wednesday. Wind at N. We set our sails and we came within three miles of New Point Comfort[83] and the wind fell calm. Here we remained.

*June 2, 1715.* Thursday. We had the wind contrary and calm and we went a fowling and killed two fishing hawks and went to see some of the planters, which treated us well.

*June 3, 1715.* Friday. We set sail and made a shift to get as far as Wicocomico[83] where we cast anchor. We had a gust of rain which wet us through.

*June 4, 1715.* Saturday. We set sail and came as far as Yorktown and we landed at Gloucester and there we supped and lay that night. This town is of one side of York river and Yorktown on the other side opposite to it.

*June 5, 1715.* Sunday. We set sail in the morning and we had a fresh gale, as much as we could carry sail. About 12 we came to Queen's Creek and about 3 we came to the landing of Williamsburg and I left the men in the boat and went up to the town which is about a mile from the landing place.

*June 6, 1715.* Monday. In the morning I hired two carts and brought my goods up to town and agreed for a lodging for myself for diet and all for twenty-six shillings per month. I hired a shop and a house for my people and I writ to my father.

*June 7, 1715.* Tuesday. I waited on Governor Spotswood[84] and he assured me of all he could do and after I had been with him some time I took my leave of him. He invited me to dinner which I accepted of and I afterwards settled Morriset in his shop. I went to my lodgings and so to bed.

Here I remained until September 6, 1715, and made several acquaintance. I also met with an old brother officer, Mr. Irwin.[85] He did me a great deal of service.

# V. Land Hunting to Germanna

*November 9, 1715.* Saturday. Williamsburg, Virginia. At eight of the clock in the morning, Mr. Clayton[86] and I waited on Governor Spotswood. We tell him we were going to the German town to know if he had any service there. We breakfasted with him and at 9 we mounted our horses, and set out from Williamsburg, the roads very good and level. About 4 of the clock we came to Mr. Roots,[87] 25 miles from Williamsburg, where we crossed York river to West Point. I reckon the river to be about one mile and a half over in this place. This river of York divides itself here where we landed, which is West Point, into two rivers, the north branch called Mattapony river and the south branch Pamunkey river. Both of these rivers are navigable for about 40 miles from the place where they fork. A quarter after five we mounted our horses and rid five miles further and came to one Mr. Austin Moor's house,[88] upon Pamunkey [Fontaine means Mattaponi] river, where we were well entertained. We had good wine and victuals and we made this day in all 31½ miles which are of the same length as the miles about London but the roads good.

*November 10, 1715.* Sunday. King William County. We remained here all this day. I went to see Mr. Moor's improvements in the marsh, where by draining he hath very good hay. My horse is run away. We are kindly received here.

*November 11, 1715.* Monday. Not being in any hopes of finding my horse, I borrowed one of Mr. Moor. About 9 of the clock we sent the horses over Mattapony river in the boat and at 10 we took our leave of Mr. Moor and his wife[89] and went in a canoe which is made of the body of a large tree, that is about three feet in diameter, which they saw off about 20 feet long and afterwards saw off a slab of it and then dig it out hollow ⌣. Six or eight men may go in one of these canoes. As we were

[ 83 ]

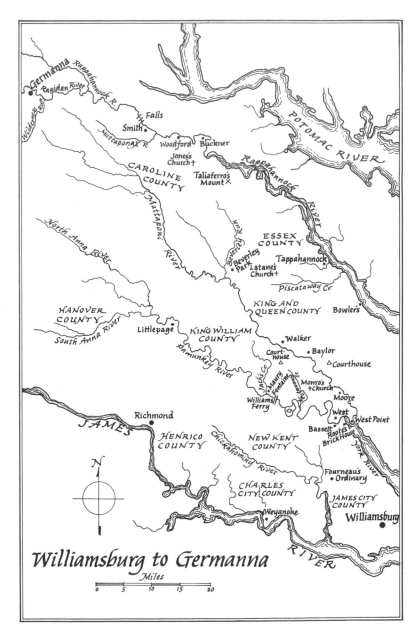

### Williamsburg to Germanna

Miles

0    5    10    15    20

This map shows the places mentioned by John Fontaine in his two journeys of 1715 and 1716 and the approximate location of his plantation.

going along the marsh I see the nest of a musk rat. This animal is about twice as big as a London rat and the same color as a beaver. It lives both in the water and on the land. I went to his nest which was made in the marsh of reeds and made about the bigness of a half hogshead. I pulled this building to pieces and found that it was made two stories high, and four rooms in it, two of a floor. The rooms were in the form of a pair of spectacles, two of those rooms above ground and two under ground ⌀⌀. So we continued on to the other side which is King and Queen County. At 11 of the clock we mounted our horses and went this day to Mr. Baylors[90] where we put up and were well entertained. He lives upon Mattapony river and is one of the greatest dealers for tobacco in the country.

*November 12, 1715.* Tuesday. About seven of the clock we breakfasted, about nine of the clock a servant of Mr. Moors brought me my horse to Mr. Baylors. About 11 we took our leaves and continued on our way, the day very windy. We see by the side of the road an Indian Cabin, which was built with posts put into the ground, the one by the other, as close as they could lay, and about seven feet high all of an equal length. It was built four square and a sort of roof upon it covered with the bark of trees. They say it keeps out the rain very well.[91] The Indian women were all naked, only a girdle they had tied about their waist, and they had about a yard of blanketing which they passed one end under the fore part of the girdle, and they pull this cloth so fastened before between their thighs and fasten the other end under the girdle behind, which covers their nakedness. Their beds were mats made of bullrushes. They lie upon them and had one blanket to cover them. All the household goods they had was a pot. We continued on our road, we see several squirrels and were on horseback till ten of the clock at night and then arrived to Mr. Robert Beverley's house[92] which they reckon from Mr. Baylors 30 miles. The roads very good. Here we were well received.

*November 13, 1715.* Wednesday. We remained here, it being blowing and showery weather. After breakfast we went to see Mr. Beverly's vineyard.[93] We see the several sorts of vines which are natural and grow here in the woods. This vineyard is situated upon the side of a hill and consists of about three acres of land. He assures us that he made this year about four hundred gallons of wine. He hath been at great expences about this improvement. He hath also caves and a wine press, but according to the method they use in Spain he hath not the right method for it, nor his vineyard is not rightly managed. He hath several plants of French vines amongst them.

*November 14, 1715.* Thursday. The weather was very bad and rained hard. We were very kindly received. We diverted ourselves within doors and drunk very heartily of the wine of his own making, which was good, but I found by the taste that he did not understand how for to make it. This man lives well, but has nothing in or about his house but just what is necessary, tho' rich. He hath good beds in his house but no curtains and instead of cane chairs he hath stools made of wood, and lives upon the product of his land.

*November 15, 1715.* Friday. Blowing weather. Mr. Beverley would not suffer us to go. He told me that the reason he had for making so large a vineyard was that about four years ago he made a wager with the gentlemen of the country, who thought it impossible to bring a vineyard to any perfection, made the following agreement with him that if he would give them one guinea then in hand they would give him ten if in seven years time he could cultivate a vineyard that would yield at one vintage seven hundred gallons of wine. Mr. Beverly gave a hundred guineas upon the above mentioned terms and I do not in the least doubt but the next year he will make the seven hundred gallons and win the thousand guineas. We were very merry with the wine of his own making and drunk prosperity to his vineyard.

*November 16, 1715.* Saturday. Mr. Beverly detained us and we went out a hunting. We see several deer but could kill none. We shot some squirrels and partridges, and went round a great tract of land that belongs to him and returned home. We passed the time very agreeably and so to bed.

*November 17, 1715.* Sunday. About ten of the clock we mounted our horses, Mr. Beverly with us and we went about seven miles to his parish church where we had a good sermon from a French man named Mr. De Lattiny,[94] who is minister of this parish. After dinner we returned to Mr. Beverly's house, and finished the day there.

## November 14 to November 20, 1715

*November 18, 1715.* Monday. Mr. Beverly's son[95] hindered us from proceeding on our journey this day, by promising to set out with us the next morning. So we took our guns and went a hunting. We killed some squirrels and partridge, but did no hurt to the wild turkies nor deer though we see several. Today we went to some of the planters houses where we diverted ourselves for some time and so returned to our friend's house and passed away the evening merrily.

*November 19, 1715.* Tuesday. In the morning about nine of the clock, we mounted our horses and took our leave of Mr. Beverly. His son came along with us. About eleven it rained hard until twelve, and about three we came to a place upon Rappahannoc River, called Taliaferro's Mount,[96] from whence we had a feeble view of the Appalachian Mountains, but a fine view of the river, which is navigable for large ships, and several fine islands in it. When we had satisfied our sight we continued on our journey and about six we arrived at one Mrs. Woodford's[97] who lives upon Rappahannoc river in a very agreeable place. This day we made 30 miles. This place is ten miles below the falls of Rappahannoc river and forty miles from the German settlement where we design to go.[98] We see upon the river abundance of ducks, geese and water pheasants. We were kindly entertained here.

*November 20, 1715.* Wednesday. At seven in the morning we took our leave of Mrs. Woodford. The gentlewoman gave us provisions with us and we put on our way and about 5 miles from Mrs. Woodfords we came upon a tract of three thousand acres of land which is in the disposal of Mr. Beverly, which he told me when I was at his house he would sell me at the rate of £7:10 per hundred acres. I rid over part of the land and found it to be well timbered and good. It fronts upon the river of Rappahannoc about half a mile, where vessels of 100 tons or sloops may come; and five miles above it I see a small river which runs through the heart of the land which river they call Massaponax,[99] and fit for to set mills upon. I would have agreed for this tract of land but that Mr. Beverly would not dispose of it as commonly land is disposed of, but would have the deeds made to me for nine hundred and ninety nine years, which I would not, but insisted on having it for me and my heirs for ever. So I did not buy the land of him. We continued on our way until we came five miles above this land, and there we went to see the Falls of Rappahannoc river, and the water run with such violence over the rocks and large stones that are in the river that tis almost impossible for boat or canoe to go up or down in safety. After we had satisfied our curiosity, we continued on the road. About five we crossed a bridge that was made by the Germans and about six we arrived to the German settlement. We went immediately to the minister's[100] house. We found nothing to eat but lived on our small provisions and lay upon good straw. We passed the night very indifferently.

*November 21, 1715.* Thursday. Our beds not being very easy, as soon as 'twas day we got up. It rained hard, but notwithstanding we walked about the town which is pallisaded with stakes stuck in the ground, and laid close the one to the other, of substance to bear out a musket shot. There is but nine families and they have nine houses built all in a line, and before every house about 20 feet from the house they have small sheds built for their hogs and hens, so that the hog stys and houses make a street. This place that is paled in is a pentagon, very regularly laid out, and in the very centre there is a blockhouse made with five sides which answers to the five sides of pales or great inclosure. There is loop holes through it, from which you may see all the inside of the inclosure. This was intended for a retreat for the people in case they were not able to defend the pallisadoes if attacked by the Indians. They make use of this Blockhouse for divine service. They go to prayers constantly once a day and have two sermons a Sunday. We went to hear them perform their service, which was done in their own language which we did not understand, but they seem to be very devout and sing the Psalms very well. This town or settlement lies upon Rappahannoc river 30 miles above the Falls and 30 miles from any Inhabitants. The Germans live very miserably. We would tarry here some time but for want of provisions we are obliged to go. We got from the minister a bit of smoked beef and cabbage, which was very ordinary and dirtily drest. We made a collection between us three of about thirty shillings for the minister, and about 12 of the clock we took our leave of them and set out to return, the weather hazy and small rain. In less than three hours we see 19 deer. About 6 of the clock we arrived at Mr. Smith's house[101] which is almost upon the Falls of Rappahannoc river. We have made this day 30 miles. He was not at home, but his housekeeper entertained us well. We had a good turkey for supper and beds to lie on.

*November 22, 1715.* Friday. At seven in the morning we mounted our horses and we met upon the road with two huntsmen. We went with them in the woods and in half an hour they shot a buck and a doe and took them on their horses. So we left them and continued on our road and about four of the clock we arrived at one Mr. Buckner's house[102] who lives upon Rappahannoc river, where we tarried that night. We had good punch and were very merry.

*November 23, 1715*. Saturday. At eight in the morning breakfasted and got our horses and continued on our road. About 11 we met with Mr. Beverly and went with him to see a piece of land he had to sell containing 500 acres. It lies upon Rappahannoc river, it fronts one mile on the river and on one side of it there is a large creek navigable for sloops, and there is an old house on the land, and 100 acres of cleared land about it, and the other 400 acres had wood growing on it, but all the large timber is cut down. He asked £15 per hundred acres for it, but I thought that too dear and we could not agree. We see several turkies in our way, but had no arms with us. About seven o clock at night we arrived at Mr. Beverly's house. We made this day about 38 miles.

*November 24, 1715*. Sunday. At 8 in the morning we got a horseback, and took our leave of Mr. Beverly and his son, who left us and so we put on our journey till we come to Mr. Thomas Walker's house[103] upon Mattapony river. Here we set up that night and were well entertained and made in all this day 25 miles.

*November 25, 1715*. Monday. My horse proving lame I was obliged to leave him at Mr. Walkers. I hired a horse and from thence we went to King and Queen Court House, where we dined and tarried there until four in the afternoon and were invited by Captain Story[104] to his house. We went with him and tarried all night. We had but indifferent entertainment.

*November 26, 1715*. Tuesday. In the morning we crossed York river Ferry to the Brick house.[105] About one we put up at Fourrier's ordinary,[106] where we dined. At two we set out from thence and at 5 in the afternoon we arrived at Williamsburg.

This journey going and coming from the German settlement comes to 292 miles[107] besides ferriages and cost me about £3:10:0.

# VI. The Indians at Fort Christanna

From November 1715 to October 1716 I remained at Williamsburg and put out notes [advertised] for my horse and in some months after I got him, but in the meantime which is February 7, 1715/16 I bought a horse which cost me £10 and March 20, trucked [traded] the horse which cost me £10 for another which I gave forty shillings in money to boot and the Governor proposed a journey to his settlement, on Meherrin river called Christanna.[108]

*April {13,} 1716.* Williamsburg. The first day. Governor Spotswood and I set out from Williamsburg about 8 of the clock in the morning and we went to James Town, in a four wheeled Chaise, which is situated close upon James River, eight miles from Williamsburg. This town chiefly consists in a church, a Court House[109] and three or four brick houses. This was the former seat of the Governor but now 'tis removed to Middle Plantation which they call Williamsburg. The place where this town is built is on an island[110] all surrounded with water and was fortified with a small rampart with embrasures, but now is all gone to ruin. Our horses were ferried over the river before us. We left the Chaise at Jamestown and about 10 of the clock we were in the ferry boat and crossed the river. They reckon this place to be about two miles broad. When we arrived to the other side of the river, we mounted our horses and set on the journey. It rained all this day very fast and we were well wet. About two of the clock we put into a planter's house and dined upon our own provisions and fed our horses, and about three we mounted our horses and came to a place called Simmons' Ferry[111] upon Nottoway River. There was a great fresh in the river so that we were obliged to swim our horses over and we passed in a canoe. Then we mounted our horses and put on till we came to one Mr. Hicks[112] his plantation upon one of the branches of Meherrin River called

Herrin Creek.[113] The man of the house was not at home, so we fared but indifferently. We made in all this day 65 miles.

*April {14,} 1716.* The second day. In the morning we set out with a guide for Christiana. For this house is the most outward settlement on this side of Virginia which is the south side. We have no roads here to conduct us, nor inhabitants to direct the traveller. There were several Indians that met us and about twelve we came to Meherrin River opposite to Christianna Fort. We see this day several fine tracts of land and plains called Savannas which lie along by the river side, much like unto our low meadow lands in England. There is neither tree nor shrub that grows upon those plains, nothing but good grass, which for want of being mowed or eat down by the cattle grows rank and coarse. Those places are not miry, but good and firm ground. Those plains are subject to inundations after great rains and when the rivers overflow, but there is seldom above 6 or 8 inches water over them, which may be easily prevented by ditching it. In about half an hour after twelve we crossed the river in a canoe and went up to the fort which is built upon a rising ground. It is an inclosure of five sides, made only with pallisadoes, and instead of five bastions, there are five houses which defend the one the other—each side is about one hundred yards long. There are five cannon here, which fired to welcome the Governor. There are 12 men continually here to keep the place. After all the ceremony [was] over we came into the fort and we were well entertained. The day proving wet and windy, we remained within doors and we employed ourselves reading of Mr. Charles Griffiths[114] his observations on the benefits of a solitary life. We reckon that we made this day 15 miles. In all from Williamsburg 80 miles.

*April {15,} 1716.* The third day. Christanna Fort. About 9 in the morning we got up and breakfasted. Mr. Griffiths who is an Englishman, he is employed by the government to teach the Indian children and to bring them to Christianity. He remains in this place and teaches them to read the Bible and Common Prayers, as also to write, and the English tongue. He hath had good success amongst them. He hath now been a year amongst them. He told the Governor that the Indian Chiefs or Great Men, as they style themselves, were coming to the Fort to compliment him. These Indians are called Saponey Indians,[115] and are always at peace with the English. They consist of about 200 persons, men, women and children

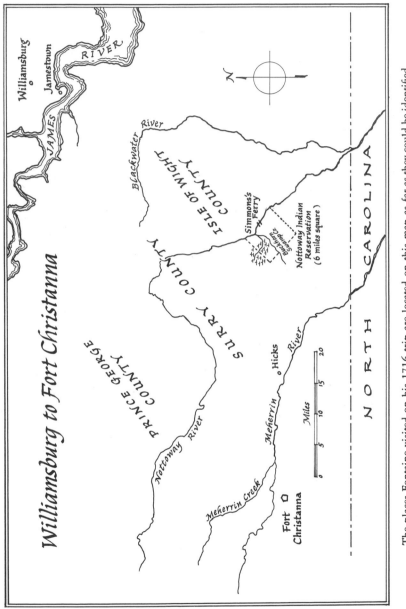

## Williamsburg to Fort Christanna

Williamsburg
Jamestown
JAMES RIVER
Blackwater River
ISLE OF WIGHT COUNTY
Simmons's Ferry
Nottoway Indian Reservation (6 miles square)
PRINCE GEORGE COUNTY
SURRY COUNTY
Nottoway River
Hicks
Meherrin River
Meherrin Creek
Fort Christanna
NORTH CAROLINA

Miles
0  5  10  15  20

N

The places Fontaine visited on his 1716 trip are located on this map as far as they could be identified.

and live within musket shot of this fort and are protected by the English, and under covert of this fort from the insults of the other Indians, who are at difference with the English. Those Indians pay a tribute to the Governor every year to renew and confirm the peace and shew their submission. This nation hath no king at present, but are governed by twelve of their old men, which have power to act for the whole nation, and they will stand to every thing that those twelve men agree to, as their own act. Those twelve men came to the Fort about 12 of the clock, and brought with them several skins, and as soon as they came to the Governor they laid them at his feet, and then all of them as one man made a bow to the Governor, and then desired an interpreter, saying they had something to represent to him. Notwithstanding some of them could speak good English, yet when they treat of any thing that concerns their nation, they will not treat but in their own language, and that by an interpreter, nor will not answer to any question made to them without it be in their own tongue. So the Governor got an interpreter, after which they stood silent for a while, and after they had spit several times upon the ground one of them began to speak and assured the Governor of the satisfaction they had of seeing him amongst them and assured him of the good will they had towards the English— and that some of the English had wronged them in some things which they would make appear, and desired he would get justice done to them, that they depended on him for it; which the Governor promised he would, and thanked them for the good opinion they had of his justice towards them. Whereupon they all made a bow and so sat down on the ground all round the Governor.

The first complaint they made was against another nation of Indians called Genitos,[116] had surprised a party of their young men that had been out a hunting and murdered 15 of them without any reason, and desired the Governor to assist them to go out to war with these Genitoes Indians until they had killed as many of them, but this the Governor could not grant them, but told them he would permit them to revenge themselves, and help them to powder and ball, at which they seemed somewhat rejoiced. They also complained against some of the English, who had cheated them, but the Governor paid them for what they could make out they were wronged of by these English, which satisfied them. Afterwards the Governor made them several presents and so dismissed them.

About three of the clock came fifty of the young men with feathers in their hair, and run through their ears, and their faces painted with blue and vermilion, and their hair cut in many forms. Some left one side of their hair on, and others had their hair cut on both sides and on the upper part of the head, made it stand like a cock's comb, and they had blue and red blankets wrapped about them. They dress themselves after this manner when they go to war the one with the other so they call this their war dress, which really is very terrible and makes them look like so many furies. Those young men made no speeches, only walked up and down and seemed to be very proud of their most abominable dress.

After this came the young women. They have all long straight black hair which comes down to their waist. They had each of them a blanket tied about their waists, and it hung down about their legs like a petticoat. They have no shifts or any thing to cover them from their waists up, but go naked. Others of them there was that had two deer skins sewed together and they threw it over their shoulders like a mantle. They all of them grease their bodies and head with bear's oil, which with the smoke of their cabins gives them an ugly hue. They are very modest and very true to their husbands. They are straight, well limbed, good shape and extraordinary good features as well the men as the women. They look wild and are mighty shy of an Englishman and will not let you touch them. The men marry but one wife and cannot marry any more until she die or grow so old that she will not bear any more children. But when she hath done bearing, then the man may take another wife, but is obliged to keep them both and maintain them. They take one another without ceremony.

Here are some of the Indian words.[117]

| | |
|---|---|
| The Sun | My[118] |
| Come here | Kihoe[119] |
| Stay | Monotisnock[120] |
| Is this the way to the horse head | Hodke tock ire chunkete posse[121] |
| Brother | Ohenopse[122] |
| Presently | Inking[123] |
| My dear wife | Mihu mima Mikito[14] |
| snake | moka[125] |
| gun | mikta[126] |
| Powder horn | Tabike[127] |
| Shot bag | Miktoke[128] |
| Stockings | Honis[129] |
| Breeches | Lonoughte[130] |
| Coat | Opockhe[131] |

| | |
|---|---|
| shirt | Opockhe hassa[132] |
| wig | Machneto dufas[133] |
| Hat | Apato Bokso[134] |
| Shoes | Makasoons;[135] agohele[136] |
| Otter | Mosnukhe[137] |
| Sword | Impough[138] |
| powder | Mahinkt[139] |
| Shot | Mankey[140] |
| water | Money[141] |
| How d'ye do? | Jog de log[142] |
| Will you kiss me? | Ke ly pomerin[143] |
| Yes | Keneha[144] |
| Come to bed | Conopanan[145] |
| What you please | Ikiron[146] |
| No | Metaugh[147] |
| My service to you[r?] queen | Kenepaskiniwiky[148] |
| I am going to be sured [saved or served?] | Joquahingnomotsonan[149] |
| I thank you sir | Ketemaghketersinaw[150] |
| You are very welcome | Mecouremechin[151] |
| One | Nacout[152] |
| Two | Tock[153] |
| Three | Nos[154] |
| Four | Jow[155] |
| Five | Prance[156] |
| Six | Quiock[157] |
| Seven | Tappons[158] |
| Eight | Massons[159] |
| Nine | Ketaugh[160] |
| Ten | Metough[161] |
| Eleven | Os nacout[162] |

And so add *Os* all along until you come to 19.

| | |
|---|---|
| Twenty | Takabosque[163] |

*April 16, 1716.* At Christiana. The fourth day. In the morning I rid out
with the Governor and some of the people of the fort to view the lands
which were not yet taken up. We see several fine tracts of land, well
watered and good places to make mills on. I had a mind to take some of it
up, so I asked the Governor if he would permit me to take up 3000 acres

of land. He gave me his promise for it.[164] I went through the land I designed to take up and viewed it. It lies upon both sides of Meherrin River, and I design to have it in a long square, half one side and half the other, so that I shall have at least three miles of the river in the land. I am informed that this river disgorgeth itself into the Sound of Currytuck[165] but this river tho' large and deep is not navigable because of the great rocks it falls over in some places. There is a great deal of fish in this place. We had two for dinner about 16 inches long which are very good and firm. I gave ten shillings to Captain Hicks[166] for his trouble of shewing me the land, and he promises me he will assist me in surveying of it. We see several turkies and deer, but we killed none. We returned to the Fort about 5 of the clock.

[*April 17, 1716.*] The fifth day. After breakfast I went down to the Saponey Indian town, which is about a musket shot from the fort. This town lieth in a plain by the river side. I walked round the town to view it. The houses join all the one to the other and altogether make a circle. The walls of their houses are large pieces of timber, which are squared and being sharpened at the lower end, they are put above two feet in the ground and about seven feet above the ground. They laid them as close as they could the one to the other, and when these posts are all fixed after this manner then they make a sort of a roof with rafters and cover the house with oak or hickory bark, which they strip off in great flakes, and lay it so closely that no rain can come in. Some of their houses are covered in a circular manner which they do by getting long saplings and stick each end in the ground and so cover them with bark, but there is none of the houses in this town so covered.[167] There is three ways of coming into this town or circle of houses which are passages of about 6 feet wide between two of the houses. All the doors of the houses are on the inside of the ring and it is very level withinside which is in common with all the people to divert themselves. There is also in the centre of the inside circle a great stump of a tree. I asked the reason they left that stand, and they informed me it was for one of their head men to stand on when he had any thing of consequence to relate to them, that being raised, he may the better be heard.

The Indian women bind their children to a board that is cut after the shape of the child. There is two pieces at the bottom of this board to tye the child's legs to, and a piece cut out behind so that all that the child doth falls from him and he is never dirty nor never wants to be changed. The head or top of the board is round, and there is a hole through the top of it, through which there is a string so that when the women are tired holding of them or have a mind to work they hang the board on which the children are tied to the limb of a tree or to a pin in a post for that purpose, and there the children swing about and divert themselves and are out of the reach of any thing that may hurt them. They keep those children this way until they are almost two years old, which I believe is the reason they are all so straight, and so few of them that are lame or odd shaped. Their houses are pretty large, never have no garrets nor no other light than the door and the light that comes in from the hole in the top of the house, which is to let out the smoke. They make their fires always in the middle of the houses. The chief of their household goods is a pot and wooden dishes and trays they make themselves. They seldom have any thing in their houses to sit upon, but sit commonly on the ground. They have small divisions in their houses to lie in. This is made with mats which they make of bullrushes. They also have bedsteads which raise them about two feet off the ground, upon which they lay bear and deer skins instead of a quilt. All the covering they have is a blanket. Those people have no sort of tame creatures, but live altogether upon their hunting and corn, which their wives cultivate. They live as lazily and miserable as any people in the world.

Between the town and the river upon the river side there are several little huts built with wattles in form of an oven with a small door in one end of it. These wattles are plaistered without side with clay very close, and they are big enough to hold a man. They call those houses sweating houses, for when they have any sickness they get 10 or 12 pebble-stones which they make very red in a fire and when they are red hot they carry them in those little huts and the sick man or woman goes in naked, only a blanket with him and they shut the door upon them and there they sit and sweat until they are no more able to support it and then they go out naked and immediately jump into the water over head and ears. This is the remedy they have for all distempers.

[*April 18, 1716.*] The sixth day. Christiana. The Governor sent for all the young boys, and they brought with them their bows, and he got an axe which he stuck up and made them all shoot by turns at the eye of the axe, which was about 20 yards distance. The Governor had looking glasses and knives which were the prizes the boys shot for. They were very dexterous at this exercise and very often shot through the eye of the axe. This diversion continued about an hour.

The Governor asked the boys to dance a war dance so they prepared for it and made a great ring. The musician being come he set himself in the middle of the ring, and all the instrument he had was a piece of a board and two small sticks. The board he set upon his lap and began to sing a doleful tune, and by striking on the board with his sticks he accompanied his voice and made several antic motions, and sometimes shrieked hideously, which was answered by the boys. According as the man sung so the boys danced all round endeavouring who could outdo the one the other in antic motions, and hideous cries. Their motions answered in some way to the time of the music. All that I could remark by their actions was that they were representing how they attacked their enemies, and would relate the one to the other how many of the other Indians they had killed, and how they did it, making all the motions in this dance as if they were actually in the action. By this lively representation of their warring one may see the base way they have of surprising and murdering the one the other and their inhuman way of murdering all their prisoners, and what terrible cries they have when they are conquerors. After the dance was over the governor treated all the boys, but they are so little used to have a belly full that they rather devoured their victuals than any thing else. So this day ended.

[*April 19, 1716.*] The seventh day. Christiana. After breakfast we assembled ourselves, and read the Common Prayer. There was with us eight of the Indian boys who answered very well to the prayers and understand what is read. After prayers we dined and in the afternoon we walked abroad to see the land which is well timbered and very good. We returned to the Fort and supped. Nothing remarkable.

[*April 20, 1716.*] The eighth day. Christiana. About ten in the morning there came to the fort ten of the Meherrin Indians[168] to trade, laden with beaver, deer and bear skins, for our Indian Company[169] have goods here for that purpose. They delivered up their arms to the white men of the fort, and left their skins and furs there also. Those Indians would not lie in the Indian town but went in the woods where they lay until such time as they had done trading.

The Governor and I we laid out an avenue about half a mile long, which gave us employment enough this day.[170]

*April* [21,] *1716.* Christiana. The ninth day. About seven in the morning we got a horseback and were just out of the fort when the cannon fired. We passed down by the Indian town, where they had notice that the Governor was returning, so they got twelve of their young men ready with their arms, and one of their old men at the head of them, and assured the governor they were sorry he would leave them, but that they would guard him safe to the Inhabitants, which they pressed upon him so that he was forced to accept of it. They were all a foot, so the governor to compliment the head man of the Indian party lent him his lead horse, but after we had rid about a mile we came to a ford of Meherrin River, and we put in, but being mistaken in our water mark, we were sometimes obliged to make our horses swim, but got over safe. The Indian Chief seeing that, he unsaddles his horse, and strips himself all to his belt and clout that covered his nakedness, and forded over the river leading his horse after him. The fancy of the Indian made us all merry for a while. The day being warm and the Indian not accustomed to ride, before we went two miles, the horse threw him down, but he had courage enough to mount again, and by the time we had got a mile further he was so terribly galled that he was forced to dismount and desired the Governor to take his horse, and could not imagine what good they were for, if it was not to cripple the Indians. We were forced to ride easy that we make [might] keep company with our Indian Guard, who accompanied us as far as a river called Nottoway river, which taketh its name from the Nottoway Indians,[171] who formerly lived upon this river. This place is about 15 miles from the fort. Here we parted with our guard of Indians and the Governor ordered them to have a pound of powder, and shot in proportion, to each man. So they left us. We crossed this river and rid fifteen miles farther until we came to a poor planter's house, where we put up for that night. They had no beds in the house, so the Governor lay upon the ground and had his bear's skin under him. I lay upon a large table in my cloak, and thus we fared until day which was welcome to us.

*April* [22,] *1716.* The tenth day. On our way to Williamsburg. At 5 we got up and at 6 we mounted our horses and we took a guide who pretended to know the way and bring us a short cut, but instead of that he brought us out of our way about seven miles. When we found that he was lost, we dismissed our guide. The sun shined out clear, so the Governor he conducted us and about four of the clock we came to James River and took the ferry and about 6 of the clock we mounted our horses and went to Williamsburg, where we arrived about 8 of the clock. I supped with the Governor, and being well tired, after went to my lodgings and to bed. This journey coming and going comes to one hundred sixty miles.[172]

# VII. Over the Blue Ridge

*August 20, 1716.* [Monday]. Williamsburg, Virginia. In the morning got my horses ready and what baggage was necessary and I waited on the Governor who was in a readiness for an expedition over the Appalachian Mountains. We breakfasted and about ten got on horseback, and at four came to the Brick house[173] upon York river, where we crossed the ferry, and at 6 we came to Mr. Austin Moors house [174] upon Mattapony river in King William County. Here we lay all night well entertained.

*August 21, 1716.* [Tuesday]. King William County. At ten we set out from Mr. Moors and crossed the river of Mattapony and continued on the road, fair weather, and were on horseback till nine of the clock at night before we came to Mr. Robert Beverly's house,[175] where we were well entertained and remained here this night.

*August 22, 1716.* [Wednesday]. Essex County. At nine in the morning we set out from Mr. Beverly's. The Governor left his chaise here, and mounted his horses. The weather fair we continued on our journey until we came to Mrs. Woodford's[176] where we lay and were well entertained. This house lies on Rappahannoc river, ten miles below the Falls.

*August 23, 1716.* [Thursday]. Mrs. Woodford's. Here we remained all this day and diverted ourselves and rested our horses.

*August 24, 1716.* [Friday]. Mrs. Woodford's. In the morning at seven we mounted our horses, and came to Mr. Austin Smith's house[177] about ten, where we dined and remained till about one of the clock. Then we set out, and about nine of the clock we came to the German town,[178] where we set up that night. Bad beds and indifferent entertainment.

*August 25, 1716.* [Saturday]. Germantown. After dinner we went to see the mines,[179] but I could not observe that there was any good mine. The Germans pretended that 'tis a silver mine. We took some of the ore and endeavoured to run it, but could get nothing out of it and I am of opinion it will not come to any thing, not as much as lead. There are many of the gentlemen of the country concerned in this work. We returned and to our beds, hard beds.

*August 26, 1716.* [Sunday]. Germanna. At seven we got up and several gentlemen of the country that were to meet the governor at this place for the expedition, came here, as also two companies of Rangers, consisting each of 6 men and an officer[180] to each company, as also four Meherrin Indians. In the morning I diverted myself shooting at a mark with the other gentlemen. At twelve we dined and after dinner we mounted our horses and crossed Rappahannoc river that runs by this place and went to find some convenient place for our horses to feed in and to view the land hereabouts. Our guide left us and we went so far in the woods that we did not know the way back again, so we hallooed and shot, and in half an hour after sunset the guide came to us, and we came to cross the river by another ford higher up. The descent to the river being steep and the night dark, we were obliged to dismount and lead our horses down to the river side through the bushes, which was very troublesome and the greatest part of our company dismounted, the bank being steep and went into the water to mount their horses where they were up to the crotch in the water. After we forded the river and came to the other side where the bank was steep also and one of our company going up, his horse fell back upon the top of him in the river, but he received no other damage than being heartily wet which made sport for the rest. A hornet stung one of the gentlemen in the face, which swelled prodigiously, and about ten we came to the town, where we supped, and to bed.

*August 27, 1716.* [Monday]. Germanna. At ten we got our tents in order, and getting of our horses shod.[181] About twelve I was taken with a violent headache, and pains in all my bones so that I was obliged to lie down and was very bad that day.[182]

*August 28, 1716.* [Tuesday]. Germanna. About one in the morning I was taken with a violent fever and it continued till twelve. At six at night my fever abated and I began to take the bark,[183] and had one ounce divided into eight doses, and took two doses. By ten of the clock that night the fever abated, but great pains in my head and bones.

*August 29, 1716.* [Wednesday]. Germanna. In the morning we got all things in readiness and about one we left the German town for to set out on our intended journey. At five in the afternoon the governor gave orders to encamp near a small river three miles from Germanna, which we called Expedition Run.[184] Here we lay all night. This first encampment was called Beverly Camp in honour of one of the gentlemen in our company.[185] Here we remained this night. We made great fires and supped and drunk good punch. By ten of the clock I had taken all of my ounce of Jesuit's Bark, but my head was much out of order.

*August 30, 1716.* [Thursday]. Beverly Camp. In the morning about seven of the clock the trumpet sounded to awake all the company, and we got up. One Austin Smith,[186] one of the gentlemen with us, having a fever returned home, and left us at nine in the morning. We sent our servants and baggage before us. We all lay on the ground. We had tents, but we found by the pains in our bones that we had not good beds to lie on. We remained here because two of the governor's horses strayed and at half an hour after two we got the horses, and at three we mounted and half an hour after four, we came up with our baggage (three miles) to a small river which we called Mine River, because there was an appearance of a silver mine by it, and we made about three miles more until we came to another small river, which is at the foot of a small mountain, so we encamped here and called this Mountain Run,[187] and our camp we called Todd Camp.[188] We had here good pasturage for our horses, and venison in abundance for ourselves which we roasted before the fire on wooden forks, and so we went to bed in our tents. Made 6 miles this day.

*August 31, 1716.* [Friday]. From Todd's Camp. At eight in the morning, we set out from Mountain river, and about five miles from this place we came upon the upper part of Rappahannoc river. One of the gentlemen and I, we kept out on one side of the company about a mile to have the better hunting. I see a deer, and off my horse I shot him, but my horse threw me, a terrible fall, and run away. We run after and with a great deal of difficulty we got him, but we could not after find the deer we shot and we lost ourselves for about two hours before we could come upon the track of our company. About five miles farther we crossed the same river again, and two miles farther we met with a large bear and one of our company shot him and I got the skin. We killed several deer, and about two miles from the place where we killed the bear we encamped upon Rappahannoc river[189] and from our encampment we see the Appalachian Hills very plain. We made large fires, pitched our tents and cut boughs to lie upon, and had good liquor and at ten we went to sleep. We always kept one Sentry at the governor's tent door. We called this A[?] Smith's Camp.[190] We made this day fourteen miles straight way.

*September 1, 1716.* [Saturday]. Smith's Camp. About eight we mounted our horses, and we made about six miles of our way through a very pleasant plain which lies where Rappahannoc River forks. There is the largest timber that ever I see, the finest and deepest mold, and good grass upon it. We had some of our baggage put out of order and some of our company dismounted by the Hornets that stung the horses. This was some hindrance and did a little damage, but afforded a great deal of diversion. We killed three bears this day, which exercised the horses as well as the men. About five of the clock we came to a run of water at the foot of a hill where we pitched our tents. We see two bears, but did not pursue them. We killed some deer. We called this Dr. Robinson's Camp,[191] and the river Blind Run.[192] We had good pasturage for our horses, and every one was cook for himself and we made our beds with bushes as before. We made this day about 13 miles in our way.

*September 2, 1716.* [Sunday]. Dr. Robinson's Camp. At nine we were all on horseback, and about five miles off we crossed almost the head of Rappahannoc River, where it is very small. We had a very rugged way. We passed over a great many small runs of water which were some very deep and others very miry. Several of the company were dismounted, some down with their horses and sometimes under them, others thrown off. We see a bear running down a tree, but it being Sunday we did not endeavour to kill any thing. At five we encamped by a small river we called White Oak River,[193] and called our camp Taylor's Camp.[194]

*September 3, 1716.* [Monday]. Taylor's Camp. About eight were on horseback, and about ten we came amongst a thicket that was so well laced together that in getting through it tore off a great deal of our baggage and our clothes all to rags, and the saddles and holsters off. And had a great deal of trouble to get through this place. About five of the clock we came to the head almost of James River. Here we encamped. This place lies at the foot of the great mountains.[195] We called this camp Colonel Robertson's Camp.[196] We made all this day but eight miles.

*September 4, 1716.* [Tuesday]. Colonel Robertson's Camp. We had two of our men sick with the measles and one of our horses poisoned by a rattlesnake. We remained here till about twelve, and took the heaviest of our baggage, and our tired horses and the sick men and made as convenient a lodge for them as we could and left with them people to guard them and hunt for them, and so we set out. The sides of the mountains are so full of vines and briars that we were forced to clear most of the way before us. We crossed one of the small mountains this side the Appalaches. From the top of it there is a fine prospect of the plains below. We were obliged to walk up the most of the way, there being abundance of loose stones on the side of the hill. I killed a large rattlesnake here, and the other people killed three more. We made about four miles and so we came to the side of James River where a man may jump over it and here we encamped and pitched our tents,[197] and as the people were lighting the fire there came out of a large log of wood a prodigious snake which they killed. We called this "rattlesnake camp," but this camp was otherwise called Brooks Camp.[198]

*September 5, 1716.* [Wednesday]. Brooks Camp. At nine we were mounted, a fair day; we were obliged to have axemen to clear the way in some places. We followed the windings of the top of James River, observing that it came from the very top of the mountains. We killed two rattlesnakes. In our way up this hill it is in some places very steep and in others so that we could ride it up. About one of the clock we came to the top of the mountain; which is about four miles and a half, and came to the very head spring of James River[199] where it runs no bigger than a man's arm, from under a large stone. We drunk King George's health here and all the Royal Family. This is the very top of the Appalachian Mountains. About a musket shot from this spring there is another which rises and runs down on the other side. It goes westward. We thought we could go down that way but met with such prodigious precipices that we were obliged to return to the top again. We found some trees which had been formerly marked, I suppose by the Northern Indians, and followed those trees and found a good safe descent. Several of the company were for returning but the Governor persuaded them to continue on. About five we were down on the other side and continued our way for about seven miles further until we came to a large river where we encamped by the side of it.[200] We made this day 14 miles. I being somewhat more curious than the rest went on a high rock on the top of the mountain to see fine prospects and I lost my gun. We see when we were over the mountains the feeting of several Elks and Buffaloes and their beds. We eat very good grapes, and see a vine which bore a sort of wild cucumber, and a shrub which bore a fruit like unto a currant. We called this place Spotswood Camp.

*September 6, 1716.* [Thursday]. Spotswood Camp (Our Governor). We crossed this river which we called Euphrates.[201] It is very deep and the main course of the water is north. It is four score yards wide in the narrowest place and about two foot and ½ water from side to side. We drank some healths on the other side and returned, after which I went a swimming in it. It being deep in several places, no place of it fordable as we could see only the place we forded. I got some grass hoppers and fished. And another and I we catched a dish of fish. We took some perch and a fish they call Chubb. The others went a hunting and killed deer and turkies. The Governor had graving irons but could not grave any thing the stones were so hard. I graved my name on a tree by the river side and the governor buried a bottle with a paper enclosed in which he writ that he took possession of this place in the name and for King George 1st of England. We had a good dinner. After dinner we got the men all together and loaded all their arms and we drunk the King's health in Champagne, and fired a volley; the Prince's health in Burgundy, and fired a volley; and all the rest of the Royal Family in Claret, and a volley. We drunk the Governor's health and fired another volley. We had several sorts of liquors, namely Virginia Red Wine and White Wine, Irish Usquebaugh, Brandy, Shrub, two sorts of Rum, Champagne, Canary, Cherry punch, Cider, Water &c. I sent two of the Rangers for to look for my gun which I dropped in the mountains. They found it and at night brought it to me. I gave them a pistole for their trouble. The highest of the mountains we called it Mount George, and the one we crossed over Mount Spotswood.[202]

*September 7, 1716.* [Friday]. Spotswood Camp, the other side the

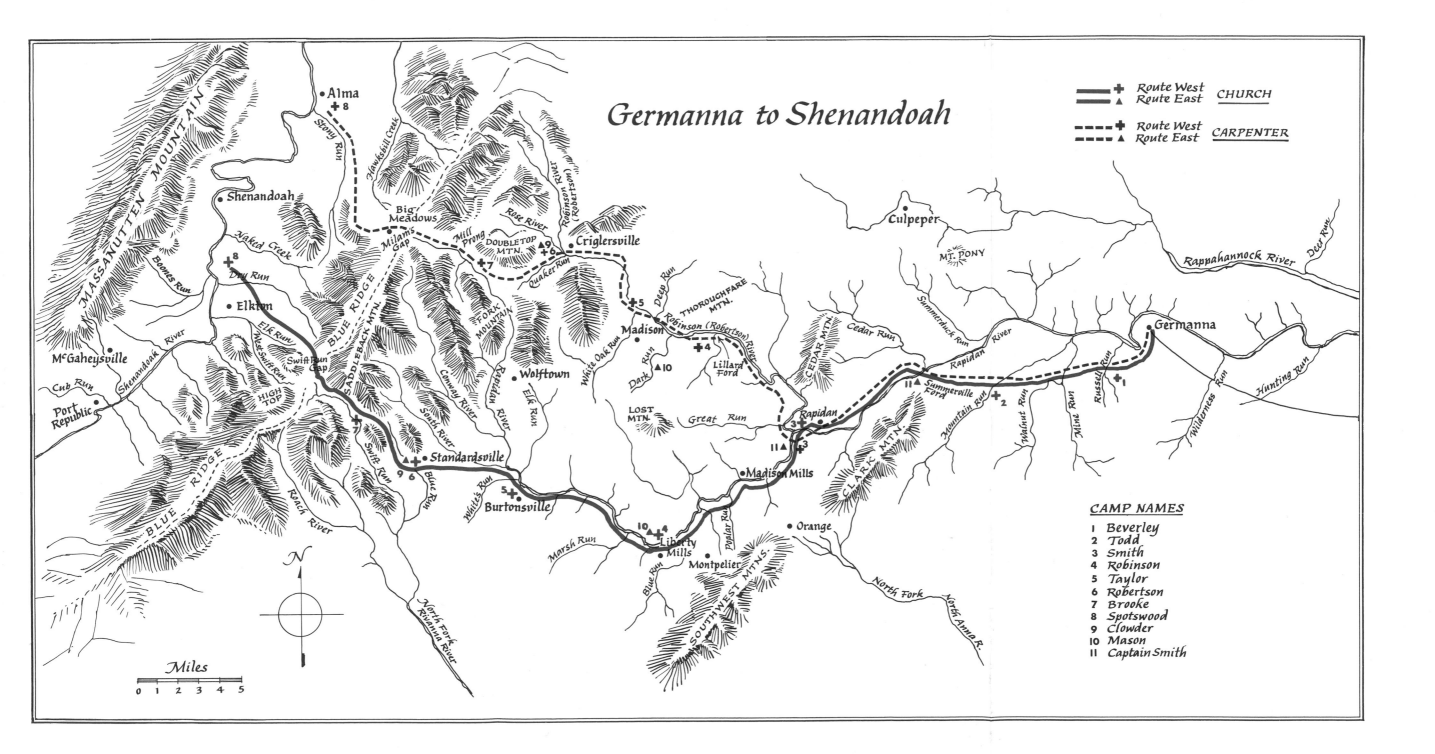

# Germanna to Shenandoah

Route West ┼
Route East ▲ **CHURCH**

Route West ┼
Route East ▲ **CARPENTER**

**CAMP NAMES**

1 Beverley
2 Todd
3 Smith
4 Robinson
5 Taylor
6 Robertson
7 Brooke
8 Spotswood
9 Clowder
10 Mason
11 Captain Smith

Miles
0 1 2 3 4 5

Appalaches. At seven in the morning mounted our horses and we parted with the rangers, who were to go farther on, and returned homewards. We repassed the Mountains and at five in the afternoon we came to Hospital Camp where we left our sick men and heavy baggage and found all things well and safe. We encamped here, and called it Captain Clouders Camp.[203] Here we remained this night. 16 miles.

*September 8, 1716.* [Saturday]. Clouder's Camp. This side the mountains. At nine all on horseback. We see several bears and deer, and killed some wild turkies. We made 27 miles this day and came to a run side where we encamped and we called this place Mason's Camp.[204] We had good forage for our horses and lay as usual. Made twenty miles this day.

*September 9, 1716.* [Sunday]. Mason's Camp. Set out at nine of the clock and before twelve we see several bears. We killed three, one of which attacked one of our men that was riding after him and narrowly missed him, tore his things that he had behind him off of his horse, and would have destroyed him had he not been immediately helped by other men and our dogs. Some of the dogs suffered in this engagement. At two we crossed one of the branches of the Rappahannoc River and at five encamped on the side of the Rapid Ann on a tract of land Mr. Beverley hath design to take up.[205] We made this day 23 miles and called this Captain Smith's Camp.[206] We eat part of one of the bears which tasted very well and would be good if one did not know what it was. It may pass for veal. We were very merry and diverted ourselves with our adventures.

*September 10, 1716.* [Monday]. Captain Smith's Camp. At eight we were on horseback; at ten as we were going up a small hill Mr. Beverly and his horse fell down, they both rolled to the bottom. There was no bones broken of neither side. At twelve as we were crossing a run of water Mr. Clouder fell in the water so we called this place Clouder's run. At one we arrived to a large spring where we dined and drunk a bowl of punch. We called this Fontaine's spring. About two we got a horseback and at four we came to Germanna. The Governor thanked the Gentlemen for their assistance in the expedition. Mr. Mason left us at five.[207] I went and swam in the Rappahannoc river and returned to the town.

*September 11, 1716.* [Tuesday]. Germanna Town. After breakfast all our company left us excepting Dr. Robinson and Mr. Clouder.[208] We walked all about the town and the Governor settled his business with the Germans here, and accommodated the minister and the people, then to bed.

*September 12, 1716.* [Wednesday]. Germanna town. After breakfast went a fishing in Rappahannoc and took seven fish which we had for dinner. After which Mr. Robinson and I we endeavoured to melt some ore in the smiths forge, but could get nothing out of it. About four Dr. Robinsons and Mr. Clouders' boys were taken violently ill with a fever. Mr. Robinson and Mr. Clouder left us and left their boys here.

*September 13, 1716.* [Thursday]. Germanna town. About eight of the clock we mounted our horses and went to the mine, where we took several pieces of ore and at nine we set out from the mine, our servants being gone before, we set after them, and about three we lit in the woods and there the governor and I dined. After we mounted and continued on our road. I killed a black snake which was about five feet long. We continued on and about six we arrived at Mrs. Woodfords who lives on Rappahannoc River where we continued this night.

*September 14, 1716.* [Friday], from Mrs. Woodfords. At seven we sent our servants and baggage before and at ten we mounted our horses. We killed another snake about four feet 9 inches long, and at twelve of the clock we came to the church[209] where we met with Mr. Buckner,[210] where we remained till about two to settle some county business—then we mounted our horses and see several wild turkies on the road, and at seven we came to Mr. Beverly's house, which is upon the head of Mattapony river, where we were well entertained. My boy was taken with a violent fever and very sick.

*September 15, 1716.* [Saturday], from Mr. Beverly. At seven my servant was somewhat better. I sent him away with my horses and here the governor took his chaise and I with him. At twelve we came to a Mill dam which we had a great deal of difficulty to get the chaise over. We got into the chaise and continued on our way and about five arrived at Mr. Baylor's.[211] Here we remained all night.

*September 16, 1716.* [Sunday]. Mr. Baylor upon Mattapony. My boy was so sick that I was obliged to leave him here and the Governor's servants took care of my horses. At ten we sent the caleche over Mattapony river. It being Sunday we came to the church in King William County, where we had a sermon from Mr. Monroe.[212] After sermon we continued our journey until we came to Mr. West's plantation,[213] where Colonel Basset[214] waited for the Governor with his pinnace and other boats for his servant. We arrived at his house by five of the clock. We were nobly entertained here where we remained all night.

*September 17, 1716.* [Monday]. Colonel Basset. Mattapony River. At ten we left Colonel Basset and at three we arrived at Williamsburg where I dined with him and so went to my lodgings and to bed, being well tired as well as my horses. I reckon that from Williamsburg to the Euphrates River is in all 219 miles, so that our journey going and coming 438 miles in all.[215]

# VIII. New York and Back

*October 14, 1716.* Williamsburg Virginia. I settled my business and left all my things in the hands of Major Holloway[216] designing with God's blessing for New York. I went to dine with the Governor and took my leave of him and of all my acquaintance.

*October 15, 1716.* On the road to Hampton. I got my things in readiness and mounted and came down to Hampton, which is forty miles from Williamsburg. About 6 of the clock I arrived here and went to my friend Mr. Irewin[217] where I lodged and supped.

*October 16, 1716.* At Hampton in Virginia. I sent away my horses to Williamsburg and writ to Major Holloway. I went to see several of my acquaintances and Mr. Michael Carney[218] who designed for New York so we agreed about what provisions we should put in for our voyage and I returned to Mr. Irewins where I lay.

*October 17, 1716.* At Hampton in Virginia. This town lies in a plain within ten miles of the mouth of James River and about one mile inland. From the side of the main river there is a small arm of the river that comes on both sides of this town and within a small matter of making it an island. It is a place of the greatest trade in all Virginia, and commonly where all men of war lie before this arm of the river which comes up to the town. It is not navigable for large ships by reason of a bar of sand which lies between the mouth or coming in and the main channel, but all sloops and small ships can come up to the town. This is the best outlet in all Virginia and Maryland and when there is any fleet made, they make up here and can go out to sea with the first start of a wind. There are about one hundred houses here but very few of any note. There is no church in this town. They have the best oysters and fish of all sorts here of any place in the colony. The inhabitants of this town drive a great trade with New York and Pennsylvania, and are also convenient to trade with Maryland. They do not reckon this town very healthy because there are great mud banks and wet marshes about it which have a very unwholesome smell at low water. There is good fowling hereabouts. We met at Mr. Irewin's where we were very merry and supped well and to bed.

*October 18, 1716.* At Hampton in Virginia. Mr. Carney and I spoke to the master of the sloop for our passage and bought provisions for ourselves and sent our clothes on board the sloop, he being in a readiness to sail. I met with all my acquaintance here and took my leave of them and went to Mr. Irewin's where I lay.

*October 19, 1716.* On board the sloop for New York. At eleven in the morning the wind being at N E we hoisted anchor. By one we were in the Bay of Chesapeake and passed Point Comfort[219] which makes the entrance of James River. At four we were between the two Capes of Virginia Cape Henry and Cape Charles. Weather fair, we kept within ten leagues of the shore and so steered our course all night.

*October 20, 1716.* On board the sloop. Wind continued at N E, weather fair. We kept in sight of the shore and sounded and found fourteen fathoms water, white sand, and see several flocks of ducks and geese, going to the southward. We have a smooth sea but a great swell. There is no harbor all along this coast from Cape Charles till you come to the mouth of the Bay of Delaware which goes up to Philadelphia.

*October 21, 1716.* On board the sloop at sea. Wind at N E until one of the clock and then it came about N W and blew very hard, so we sounded and found but ten fathoms water. The wind continued to blow so we came to an anchor, and about four we see a sloop coming from the sea. She came to an anchor by us, here we remained all night, and the wind blew very hard, still in sight of the land and somewhat to the northward of Delaware Bay. There is great banks of sand lies off here which are very dangerous. We can see the breakers on them.

*October 22, 1716.* On board the sloop at sea. In the morning about

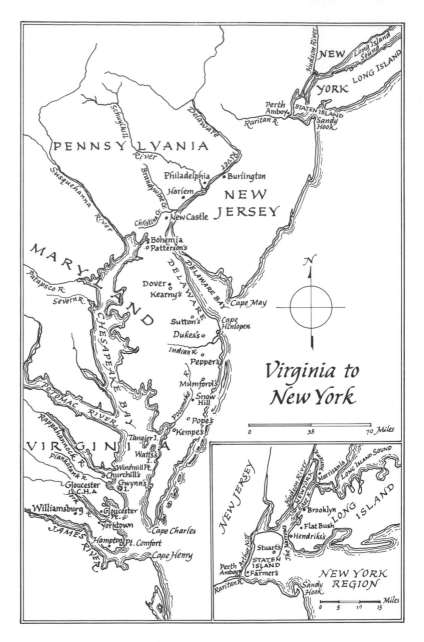

This map identifies most of the places mentioned by Fontaine on his journey
to New York in the fall of 1716.

seven of the clock we rose our anchor and set our sails. Wind at N W, a stiff gale and great sea. We split our jib and foresail about 12 of the clock; and we twined all day. About three we were up with Sandy Hook which is the Cape land of New York Port. It is a low land, sandy and few trees upon it. About sun set we came to an anchor under Sandy Hook in seven fathom water and about 3 miles from shore.

*October 23, 1716.* In the sloop at anchor under Sandy Hook. The weather was so foggy all day that we could not see the shore nor landmarks, so we could not hoist our anchor, for this is a very dangerous bay to come up without one has fair weather to see the landmarks. There are several banks and shoals of sand here very dangerous. There is a great deal of wild water fowl on those shoals of all sorts. I observe the ducks, geese and other fowl are a great deal sooner here than with us in Virginia.

*October 24, 1716.* Weather calm, but such a fog that we could not see half a mile off. We had a mind to go ashore, but the master and sailors were afraid that they could not find the sloop again with the boat, so we consented to remain on board. This fog we have here is occasioned by the burning of the woods, for in this time the inhabitants set the woods on fire; as also the Indians go about this time of the year a fire hunting.

*October 25, 1716.* Off Sandy Hook. We are still at anchor, weather very foggy, so that the master will not venture up with his sloop. About twelve it cleared up so that we could see the land. We got the boat and the men landed us in Staten Island; so we were obliged to walk about four miles a foot, not being able to hire any horses. This island is most high land and rocky and the land that is good is mixed with small stones. There are some good improvements here, this place is mostly inhabited by Dutch people. Their houses are all built with stone and lime. There are some hedges as in England. The chief increase of this place is wheat and cattle. They breed large horses here. About five of the clock we came to the Ferry between Long Island and Staten Island which is about one mile broad. The main body of New York River comes this way between these two islands. We crossed the ferry and came upon Long Island.[220] There is a small sort of village here, where, it being late, we put up at one Harris Hendrick's house,[221] a Dutchman. We were well lodged and supped well.

*October 26, 1716.* Long Island. About eight of the clock in the morning we hired two horses to go to New York. It is about eight miles of [from] this ferry by land, but not near so much by water. This island is very plain ground in general, bears extraordinary good grass, and is an excellent place for cattle. It produceth wheat and all English grain in abundance. The chief part of the Inhabitants here are Dutch and some French amongst them. There are several good improvements here and many fine villages. They have destroyed most of the woods in this island. They have besides the plentiful produce of the Island, all the advantages of fishing and fowling that can be wished for. About eleven we came to the ferry which goes over to New York. There is a fine village[222] upon this island opposite to New York. The ferry is about a quarter of a mile over, and water runs very rapidly here, and there is good convenient landings on both sides. About 12 we landed at New York. We went and agreed for our lodgings to a dutchwoman called Schuyler[223] and then I went to see Mr. Andrew Freneau[224] at his house. He received me very well, after which I went to the tavern and about ten at night I went to my lodgings and to bed.

*October 27, 1716.* New York town. About nine I went and breakfasted at the Coffee House[225] and at eleven I waited on Governor Hunter,[226] where I was received very kindly. He invited me to dinner with him. I dined with him. After dinner I walked with him about the fort,[227] wherein he lives. It is a small square, situated upon a height above the town and commands it. The one side of it fronts the harbour, and hath a small curtain, and two bastions, and the land side hath but two half bastions to it, so that 'tis a square composed of two whole and two half bastions. There is a ravelin towards the land, that lies one side of the gate. It is but a weak place and badly contrived. There is a regiment of men in this place,[228] and the Governor hath always a guard, but this is all the duty they have which is very little. From the Governor's I went to see the Mayor of the town, one Dr. Johnson,[229] and was kindly received; from thence to Colonel Delorty,[230] and at night I went to the tavern, and was there with the Irish Club until ten, and so to bed.

*October 28, 1716.* Sunday. New York. About eight in the morning Mr. Carney and I we hired horses, and went about seven miles in the country to one Colonel Morris's,[231] who lives out of town. This man is Judge or Chief Justice of this Province, a very sensible and good man. We remained with him all night, were well received, and see a great many fine improvements about him that he had made. He shewed us several rare collections he had made. He lives upon the river[232] that comes down to York town.

*October 29, 1716.* Monday. New York. About ten of the clock we left Colonel Morris's, crossed the river,[233] about 12 we arrived to New York. The roads are very bad and stony, and no possibility for coaches to go only in the winter when the snow fills all up and makes all smooth, then they can make use of their wheel carriages. There is but two coaches belonging to this province though many rich people, because of the badness of the roads. About two we were invited to dinner by Mr. Hamilton[234] and Mr. Lane.[235] We dined with them, then I visited Mr. Freneau, was kindly received. We had a great deal of discourse with him about the trade of Virginia. From thence I walked round this town. There is here three churches, the English church,[236] the French[237] and the Dutch church.[238] There is also a place for their assembly to sit,[239] which is not very fine, and where they judge all matters. The town is compact, the houses for the most part built after the dutch manner, with the gable ends toward the street. The streets are of good breadth, the town is built close upon the river, and there is a fine quay that reigns all round the town built with stone and piles of wood outside. There are small docks for cleaning and building small ships. The ships at high water come up to the quay to lade and unlade. The river is frozen in the winter, sometimes all over and such abundance of ice comes down that it often cuts the cables of the ships, but cannot hurt them near the quay. The place the town is built on rises as it goes from the water, so it is amphitheatre like. The French have all the privileges that can be in this place and are the most in number here.[240] They are of the council, of the parliament, and in all other employments here. Their chief commodities are Beef, Flour, Pork, Butter and Cheese, which they send to the West Indies and sometimes to Lisbon. They are very cold and all amongst the snow frozen for four months of the year and very hot in the latter part of the summer. They have plenty of all sorts of fish, oysters and water fowl. They drive a great trade with the Norwood [Northern] Indians, for skins and furs.

*October 30, 1716.* Tuesday. New York. At ten of the clock went to the Coffee House and at two of the clock went and dined with the Governor, from thence went to see Colonel Ingoldsby,[241] from thence to the Irish club, where I remained till ten and so home to my lodgings.

*October 31, 1716.* Wednesday. New York. At ten went to the Coffee House and walked upon their Exchange[242] which is a small place that is planked, and pillars of wood all round it, over which it is covered, and supported by the pillars, but the place is open on all sides. At twelve met with Mr. Andrew Freneau. He invited me to dinner with him. I remained with him till four of the clock and then I went to the Coffee House where I continued till six and then met with Mr. Freneau and went to the French club, where they treated me and at ten I went home and to bed.

*November 1, 1716.* Thursday. New York. At eleven to the Coffee House, dined at the tavern, from thence to Mr. Freneau and at 6 to the tavern and at nine went home.

*November 2, 1716.* Friday. New York. At nine of the clock breakfasted at the Coffee house. At two I went and dined at the tavern, from thence to Mr. Freneau, and at 6 to the tavern and at nine went home, and writ to my Cousin Arnaud in London and so to bed.

*November 3, 1716.* Saturday. New York. At eight to the Coffee House breakfasted, at one went to the tavern and dined, informed myself about one Maxwell. Mr. Fooks[243] [had] recommended [him] to me and they informed me he was very much in debt, had been a long time in prison there, and that he is now gone to South Carolina and calls himself instead of his right name James Maxwell, Joseph Mitchell.[244] From the tavern I went to the Coffee House where I remained till four. Thence I went home to writ to Mr. Fooks in Dublin about this Maxwell and to bed.

*November 4, 1716.* Sunday. New York. At ten went to Mr. Freneau and went with him to church. I returned to his house and dined with him. At half an hour after two we went to church again which is after Calvin's way. The church is very large and beautiful.[245] Within there was a very great congregation. After service I went home and to bed.

*November 5, 1716.* Monday. New York. At ten in the morning went to Mr. Freneau to carry him a memorandum of the prices of goods. I went and dined at the Coffee house. From thence went to the French club at the tavern where we drank all loyal healths. At ten went home and to bed.

*November 6, 1716.* Tuesday. New York. About ten went to visit Mr. Delancy[246] and from thence went to Mr. Freneau where I remained till eleven, and so to the Coffee House. The Postmaster general Mr. Hamilton invited me, I dined with him. At three I returned to the Coffee House. At 6 the Collector Mr. Byerly[247] and some others we went to the tavern and there we remained till ten and from thence to bed.

*November 7, 1716.* Wednesday. New York. At eight went to the Coffee House. At ten waited on Governor Hunter and drank tea with him. From thence I waited on Mr. Birchfield[248] Surveyor General, and I dined with him and took my leave of him. He made me some promises of service if any opportunity should offer. At four I went to the Coffee House and met with Mr. Freneau. At six we went to the French club and at ten to bed.

*November 8, 1716.* Thursday. New York. At ten waited on Governor Hunter, breakfasted with him, at two dined with him. I took my leave of the Governor, at four left him, went to my lodgings and supped there, and at eight to bed.

*November 9, 1716.* Friday. New York. At five of the clock in the morning got all our things in readiness in the ferryboat and set out for Amboy, wind contrary. It blew hard, so that at nine we were forced back again, so we hired two horses Mr. Carney and I, and went seven miles out of town to Colonel Morris's where we dined and returned to York town and lay at our lodgings.[249]

*November 10, 1716.* Saturday. New York. At eight in the morning I bought a horse of Mr. Lancaster Sims[250] paid him £8 for him. At ten crossed the ferry from New York to Long Island, there we mounted our horses and passed by a fine village called Flat Bush. At twelve we arrived at Hanse Hendrick's house.[251] The ferryman endeavoured to cross the ferry from thence to Staten Island, was put back. At three of the clock we see a ship called the Caesar gally run aground upon White Bank.[252] We dined here in Long Island at Hendrick's and about five we got in the ferryboat and with much difficulty got over to Staten Island, then we mounted our horses and came to one Stewards,[253] an Inn, on the road, and about seven miles from the ferry we supped and lay here all night.

*November 11, 1716.* Sunday. Staten Island. At seven in the morning we set out from Stewards, and at 12 of the clock, we came to one Colonel Farnier's house,[254] where the ferry is kept, so we got ferried over to Amboy, which is a small village and the Governor[255] hath a house here and gardens. This is an agreeable little place, surrounded of two sides by the water.[256] After dinner we went to church. The church is very small and much out of repair.[257] The wind blew very hard and we were not able to ferry over our horses, so we were obliged to remain here this night.

*November 12, 1716.* Monday. Amboy village. The wind continued blowing very hard at N W. We could by no means get over the ferry. In the morning we took a walk abroad in the country about here, which is very agreeable. At two we returned to our inn and dined and met with two gentlemen of New York, Justice Johnston[258] and Mr. Bickly,[259] two lawyers. We drunk till ten, and to bed.

*November 13, 1716.* Tuesday. Amboy. At ten we crossed the ferry, we mounted our horses. About two we dined, at three we mounted and continued on our way until seven. We made but 32 miles this day. We had bad entertainment.

*November 14, 1716.* Wednesday. On the road. At half an hour after seven we set out from our lodgings and within one mile of Burlington I met with Mr. John Ballaguier.[260] At 11, we came to Burlington, where we dined. This is a very pretty village and there is a river[261] passes through it navigable for sloops. At half an hour after twelve we set out for Philadelphia. The distance is twenty miles from Burlington. The roads are good here. At six we arrived at Philadelphia, and I waited on Mr. Samuel Peres[262] and gave him Mr. Freneau's letter. He had no service for me.

*November 15, 1716.* Thursday. Philadelphia. At eight of the clock went to view the town which is situated upon Delaware River upon rising ground and built very regular. The houses most brick after the english fashion. The streets are very large and regular, the houses most brick. There are many convenient docks for the building sloops and ships here.

They have a great trade to all the Islands belonging to the english, as also to Lisbon and the Madeira Islands. The produce of the country is chiefly wheat, barley and all English grain, beef, butter, cheese, flax and hemp. The inhabitants are most part quakers and they have several good meetings. There is some English churches here. There are all sorts of trades established in this town, and money that is not milled goes for six shillings and four pence the ounce. At twelve of the clock we left the town and crossing the ferry[263] about two miles out of the town we had a great shower. At five of the clock we got to Harlem,[264] the roads not very good here. This place is a small village, but well situated on Delaware River, sixteen miles from Philadelphia. We lay here all night, good entertainment.

*November 16, 1716.* Friday. Harlem, Pennsylvania. At eight of the clock set out from Harlem. We crossed two ferries,[265] and at one of the clock came to Newcastle. After dinner walked about the town. There are a great many good brick houses, but a place of no trade, tho' situated upon Delaware River. We remained here all this day and were well entertained and lodged.

*November 17, 1716.* Saturday. New Castle, Delaware. About eight of the clock we set out from Newcastle [for Bohemia landing. About fifteen miles on the way we came to the division line between Pennsylvania (that is, the Three Lower Counties, or Delaware) and Maryland. At three we reached[266]] Bohemia landing[267] in hopes to find a sloop there, but we were disappointed. There is two or three houses here, but no entertainment. So we were obliged to go four miles further till we came to Mr. Patterson's,[268] a house of entertainment. Here we remained this night.

*November 18, 1716.* Sunday. At Patterson's in Maryland.[269] Here we remained all day, there being nothing to be seen here but trees. We are 60 miles from Philadelphia. A fair day.

*November 19, 1716.* Monday. Maryland. At eight of the clock set out from Patterson's house, and at twelve arrived at the Court House.[270] This is the County of Kent. Here we baited our horses, had but indifferent entertainment. About three Mr. Carney and I went to his brother's house[271] who lives here. Here we put up and remained all night. We reckon that we made this day 33 miles.

[ 119 ]

*November 20, 1716.* Tuesday. Maryland. It being rainy we remained here where we lay and were well entertained. This gentleman hath an extraordinary good tannery which turns to account.

*November 21, 1716.* Wednesday. Maryland. At nine in the morning we set out from Mr. Carney's brothers and at one we came to one Sutton's house, [272] about 28 miles from Mr. Carney's plantation, and dined at three. There were about eight rogues that were drinking there, being resolved to fall upon us and rob us. My comrade, going out, not expecting any thing was knocked down. He endeavoured to defend himself with his sword, but with their stakes they broke it to pieces. They endeavoured to serve me after the same manner, but I defended myself and my friend until we got to our horses and with a great deal of trouble got away from them, and put on forward on the road about six miles to avoid them, and put up, it being dark, in a poor man's house. About ten o'clock at night they came to steal our horses, and endeavour to surprise us, but when they see we were prepared for them, after some few injurious words and threats they made off. This is Sussex County. We set up all night on our guard.

*November 22, 1716.* Thursday. Sussex County, Maryland. Being threatened with an assault in the morning, we thought convenient at two of the clock to get our horses. We took a guide and by 6 of the clock, we got twelve miles off out of this county and arrived at one Duicks house.[273] We breakfasted here and about ten set out and came to the Indian Creek.[274] This part of the country is hardly inhabited, and what people are here make it their business to rob all passengers. We were detained at this creek for two hours, for the want of a canoe. We got one at last, and swim our horses over. Afterwards we mounted our horses and went three miles farther, until we came to one Pepper's house,[275] where we lay all night.

*November 23, 1716.* Friday. Maryland. At seven in morning got on horseback, a fair day. We rid sixteen miles through the forest, no inhabitants all the way. At the end of the sixteen miles we came to one Mumfords,[276] where we eat a bit. At two we mounted and at five of the clock came to Snow hill,[277] being forty miles from the place we lay last night, from Pepper's. This is a small village, but few houses, and not one public house, so we put up at a private house. This village is situated upon

Pocomoke River, navigable for sloops, as far as this place. Bad beds and ordinary victuals.

*November 24, 1716.* Saturday. Maryland, Snow Hill village. At eight got a horseback, and when we were about seventeen miles on our way we called at one Mr. Pope's[278] where we took a guide, the ways being very intricate. At 5 of the clock we came to one Mr. Kemps,[279] which we reckon distant from Snow Hill about thirty five miles. We paid our guide and dismissed him. We were very well entertained, and our horses well fed, and about ten we went to bed.

*November 25, 1716.* Sunday. Accomack County, part of Virginia. At ten we breakfasted. At eleven Mr. Kemp and I rode out. At two came to his house and dined after we had viewed a fine tract of land. After dinner we went to see the shallop that we design to hire. The wind blew very hard at N W. At ten we went to bed.

*November 26, 1716.* Monday. Accomack County, Virginia. At ten Mr. Carney and I agreed with the skipper of the sloop for us and our horses for our passage to Rappahannoc river, on the other side of the bay, and are to give him forty four shillings for his trouble. We ordered him to ballast his sloop and to be in a readiness when the wind offered. At breakfast we drank of a herb called the Golden Rod, the leaf is long, it tastes and is of the color of green tea. We dined at four. After dinner we played at chequers, then we supped and drunk punch and diverted ourselves till twelve and then went to bed.

*November 27, 1716.* Tuesday. Accomack County, Virginia. At ten we breakfasted, at twelve we ballasted the shallop and hoisted the 2 horses in, put all our things on board, as also liquor, and provisions for the run. We were resolved to set out this afternoon, but the wind nor tide did not serve, and night drawing on we returned to our kind friend Mr. James Kemp, supped, and at ten went to bed, wind being stormy at N W.

*November 28, 1716.* Wednesday. Accomack County, Virginia. At eight in the morning got up, at nine we breakfasted and took our leaves of Mr. Kemp and went to one Sandford's[280] before whose house the sloop lay. The wind blew hard, and we got a canoe, and with some difficulty got on board our shallop. At ten hoisted the anchor, with the wind at N and N by E, a hard gale. At two we came to Egg Island, at five, it being but half flood we struck on Watts's shoals, where we remained thumping for an hour. After floated, and came up to Watts's Island.[281] At seven we cast anchor, and went ashore to one Joseph Bird's house.[282] We supped on our own provisions, and for want of beds, lay before the fire all night.

*November 29, 1716.* Thursday. Watts Island. At four in the morning we got up, went to the waterside and called up the shallop men. We went on board and at five we weighed anchor and hoisted our sails. The wind is at N E. We had the tide against us, but a fresh gale of wind. At seven we see the Tangier Islands, at nine of the clock came in sight of Windmill Point, which makes the north side of Rappahannoc River and Gwinns Island the south side.[283] At one we came abreast with Windmill Point, the wind changed to S W, blew fresh. We endeavoured to weather Gwinn's Island, the sea great, and we could not go to Queen's Creek[284] in Pianketank river. We met a ship and at three we spoke to her; she came from Barbadoes. At one quarter after three finding the wind fresher, we were obliged to put before it up Rappahannoc river. The wind calmed about six, so we put ashore at Mr. Churchills plantation,[285] and landed our horses with some difficulty. It was very dark, so we were obliged to lie at the negroes quarters that night.

*November 30, 1716.* Friday. Virginia. At eight mounted our horses, fasting. At ten of the clock we crossed Pianketank ferry[286] and mounted our horses, but being strangers to the road we came out of our way to Ivy river.[287] We returned to the road and passed by Gloucester County Court House. At three we came to Gloucester town upon York river. We crossed the ferry and came to York town. We went to Power's ordinary[288] where we lay all night. I accounted and found that my journey to New York and back again cost me twenty and four pounds.

*December 1, 1716.* Saturday. York Town. At nine in the morning I set out, accompanied Mr. Carney a mile off the town and there took my leave of my fellow traveller and at eleven came to Williamsburg. I went and visited the governor and my acquaintance.

*December 3, 1716.* Virginia. Set out from Williamsburg and went to my plantation in King William County[289] and put all things in order and got my servants and overseer that were all run away.

[ 122 ]

# IX. Farewell, Virginia

*December 8, 1716.* Came to Williamsburg again, and on the 11th received news from Hampton that my brother Peter[290] was arrived.

*December 12, 1716.* I went to Hampton.

*December 14, 1716.* We came all up to Williamsburg, where we took up our lodgings. My brother and I went to view the parishes and went to the plantation, so about the 29th we returned to Williamsburg. In February Peter got a presentation to Roanoke Parish[291] and preached there. We all removed there in March 1717 and lodged at Captain Harwood's.[292] I was very sick of the fever and ague. In May being somewhat better I left them and went to the plantation where I remained and B and H[293] left me on the 15th June, so all remained on my hands. I bought a servant, which cost me £11: 5 sterling.

In October 1717 my brother James and his family came to York town in the Brig.[294] I was at this time very sick, but went down to them, so we all came up in the ship to Captain Littlepages.[295] Afterwards we went to the plantation. The houses I built not being quite finished we lodged at one Mr. Suttons.[296]

About November 7, 1717, I had finished the houses and we brought all our things and came to live there; and in November we sheathed the ship [which had sprung a leak during the passage, and when she was repaired[297]] and fitted her out for a voyage, proposed to sell her, but could not. We afterwards freighted her for Bristol, and in January 1717/18 she fell down the river.

Bought twenty one head of cattle, one horse, one servant and eleven hogs, and left the management of all to my brother James.

I was very sick for about five months, and all our family, so had a great deal of trouble.

# Farewell, Virginia

*March 27, 1718.* Received a letter from Mr. Matthew Maury[298] that he was at Captain Eskridge's house[299] with his goods, where he would wait for me. I was not well and the weather wet and rainy, but I set out and crossed the ferry at Mr. Baylor's[300] and rid afterwards seven miles in the rain and an hour in the night. Came to one Bridgworths[301] where I lay.

*March 28, 1718.* I was sick next morning but set out fasting, it being a windy day, and got eight miles on my way, but my fever increased so much, and the pains in my head and bones, that I could not ride, but was forced to alight. About ten I came to a poor widow's house where I was for about two hours senseless. About four of the clock I was taken with a violent vomiting and my fever abated something. Then I got on horseback and about 6 came to Bowlers his ferry[302] on Rappahannoc, where I lay but badly entertained all night.

*March 29, 1718.* Crossed the river and at seven came to Captain Eskridge's house. Mr. Maury was gone. Being very sick, I remained here for 3 days.

*April 1, 1718.* I mounted my horse and came this day as far as Mr. Naylors house[303] where I lay.

*April 2, 1718.* Crossed the river in a small boat, was in danger of being drowned and came to Mr. Baylors, where I lay this night.

*April 3, 1718.* Went home. In all, I made going and coming 135 miles.

*April 22, 1718.* I went down to Williamsburg to Mr. Maury, and hired a Flat, after I had bought the Rum and Molasses he wanted.

*April 25, 1718.* The goods were embarked and we went out of Queen's Creek, and went to the Oyster Banks, where we took in a great many oysters, and came about 6 miles up the river. We came as close the land as we could and stuck an oar in the mud, and tied our flat to it, where we lay till 'twas day. A cold place.

*April 26, 1718.* Took up our oar and rowed about four miles. The wind at N W, blew very hard. We were blown in on the flats, and sea was so high, and no possibility of landing, so that we were obliged to throw what oysters we had overboard to lighten the boat. Shipped a great deal of water, and having no anchor we were like to drive on the mud and loose the flat. About two of the clock the weather calming, we set out again and made about five miles, but the wind came to N W such a violent storm that we were obliged to put before the wind, and when we had gone back a mile, we ran the flat ashore upon the strand, where we thumped mightily. The wind continued very hard, but the tide being fallen, we unloaded the goods, expecting that when the boat would float, she would beat to pieces, so that about twelve at night, we had all our goods on shore, but there being no house near, we lay upon the strand all night. It rained hard and wet us to the skin, but the wind abated, and when the tide came in, we halled our flat up as far as we could and received no damage but being wet both with fresh and salt water.

*April 27, 1718.* About 6 in the morning, being Sunday, we put the goods on board and half an hour after the wind blew hard at northwest, so that about 12 it abated and we set out and reached West Point about nine of the clock.

*April 28, 1718.* Came to Captain Littlepages,[304] and the [29th] came to Philip Williams his ferry,[305] where we landed the goods.

I remained here to June 6, 1718, and then went down to Williamsburg and settled my business with Mr. Irewin and Major Holloway and June 16 passed at West Point, where I spake to Captain Brunnequil[306] and agreed with him for my passage.

*August 4, 1718.* Received a letter from Mr. Freneau[307] that there was a ship consigned to me. I got my things on shore, left my fowls with the master, paid him 22 shillings for the charges I had put him to, and as I understood, in going home, he foundered and they all perished, so that I have great reason to return God thanks for my preservation at this time, for I was fully resolved to go with him had not I been prevented by Mr. Freneau's letter, which came to my hands four days before he [Captain Brunnequil] sailed for England.

I landed my goods and came to York town, from thence to Williamsburg and so to my plantation on August 10, 1718.

*July 17, 1718.* I made over the deeds of the land to my brother James, in order to go for England.

*December 19, 1718.* Received news of the arrival of the Henry and Margaret, consigned to me.[308] I went immediately to the ship, and entered her and landed the goods, and sold the most part of them and kept the ship here till June 7, 1719, when we set sail out of James River. On July 18 we came to Weymouth, and July 19 we came to Cowes in the Isle of Wight, where I remained three days and on July 22, 1719, I left Cowes, and crossed the Bay to Southampton.

*July 23, 1719.* I set out in the stage coach for London, arrived about eight of the clock at London. I took a Hackney Coach and went to Mr. Arnaud's at Islington, where I remained until November 24, 1719, about the business of the cargo, and doing what I could for another voyage, but all to no purpose, so on November 24, I left London. My horse tired at Coventry.

*November 27, 1719.* I took the stage coach and came to Chester. November 29 and November 30 hired three horses for Holyhead.

*December 1, 1719.* Lay at Bangor.

*December 2, 1719.* Arrived at Holyhead, remained at Holyhead and went upon the top of a hill from whence I could see Ireland.

*December 5, 1719.* I embarked and December 6 arrived in the Bay of Dublin. I took the wherry and landed by twelve at Assins quay and came to Stephens Green.[309]

End of the Journal of John Fontaine. Copied by Ann Maury. Begun in Duke Street Liverpool on October 8, 1840. Finished at Ham Common Surrey on November 13, 1840.

# APPENDIX

## Fontaine Genealogy

# Appendix

## FONTAINE GENEALOGY

Jacques (James) Fontaine (b. Apr. 7, 1658, Jenouillé, France; d. 1728, Dublin) m. Feb. 8, 1685/86, Barnstaple, England, Anne Elizabeth Boursiquot (d. Jan. 29, 1720/21, Dublin)

1. James (b. 1686, Taunton, England; d. 1746, Northumberland Co., Va.)

    (1) m. 1711, Diocese of Cork and Ross, Ireland, Lucretia Desjarrie (d. ca. 1735, King William Co., Va.)

        i. Elizabeth (b. 1717) m. William Barret

        ii. Lucretia (b. 1719)

        iii. James (b. 1721) m. ca. Sept. 1, 1752, Carmarthen, Wales, Ann Fontaine (b. Dec. 6, 1729, London; d. 1753)

            a. John (b. 1753; d. 1785)

        iv. Jane (b. 1725)

        v. John

        vi. Ann (b. 1728) m. Thomas Owen

    (2) m. ca. 1737–1738, Elizabeth Harcum

        vii. Levenah (b. Dec. 28, 1739)

        viii. Mary Ann (b. Aug. 26, 1743)

        ix. William (b. Feb. 5, 1744/45)

2. Aaron (b. 1688, Taunton; d. 1699, Cork)

3. Mary Ann (b. Apr. 12, 1690, Taunton; d. Dec. 30, 1755, Charles

City Co., Va.) m. Oct. 20, 1716, Dublin, Matthew Maury (d. 1752, King William Co., Va.)

    i. James (b. Apr. 8, 1718, Dublin; d. June 9, 1769, Va.) m. Nov. 11, 1743, Mary Walker (b. Nov. 22, 1724; d. Mar. 20, 1798)

    ii. Mary (b. 1725) m. Daniel Claiborne

    iii. Abraham (b. Apr. 7, 1731) m. Susanna Poindexter

4. Peter (b. 1691, Taunton; d. Aug. 1759, Charles City Co., Va.)

    (1) m. Mar. 29, 1714, Dublin, Elizabeth Fourreau (b. ca. 1700)

        i. Mary Anne (b. 1718) m. Isaac Winston

        ii. Peter (b. 1720) m. Apr. 20, 1749, Elizabeth Winston

    (2) .m. Sarah Wade

        iii. Moses (b. 1742) m. ————— Ballard

        iv. Sarah (b. 1744) unmarried

        v. Elizabeth (b. 1747) m. William Mills

        vi. Joseph (b. 1748)

        vii. Aaron (b. Nov. 30, 1753; d. Apr. 1823) m. (1) May 19, 1773, Louisa County, Va., Barbara Terrell (b. 1756; d. 1796); (2) Louisville, Ken., Mrs. Elizabeth Whiting Thruston

        viii. Abraham (b. Apr. 9, 1756; d. 1832) m. Sarah Ballard

5. John (b. Apr. 28, 1693, Taunton; bur. Nov. 26, 1767, Newchurch, Wales) m. 1728, London, Mary Magdalen Sabatier (bur. Aug. 25, 1781, Newchurch)

    i. Ann (b. Dec. 6, 1729, London; d. 1753) m. ca. Sept. 1, 1752, Carmarthen, Wales, James Fontaine (b. 1721)

        a. John (b. 1753; d. 1785)

    ii. James (b. June 15, 1731, London; d. 1801) m. Lucretia Lemoine. No children.

    iii. John (b. Jan. 3, 1732/33, London; d. y.)

    iv. John (b. Mar. 4, 1733/34, London) unmarried

        a. Illegitimate son Joseph (later alias Thompson) by Mary Bradneck

v. David (b. July 30, 1739, London; d. ca. 1800) m. ca. 1770 Mary M. Plowman

    a. Sophia (b. Jan. 1773; d. July 1859) m. 1802 John Patrick (b. 1774; d. Sept. 19, 1841)

    b. George David (b. 1774; d. 1829) m. E. Smith

    c. James (b. 1778; d. May 9, 1826) m. Dec. 15, 1802, Hornsey, Frances Elizabeth Sheppard (b. Nov. 11, 1779)

    d. John

    e. William

    f. Ann

vi. Mary (b. Nov. 13, 1741, London; d. y.)

vii. William (b. Nov. 15, 1742, London; d. ca. 1794, Carmarthenshire) m. Jan. 27, 1766, Newchurch, Margaret Howell

    a. William of St. Peter's m. July 23, 1786, Mary Jenkins, widow, of Newchurch

    b. Mary Magdalene m: (1) David Thomas of Abergwish; (2) Sept. 1795, John David of Newchurch

    c. John (bapt. May 2, 1773)

    d. Margaret m. Apr. 1801, John David of Newchurch

    e. James (bapt. 1791) m. 1809 Phoebe Williams

viii. Daniel )
ix. Moses ) twins; d. y.

6. Moses (b. 1694, Taunton; bur. Feb. 19, 1766, Newchurch) unmarried.

7. Francis (b. Sept. 16, 1697, Cork; d. 1749, York Co., Va.)

    (1) m. 1720, London, Mary Glanisson

        i. Francis (b. 1721) m.

        ii. Mary (b. 1724) m.

        iii. John (b. 1726) m.

iv. Thomas (b. 1730)

(2) m. ca. 1735, Virginia, Susanna Brush (d. 1756, York Co., Va.)

    v. James Maury (b. 1738) m. 1771, Gloucester Co., Va., Alice Burwell (d. 1775)

    vi. Judith Barbar (b. 1740) m. Philip Moody

8. Elizabeth (b. Apr. 3, 1701, Bear Haven; d. ca. 1764) m. Oct. 31, 1729, London, Daniel Torin (b. ca. 1707, Wandsworth; bur. June 1, 1767, Wandsworth)

    i. Abraham Berchere (b. ca. 1730; d. 1760) m. July 1754, Carmarthen, Mary Richards, widow

    ii. Samuel (will, 1768–1769) unmarried

    iii. Mary (d. y.)

NOTES TO INTRODUCTION

# Notes to Introduction

1. Ann Maury, ed., *Memoirs of a Huguenot Family: Translated and Compiled from the Original Autobiography of the Rev. James Fontaine, and Other Family Manuscripts, Comprising* [that is, including] *an Original Journal of Travels in Virginia, New-York, etc. in 1715 and 1716* (New York, 1853), pp. 193–228. The three sections of the *Memoirs* are cited hereafter as James Fontaine, *Autobiography* (pp. 13–244); John Fontaine, *Journal* (pp. 245–310); or Fontaine Family, *Letters* (pp. 311–443). James Fontaine became a justice of the peace for county Cork, Nov. 20, 1702. Cork Historical and Archaeological Society *Journal*, 3 (1897):61. See also note 52 below.

2. Fontaine Family, *Letters*, pp. 311–24.

3. James Fontaine, *Autobiography*, pp. 39–40, 51, 54.

4. Same, pp. 58–101, 113.

5. Same, pp. 113–28.

6. Same, pp. 128–33.

7. Same, p. 143; Huguenot Society of London *Proceedings*, 7 (1901–4): 35; 17 (1942–46):375.

8. James Fontaine, *Autobiography*, pp. 123–27, 135, 142, 143–47, 156–65.

9. Same, pp. 147–52, 154–56, 165–77, 179–83; Hug. Soc. London *Proceedings*, 6 (1898–1901):423; 17 (1942–46):375; Richard Caulfield, ed., *The Council Book of the Corporation of the City of Cork* . . . (Guildford, Surrey, 1876), p. 236; Grace Lawless Lee, *The Huguenot Settlements in Ireland* (London, 1936), pp. 23, 35, 36, 39; T. A. Lunham, "Early French Refugees in Cork . . . ," Cork Hist. Archaeol. Soc. *Journal* (2), 24 (1918):10–11, 13–15.

10. James Fontaine, *Autobiography*, pp. 134, 157, 167, 170, 177–79, 181, 185.

11. Same, pp. 181–88, 219; W. Maziere Brady, *Clerical and Parochial Records of Cork, Cloyne, and Ross* . . . , 3 vols. (Dublin, 1863–64), 2:454, 503.

12. His advertisement for the school is in the *Dublin Gazette*, Aug. 9, 1709. See also L. H. Torin, "Notes on the Torin Family" (mimeographed, n.p., n.d.), p. 5 (courtesy of Mrs. L. H. Torin, Platcock, Fortrose, Ross-shire, Scotland).

13. James Fontaine, *Autobiography*, p. 231; Dublin University, Trinity College, *Alumni Dublinensis: A Register of the Students, Graduates, Professors, and Provosts* . . . *(1593–1860)*, George D. Burtchaell and Thomas V. Sadler, eds. (Dublin, 1935), p. 303.

14. It is possible, however, that the bishop of London refused to appoint Fontaine to the college because he was a dissenter. *The Official Letters of Alexander Spotswood*, R. A. Brock, ed., Virginia Historical Society *Collections*, n.s., 2 vols. (Richmond, 1882, 1885), 2:166–67; *Virginia Magazine of History and Biography* [henceforth cited as *VMHB*], 4 (1896–97):171–72; Wil-

liam Wilson Manross, comp., *The Fulham Papers in the Lambeth Palace Library: American Colonial Section Calendar and Indexes* (Oxford, 1965), xi, pp. 229–30; James Fontaine, *Autobiography*, pp. 242–43; Hug. Soc. London, *Registers of the French Non-Conformist Churches of Lucy Lane and Peter Street, Dublin*, Thomas Philip LeFann, ed. (Aberdeen, 1901), p. 90.

15. James Fontaine, *Autobiography*, pp. 231, 233–35.

16. John Watkins, *An Essay towards a History of Bideford in the County of Devon* (Exeter, 1792), pp. 59–66, 87; Joseph Besly Gribble, *Memorials of Barnstaple, Being an Attempt to Supply the Want of a History of That Ancient Borough* (Barnstaple, 1930), pp. 524–44, 601–2; Inkerman Rogers, *A Concise History of Bideford* (Bideford, 1938), pp. 21–24; W. G. Hoskins, *Devon* [A New Survey of England] (London, 1954), pp. 115–16, 208, 217–18, 238, 327–30, 335–37; W. B. Stephens, "The West-Country Ports and the Struggle for the Newfoundland Fisheries in the Seventeenth Century," Devonshire Association for the Advancement of Science, Literature, and Art *Report and Transactions*, 88 (1956) :90–101; C. Malcolm Watkins, "North Devon Pottery and Its Export to America in the 17th Century," Museum of History and Technology, Smithsonian Institution *Contributions*, Paper 13 (1960) :22–28; Inkerman Rogers, *A Record of Wooden Sailing Ships and Warships Built in the Port of Bideford* . . . (Bideford, 1947). See also Journal, note 38 below.

17. Robert Beverley, *The History and Present State of Virginia* (London, 1705), Louis B. Wright, ed. (Chapel Hill, 1947), pp. 312–13.

18. Same, p. 191; Hugh Jones, *The Present State of Virginia* . . . (London, 1724), Richard L. Morton, ed. (Chapel Hill, 1956), p. 59. See also Journal, note 117 below.

19. Spotswood, *Official Letters*, 2:

295–98; Herbert Levi Osgood, *The American Colonies in the Eighteenth Century*, 4 vols. (New York, 1924), 2:238; Richard L. Morton, *Colonial Virginia*, 2 vols. (Chapel Hill, 1960), 2:451; Jones, *Present State*, pp. 58–59. George H. Reese, formerly of the Colonial Williamsburg Research Department and an accomplished Latin scholar, supplied the translation of the motto, which has often been erroneously rendered. William Alexander Caruthers, *The Knights of the Horseshoe; a Traditionary Tale of the Cocked Hat Gentry in the Old Dominion* (Wetumpka, Ala., 1845); Curtis Carroll Davis, *Chronicler of Cavaliers: A Life of the Virginia Novelist, Dr. William A. Caruthers* (Richmond, 1953), pp. 196–253.

20. Alexander Spotswood, "Journal of . . . Travels . . . for the Public Service of Virginia, 1711–1717," *William and Mary Quarterly* [henceforth cited as *WMQ*] (2), 3 (1923) :40–45. See also Journal, notes 101, 185, 188, 190–91, 194, 196, 198, 203, 206–8 below.

21. Philip Slaughter, *A History of St. Mark's Parish, Culpeper County, Virginia* . . . (Baltimore, 1877), pp. 83–96.

22. W. W. Scott, "The Knights of the Golden Horseshoe: Their Route," *WMQ* (2), 3 (1923) :145–53. See also his *History of Orange County, Virginia* (Richmond, 1907), pp. 98–113.

23. Charles E. Kemper, "Spotswood Mileage Accounts," *WMQ* (2), 3 (1923) :171–72; "The Spotswood Expedition," same (2), 4 (1924) :123–24; "Early Explorers of the Valley of Virginia," same (2), 9 (1929) :236.

24. Randolph W. Church, "Tidewater to Shenandoah—A Cameraman Retraces Spotswood's Famous Expedition," *Virginia Cavalcade*, 1 (Winter 1951) :19–25.

25. Delma R. Carpenter, "The Route Followed by Governor Spotswood in 1716 across the Blue Ridge Mountains,"

*VMHB,* 73 (1965):405–12.

26. Charles E. Hatch, Jr., *Alexander Spotswood Crosses the Blue Ridge . . .* (Blueridge Parkway, 1968).

27. U. S. Geological Survey, *Swift Run Gap* (1965), *Fletcher* (1965), and *Big Meadows* (1965) quadrangles.

28. Journal entries, Sept. 3–5, 1716, above.

29. William Waller Hening, comp., *The Statutes at Large; Being a Collection of All the Lawes of Virginia . . .* , 13 vols. [henceforth cited as Hening] (Richmond et al., 1809–23), 4:77–79; *The Laws of Virginia: being a supplement to Hening's . . .* (Richmond, 1971), pp. 179–85.

30. Great Britain, *Calendar of State Papers, Colonial Series, America and West Indies,* Cecil Headlam et al., eds. (London, 1860–), *1720–1721,* no. 359.

31. Beverley, *History* (London, 1722), p. vii.

32. William Mayo, "A Map of the Northern Neck in Virginia . . . betwixt the Rivers Potomack and Rappahannock . . . 1737 . . . ," Public Record Office, CO/700/Va./8, Colonial Williamsburg Research Department, photocopy.

33. James Madison, *A Map of Virginia* (Richmond, 1807).

34. The distances estimated by Fontaine, Church, and Carpenter are (see also Journal, note 215 below):

### OUTWARD JOURNEY

|  | Fontaine | Church | Carpenter |
|---|---|---|---|
| Germanna |  |  |  |
| Beverley Camp | 3 | 3 | 3 |
| Todd Camp | 6 | 6 | 6 |
| Smith Camp | 14 | 14 | 12 |
| Robinson Camp | 13 | 13 | 6½ |
| Taylor Camp | [12] | 12 | 6½ |
| Robertson Camp | 8 | 8 | 6 |
| Brooke Camp | 4 | 4 | 4 |
| Spotswood Camp | 14 | 14 | 16 |
|  | — | — | — |
|  | 74 | 74 | 60 |

### COMING BACK

| Spotswood Camp |  |  |  |
|---|---|---|---|
| Clowder Camp | 16 | 18 | 20 |
| Mason Camp | 20 | 20 | 10½ |
| Capt. Smith Camp | 23 | 23 | 9 |
| Germanna | [13] | 13 | 19 |
|  | — | — | — |
|  | 72 | 74 | 58½ |

35. Edward F. Heite, archaeological historian of the Virginia Historic Landmarks Commission, in June and July 1970 kindly accompanied the editor on two trips over the alternate routes of the expedition. His excellent background in Virginia history and familiarity with early Virginia roads were of great assistance.

36. Journal entry, Sept. 5, 1716, above.

37. Scott, "Knights' Route," p. 152.

38. R. Taylor Hoskins, superintendent, Shenandoah National Park, Luray, Va., generously sent the editor topographic maps of the Swift Run Gap area made on July 9, 1936, and in the summer of 1937. Stanley W. Abbott, Williamsburg landscape architect, helped interpret the maps, and Mr. Heite and the editor used them on the ground to locate the springs.

39. U. S. Geol. Surv., *Fletcher* (1965) and *Big Meadows* (1965) quads.

40. Jones, *Present State,* pp. 58–59; Davis, *Chronicler of Cavaliers,* pp. 502–6; New York (state), *Documents Relative to the Colonial History of New York,* Edmund Bailey O'Callaghan, ed., 15 vols. (Albany, 1853–57), 5:677.

41. See Journal, notes 216, 289, 295 below.

42. See Journal, note 290 below.

43. See Journal, note 294 below.

44. See Journal, note 298 below.

45. York County, Wills and Inventories, 20 (1745–59):171–72, 177–78, Va. State Lib.; Edward Lewis Goodwin, *The Colonial Church in Virginia . . .* (Milwaukee, 1927), pp. 269, 323, 340, 341; R. A. Brock, ed., *Documents,*

*Chiefly Unpublished, Relating to Huguenot Emigration to Virginia* . . . (Richmond, 1886), p. 122; William Stevens Perry, ed., *Historical Collections Relating to the American Colonial Church,* 5 vols. (Hartford, Conn., 1870), 1: 281–83; James Fontaine, *Autobiography,* 170–71; Dublin University, Trinity College, *Register,* p. 303; *WMQ* (1), 22 (1913–14):58; [Ann Maury,] *Genealogical Chart of the Fontaine and Maury Families* (New York, [ca. 1853]).

46. James Fontaine, *Autobiography,* pp. 241–42; Hug. Soc. London, *Register of the Church of Saint Martin Orgars* . . . , William Minet and Susan Minet, eds., p. 31; R. R. James, "Huguenot Clockmakers," *Horological Journal,* 100 (July 1958):416–17.

47. James Fontaine, *Autobiography,* pp. 242–44; Hug. Soc. London, *Register Lucy Lane and Peter Street Churches,* p. 90; Brock, *Huguenot Emigration,* p. 149; Alcwyn Evans, "The British Genealogist of the Gentry of Carmarthenshire," Ms. 12359 D, p. A310, National Library of Wales; Peter Thornton and Natalie Rothstein, "The Importance of the Huguenots in the London Silk Industry," Hug. Soc. London *Proceedings,* 20 (1958–64):60–88; Hug. Soc. London, *Register of Saint Martin Orgars,* no. 553.

48. John Fontaine, Fire Insurance Policies, Dec. 10, 1742; Dec. 8, 1749; Jan. 23, 1755, Hand in Hand Insurance Records, M/S 8674/45, fol. 102; M/S 8674/63, fol. 130; M/S 8764/75 fol. 58, Guildhall Library (Miss Natalie Rothstein of the Victoria and Albert Museum called this source to the editor's attention); John Sabatier, Will, Apr. 19, 1745 (proved July 2, 1745), Seymer fol. 206, Principal Probate Registry, Somerset House; James, "Huguenot Clockmakers," pp. 416–17; Charles Edward Atkins, comp., *Register of Apprentices of the Worshipful Company of Clockmakers of the City of London, 1631–1931* (London, 1931), p. 105.

The Victoria and Albert Museum formerly had a clock with a printed label that read: "Daniel Torin and John Fontaine, at the Dial in Middle Moorfields, London, and make and mend watches and clocks of all sorts, at reasonable rates." The label was dated by hand: March, 1761" and the dial inscribed: "Daniel Torin London No. 3116." John C. Irwin of Victoria and Albert Museum to editor, Jan. 2, 1970.

49. Hug. Soc. London, *Register of the French Church, Threadneedle Street, London,* 4 vols. (Lymington et al., 1896–1916), 4:139, 150, 161, 169, 197, 206, 210; Evans, "British Genealogist," p. A310; Atkins, *Clockmaker Apprentice Register,* p. 105; Cwm Castle Title Abstract, 1752–1818 (courtesy of Miss Kathleen Busfield, London); T. M. Morgan, *The History and Antiquities of the Parish of Newchurch (Carmarthenshire),* (Carmarthen, 1910), pp. 127–32; Percy J. Williams, "Cwmcastell, Parish of Newchurch, A.D. 1914," Carmarthenshire Antiquarian Society *Transactions,* 10 (1914–15):3–4; Fontaine Family, *Letters,* p. 362; W. Marston Acres, *The Bank of England from Within,* 2 vols. (London, 1931), 1:182–83.

50. John Sabatier Will, Apr. 19, 1745; John Fontaine, Will, July 15, 1763 (proved Jan. 27, 1768), Secker, fol. 12, Principal Probate Registry; F. J. Britten, *Old Clocks and Watches and Their Makers* . . . , 7th ed. (London, 1956), p. 486; Fontaine Family, *Letters,* pp. 371–73.

51. Electoral Books, Apr. 25, 1754, Dynevar Collection 284/2, Cawder Collection 1/42, Carmarthenshire Record Office, Carmarthen; George Eyre Evans, "Burgesses of the County Borough of Carmarthen," Carmarthenshire Antiq. Soc. *Transactions,* 2 (1906–7):235; 3 (1907–8):51. For Carmarthen politics of the period, see William Spurrell, *Carmarthen and Its Neighbourhood: Notes Topographical and Historical.* 2nd edition. (Carmarthen, 1879), pp. 123–29; Sir John E. Lloyd, ed., *A History of*

*Carmarthenshire from Prehistoric Times to 1900.* 2 vols. (Cardiff, 1935–39), 2: 32–48; Peter D. G. Thomas, "County Elections in Eighteenth-Century Carmarthenshire," *Carmarthen Antiquarian,* 4 (1963):125–30; Major Francis Jones, "The Vaughans of Golden Grove," Society of Cymmrodian *Transactions,* 1964, part II, pp. 199–202.

52. In addition to the printed Fontaine Family, *Letters,* pp. 311–443, Colonial Williamsburg has some original letters, copies of some of the printed letters, and microfilm copies from the American Philosophical Society of original and printed letters, some of them in the James Maury Letter Book, 1763–1768. The Alderman Library at the University of Virginia also has copies of most of the known family letters.

53. Fontaine Family, *Letters,* pp. 376–77.

54. Same, pp. 339, 384; Dumas Malone, *Jefferson the Virginian* (Boston, 1948), pp. 40–45; Helen Duprey Bullock, ed., "A Dissertation on Education in the Form of a Letter from James Maury to Robert Jackson, July 17, 1762," Albemarle County Historical Society *Magazine,* 2 (1941–42):36–60.

55. Fontaine Family, *Letters,* p. 341; James Fontaine, Marriage Bond, Aug. 31, 1752, National Library of Wales; John Fontaine, Will, July 15, 1763.

56. G. H. Baille, *Watchmakers and Clockmakers of the World,* 3rd ed. (London, 1963), p. 111; John and Moses Fontaine to Peter [Fontaine, Jr.], Cwm Castle, June 30, 1762, Colonial Williamsburg; John Fontaine, Will, July 15, 1763; Moses Fontaine, Will, Nov. 24, 1764 (proved Aug. 1, 1766), Secker fol. 12, 1768, Principal Probate Registry.

57. Fontaine Family, *Letters,* p. 364.

58. See note 52 above; note 64 below; Journal, notes 290, 294, 298 below; *West Wales Historical Records,* 5:22; 7:207.

59. Fontaine Family, *Letters,* pp. 349–52.

60. Rev. Peter Fontaine, Will and Directions to Executors, June 30, 1757, Ms. copy of original, Colonial Williamsburg; Ann Maury says Peter died in July 1757 (Fontaine Family, *Letters,* p. 354), but she probably was mistaken because Elizabeth Carter Byrd wrote her husband William [III] from Belvidere, Aug. 16, 1759: "Our poor old good Minister Fountain has left this Staige. He died not one Shiling in debt as people say." *VMHB,* 37 (1929):248.

61. Fontaine Family, *Letters,* pp. 424–31.

62. Same, pp. 442–43.

63. John Fontaine, Will, July 15, 1763; Moses Fontaine Will, Nov. 20, 1764; James Fontaine, Will, Mar. 22, 1785, in Cwm Castle Abstract of Title.

64. Carmarthenshire Antiq. Soc. *Transactions,* 3 (1907–8):51; *Fontaine and Maury Genealogical Chart.*

65. Moses Fontaine, Will, Nov. 20, 1764; Evans, "British Genealogist," p. A310; *Fontaine and Maury Genealogical Chart;* Cwm Castle Abstract of Title.

66. Evans, "British Genealogist," p. A310; *West Wales Historical Records,* 9 (1920–23):179; 11 (1926):90.

67. James Fontaine, *Autobiography,* pp. 13, 235, 244.

68. For Miss Maury, see Anne Fontaine Maury [now Mrs. William G. Hirschfield], comp., *Intimate Virginiana; a Century of Maury Travels by Land and by Sea* (Richmond, 1941), pp. 108, 210, 252–53, 315, 319, 329. The various versions and editions of James Fontaine's *Autobiography* are:

[Ann Maury, comp.] *A Tale of the Huguenots; or, Memoirs of a French Refugee Family. Translated and Compiled from the Original Manuscripts of James Fontaine by One of His Descendants with an Introduction by F. L. Hawkes* (New York, John S. Taylor, 1838).

Ann Maury, comp., *Memoirs of a Huguenot Family* (see note 1 above).

Reprinted by same publisher, 1872, 1907. Reprinted 1853 edition (Baltimore, Genealogical Publishing Company, 1967).

James Fontaine, *Memoirs of a Huguenot Family. Translated and Compiled from the Original Autobiography of the Rev. James Fontaine* (London, Religious Tract Society, [1874]).
Follows 1853 version.

Jacques Fontaine, *Mémoires d'une Famille Huguenote, victime de la révocation de l'édit de Nantes. . . . Avec une introduction et des notes par E. Castel, pasteur.* (Toulouse, Société des Livres Religieux, 1877).
Follows 1838 version.

Jacques Fontaine, *Mémoirs d'une Famille Huguenote, victime de la révocation de l'édit de Nantes. . . . publiés pour la première fois d'après le manuscrit original.* (Toulouse, Société des Livres Religieux, 1897).
Follows 1853 version.

69. John Fontaine, *Journal,* 245. Frances Elizabeth died in 1866 and Sophia in 1891. *Fontaine and Maury Genealogical Chart;* Sophia Fontaine, Will, Feb. 14, 1891 (proved Apr. 11, 1892), Principal Probate Registry.

70. Miss Irene Scouloudi, honorary secretary, and C.F.A. Marmoy, librarian, of the Huguenot Society of London were helpful in the search for the Journal, and so was Miss Frances Leigh Williams of Delray Beach, Fla. For Mrs. Hirschfeld's book, see note 68 above.

71. James Fontaine Minor Papers, Box 5, "Writings."

72. Maury, *Intimate Virginiana,* p. 252.

73. George Patrick of London by his will of Sept. 14, 1914 (proved Dec. 7, 1916) left to his nephew Douglas John George Harley Patrick of London "the Journal of John Fontaine the Army Officer dated 1710." When the nephew died at Haslemere in 1959 the Journal had disappeared. Copy of will courtesy of Miss Busfield.

NOTES TO JOURNAL

# Notes to Journal

1. Thomas Wharton (1648–1715), first marquis of Wharton, and lord lieutenant of Ireland, 1708–10, granted the commission. James Fontaine, *Autobiography*, pp. 234–35; *Dictionary of National Biography* [henceforth cited as *D.N.B.*], s.v. "Wharton, Thomas."

2. Lt. Gen. Richard Ingoldsby (d. 1712) then commanded the forces in Ireland. Same, s.v. "Ingoldsby, Richard."

3. Christopher Fleming (1669–1723), twenty-second baron of Slane, commanded the regiment. In transcribing the Journal, Miss Maury must have mistaken "Slane" for "Shawe." James Fontaine, *Autobiography*, p. 235; John Fontaine, *Journal*, p. 245; Charles Dalton, ed., *English Army Lists and Commission Registers, 1661–1774*, 6 vols. (London, 1892–1904), 6:19, 250–51; John Bernard Burke, *A Genealogical History of the Dormant, Abeyant, Forfeited, and Extinct Peerages of the British Empire* (London, 1883), pp. 217–18.

4. By the time the regiment sailed for Spain, Capt. Charles Conyers had been replaced by Capt. Henry LaFaysille (or Fausille). Dalton, *English Army Lists*, 6:250–51.

5. Capt. Thomas Phillips. Same, 6:250.

6. A small fishing village on an island overlooking Cork Harbor. For a good early history of the harbor, see D. N. Brunicardi, "Notes on the History of Haulbowline," *Irish Sword*, 7 (1965): 19–33.

7. Lt. Col. Thomas Chester was listed as out of Col. Edward Jones's Regiment of Foot, Feb. 10, 1711. Dalton, *English Army Lists*, 6:223, 254–55.

8. Probably Belém, the old suburb of Lisbon that contains the Tower of Belém. Baedeker's *Touring Guides: Spain and Portugal* (Freiburg et al., 1959), 209.

9. England and her allies had captured Barcelona, Oct. 9, 1705, because of Admiral Shovell's naval support and the earl of Peterborough's fortunate capture of the Montjuich fortress that commanded the city. Barcelona and Catalonia remained loyal to Archduke Charles of Austria throughout the war. A. W. Ward et al., eds., *The Age of Louis XIV* in *Cambridge Modern History*, 5 (New York, 1908):416, 432; John William Fortescue, *A History of the British Army*, 6 vols. (London, 1899), 1:459–63.

10. Tarragona, a busy seaport famed for its wines, is situated about 60 miles southwest of Barcelona. With the remainder of Catalonia, it fell to the English in 1705. L. Russell Muirhead, ed., *The Blue Guides: Northern Spain with the Balearic Islands*, 2nd ed. (London, 1958), pp. 141–47; Fortescue, *British Army*, 1:462.

11. Fontaine was almost certainly suffering from chronic malaria, both then and later in Virginia (see Journal entries, Aug. 27, 1716; Mar. 1717; Mar. 28, 1718). Malaria was then endemic in Portugal, Spain, and Virginia. Fred B. Devitt, M.D., of Williamsburg has verified this statement.

Fontaine probably cut his hair because of lice.

12. The cathedral was built in the twelfth and thirteenth centuries. Muirhead, *Northern Spain*, pp. 143–45.

13. About 50 miles southwest of Tarragona on the Ebro River. Muirhead, *Northern Spain*, pp. 150–51; Fortescue, *British Army*, 1:477.

14. John Campbell (1678–1743), second duke of Argyll, was ambassador extraordinary to Spain and commander-in-chief of the English forces there. *D.N.B.*, s.v. "Campbell, John."

15. The Lords of the Treasury paid Lord Slane's regiment from Dec. 23, 1710, until it was disbanded, Aug. 4, 1712. The officers were then placed on half pay, which for an ensign was 1s. 10d. per day (more than £33 yearly). Fontaine probably received this allowance for the remainder of his life. William A. Shaw, ed., *Calendar of Treasury Books, 1712–1716*, 5 vols. (London, 1954–57), 26, pt. II:55, 365; 27, pt. II:108, 402–3; 30, pt. II:260, 339; Dalton, *English Army Lists*, 6:156.

16. The river is the Lobregat. Only the chapel and great hall of this palace remain today. Baedeker's *Spain and Portugal*, p. 177; Muirhead, *Northern Spain*, p. 72.

17. The Cathedral of Santa Cruz and Santa Eulalia is on the highest point of the Old Town that in Fontaine's day was surrounded by a wall. Same, pp. 73–75.

18. Archduke Charles of Austria (1685–1740) in 1711 was made Charles VI of the Holy Roman Empire. His young bride was Elizabeth Christina of Brunswick-Wolfenbüttel. Ward, *Louis XIV*, p. 432.

19. The Montjuich fortification surmounted an isolated ridge about 700 feet high south of the city. See note 9 above. Muirhead, *Northern Spain*, pp. 81–85.

20. Piquette, sometimes piquet or picquette, is a cheap, tart wine made by pouring water on the husks of grapes.

*Oxford English Dictionary* (1933) [henceforth cited as *O.E.D.*].

21. The Barcelonians correctly estimated the situation. England and her allies had supported the succession to the Spanish throne of the Habsburg Archduke Charles against Philip V (1683–1746), grandson of Louis XIV. When Charles became the Holy Roman Emperor, the allies decided he was more dangerous than Philip, and in the Peace of Utrecht (1713) they recognized Philip as king of Spain. Supported by the English navy, his army captured Barcelona and sold its gallant survivors into slavery. Ward, *Louis XIV*, p. 446.

22. The capital of Minorca with its San Felipe fortress and church of Santa Maria was captured by the British in 1708. Muirhead, *Northern Spain*, pp. 192–95; Fortescue, *British Army*, 1:511.

23. Fontaine closes his account of his military service with no mention of active fighting, though a skirmish could have taken place at the Barcelona embarkation. His father says that John "received several wounds himself and had wounded others, being often obliged to put his hand to his sword, but he never killed any body." James Fontaine, *Autobiography*, p. 235.

24. Small islands off St. David's Head in Wales.

25. Defoe regarded Milford Haven as one of the best harbors in all Britain. Daniel Defoe, *A Tour Thro' the Whole Island of Great Britain, Divided into Circuits or Journies . . .* , 3 vols. [London, 1724–26]. With an Introduction by G.D.H. Cole, 2 vols. (London, 1927), 2:455–56.

26. Richard Sparkes was then mayor of Haverfordwest, which Defoe described as "Strong, well Built, Clean, and Populous." John Brown, J. W. Phillips, and Fred J. Warren, *The History of Haverfordwest . . .* (Haverfordwest, 1914), p. 252; Defoe, *Tour Thro' Great Britain*, 2:456. Griff C. Morgan, present Haverfordwest mayor, and Miss Maureen Patch, Pembroke county archi-

vist, have verified Sparkes's mayoralty.

27. Peter Fontaine (1646–1714?), John's uncle, assisted his father in the church at Vaux and served as minister at Royan. Imprisoned on the Isle of Oleron for six months, he fled to England, where in 1687 he received denizations for himself, his wife Suzanna, and their six children. Peter from 1692 until his death was minister or chaplain at the Pest House, which the City of London had set aside for the use of sick and infirm refugees. It afterwards became the French Hospital of La Providence. The Committee for the Pest House spent £16 13s. 6d. in a lawsuit against Fontaine in 1700, but apparently it left no scars, for in 1705 he received £21 for his services. His brother James said that Peter was "beloved and respected by all who knew him." James Fontaine, *Autobiography*, pp. 27–28; Hug. Soc. London, *Letters of Denization and Acts of Naturalization for Aliens in England and Ireland, 1603–1800*, William A. Shaw, ed., 3 vols. (Lymington et al., 1911–32), 1:197; Hug. Soc. London *Proceedings*, 1 (1885–86):50, 338; 7 (1901–4):133; 8 (1905–8):57; 11 (1915–17):250; Brock, *Huguenot Emigration*, p. 120

28. Esther, the youngest daughter of John Fontaine's uncle Peter Fontaine, was the wife of John Arnaud, a grandson of John's great-aunt Bouquet. Arnaud was "frequently called upon, to act as umpire, when differences arose between any of the French merchants in London." James Fontaine, *Autobiography*, p. 28; *Fontaine and Maury Genealogical Chart;* Brock, *Huguenot Emigration*, p. 120.

29. There were at least two Huguenot families of this name in London about this time. Cephas Gout, formerly of Paris, was admitted a foreign journeyman weaver in 1684, and Antoine Gouet was a silk worker in Will Street, 1703. Hug. Soc. London, *Publications*, 21:126; 33:51, 52; 37:no. 65.

30. Parkgate on the eastern bank of the River Dee offered ferry service to Dublin. The trip, about 120 miles long, avoided the land journey to Holyhead, which is only 60 miles from Dublin. Probably Fontaine and Gout could not obtain a satisfactory ship. Because the Dee has silted badly, Parkgate is no longer a ferry terminal. Harold Edgar Young, *A Perambulate of the Hundred of Wiwall in the County of Chester . . .* (Liverpool, 1909), pp. 128–39; Constantina Maxwell, *Dublin under the Georges* (London, 1946), pp. 248–52.

31. Both John Macky and Defoe described the route from Chester to Holyhead about this time. [John Macky], *A Journey through England, in Familiar Letters from a Gentleman* [London, 1714] in Daniel Defoe, *From London to Land's End* [Cassell's National Library] (London, 1888), pp. 180–92; Defoe, *Tour Thro' Great Britain*, 2:463–65. See also the amusing [John Bush], *Hibernia Curiosa: A Letter from a Gentleman in Dublin . . .* (London, [1767]), pp. 1–7.

32. The ships from Parkgate or Holyhead customarily landed at Ringsend, a spit of land south of the River Liffey and of Dublin. Ringsend and its neighbor to the south, Irish Town, were popular places for sea bathing. The Ringsend car thus plied between Dublin and the two villages. John Warburton et al., *History of the City of Dublin*, 2 vols. (London, 1818), 1: chart opp. 431; 2: frontispiece map and 1173; Bush, *Hibernia Curiosa*, pp. 23–26.

33. James Fontaine with his customary enterprise in 1708 found a well-built but rundown house on St. Stephen's Green, leased it for 99 years at £10 annually, and spent £450 in converting it into a grammar school. The map in Bush (1764) showed the French Walk on the west side of the green. James Fontaine, *Autobiography*, pp. 228–32; Warburton, *Dublin*, 1: 459–63; Bush, *Hibernia Curiosa*, frontispiece; Torin, "Torin Family," p. 5.

34. John Hepburn, mathematician,

advertised that in Darby's Square, St. Warborough's Street, he taught mathematical geometry, algebra, trigonometry, navigation, astronomy, surveying, gauging, dialing, fortification, gunnery, the use of globes and instruments, and merchants' accounts. He would also board young gentlemen. Thomas Hume's *Dublin Courant,* Sept. 2, 1721; Sept. 18, 1723, National Library of Ireland (microfilm).

35. James Fontaine (1686–1746) probably was still living in Bear Haven (today Castletown Berehaven) on Bantry Bay, county Cork. He became a justice of the peace for the county in 1710 and was married to Lucretia Desjarrie the next year. He may still have conducted a fishing business, because John gives detailed reports on the Newfoundland fishery in the Journal, entries, Feb. 3, Mar. 11, 1714/15. James Fontaine, *Autobiography,* pp. 180–232; Cork Hist. and Archaeol. Soc. *Journal,* 3 (1897): 47, 62. See note 294 below.

36. John's father succinctly describes the purpose of his voyage as follows: "John, the officer, was without employment, it was therefore determined that he should make a voyage to America, travel through every part where the climate was temperate, and purchase a plantation, in such situation as he judged would prove in all respects the most advantageous." James Fontaine, *Autobiography,* p. 238.

37. In 1724 a heated controversy took place in Ireland over accepting halfpence and farthings made by one William Woods. On Sept. 22, 1724, Thomas Hume's *Dublin Courant* carried a list of Youghall merchants agreeing not to accept the coins, but Mr. Downs is not on it. Nor does the name appear in the published Youghal Council records. He might be a relative of the Mr. Downe of Barnstaple with whom James Fontaine stayed in 1685–86. See Introduction, p. 6 above.

38. The master of the "Dove" was William Shapley and her owner Thomas Smith, the Bideford merchant. In June 1714 she had arrived at Bideford from Virginia with a cargo of tobacco and in November sailed from her home port laden with mixed merchandise that included rugs, hats, stockings, textiles, haberdashery, books, paper, shoes, nails, ironmongery, wrought pewter, brass work, wool cards, 6 chairs (18s. value), one looking glass (£1), one chest of drawers (£1 5s.), and 18 Russia leather chairs (£5 6s. 8d.) (Bideford Port Books, Public Record Office, London, E190, 987/9, 15). The "Dove," sometimes called the "Virginia Dove," was a 100-ton square-stern vessel, carrying four guns, built in Virginia (probably on the Potomac) in 1699 and registered at Bideford. On May 28, 1706, she cleared the South Potomac District for Bideford with Samuel Ellis listed as master and Thomas Smith owner. Naval Office Returns, South Potomac District, CO 5/1441, p. 456, Colonial Williamsburg [microfilm], courtesy of Harold B. Gill. The "Dove" arrived at Waterford, Ireland, Jan. 1, 1708/9, with tobacco from Virginia. *Dublin Gazette,* Jan. 4, 1708/9, Trinity College Library, Dublin. The latitude and longitude figures are from London Times, *Index-Gazetteer of the World* (London, 1965), p. 423.

39. The "Dove" was taking the northern route across the Atlantic to Virginia. Until about 1650 the southern route by way of Cape Finistere, the Canaries, and the West Indies had been more frequently used. The northern route, though much shorter and avoiding the dangers of stormy Cape Hatteras, could be rough and perilous in winter. Arthur Pierce Middleton, *Tobacco Coast: A Maritime History of Chesapeake Bay in the Colonial Era* (Newport News, Va., 1953), pp. 4-7; D. W. Waters, *The Art of Navigation in England in Elizabethan and Early Stuart Times* (New Haven, 1958), p. 261.

The navigator at sea then used a combination of dead reckoning and celestial navigation in determining his course. Fontaine explains how latitude was determined by taking an observation, either of the sun (Journal, entry, Dec. 16, 1714) or of the Pole Star (May 10, 1715). See also Middleton, pp. 20–25; Waters, pp. 308–10. 592–93, plates 66. 84–85; M. V. Brewington, *The Peabody Museum Collection of Navigating Instruments* . . . (Salem, Mass., 1963).

40. In hawking, to rake is to fly along after or strike the game. Apparently the term "rake" was applied to bats also. *O.E.D.*

41. A popular name for porpoise at that time; now rare. Same.

42. Fontaine is describing the method of sighting the sun with a modified cross-staff or forestaff. Capt. John Davis (1550?–1605) had invented the backstaff about 1695; in using it the observer stood with his back to the sun and used a shadow vane to determine the reading. Though the advantages of the backstaff or Davis quadrant were recognized at once, many shipmasters continued to use the cross-staff, though sometimes equipped with a cross vane on which the shadow of the larger crosspiece would fall. Waters, *Art of Navigation*, pp. 53–55, 135–36, 204–5, 306; plates 17, 53–55, 70–71, 85; Brewington, *Peabody Museum Collection,* pp. 3, 6–9; plates 4–7. Silvio A. Bedini, assistant director, National Museum of History and Technology, and John Parry, professor of oceanographic history, Harvard University, have commented helpfully on Fontaine's descriptions of sighting the sun and Pole Star (see note 74 below).

43. An obsolete form of mire, applied to several birds. A mire-crow was a laughing gull, and a mire-duck a wild duck. *O.E.D.*

44. Thiboult may have been one of Fontaine's four servants, but it is not clear whether the quarrel arose because Fontaine or the sailors were beating him.

45. The goods probably had been damaged in the storm. William Binauld was a Huguenot refugee merchant and printer in Dublin. In 1713 he and Eliphal Dobson printed a Bible, Common Prayer Book, and Singing Psalms. *Dublin Gazette,* Oct. 24, 1713; John Fontaine, *Journal,* p. 247. See also note 51 below.

46. Appledore lies at the junction of the Taw and Torridge rivers. Barnstaple is up the Taw and Bideford up the Torridge. Ward, Locke & Co., Ltd., *Guide to Bideford, Clovelly, Westward Ho!, Barnstaple, Ilfracombe, and Northwest Devon* (London and Melbourne, 1951), pp. 14-15.

47. Bideford and Barnstaple are perceptively described in Defoe, *Tour Thro' Great Britain,* 1:259-62.

48. Thomas Smith, Bideford merchant and shipowner, and his son John are mentioned in Bideford Bridge Trust Leases, no. 21, Sept. 8, 1701, Devon County Archives (courtesy of Miss Margaret Cash) and are among 85 citizens who signed a statement in a Bideford tax suit of 1766. William Henry Rogers, "Notes on Bideford" (ms.), 3 vols., Exeter City Record Office, 1:178–205. There is also a typed copy of this set with different pagination in the Bideford City Library. See also I. Rogers, *Bideford Ships,* pp. 11, 14, 22, 23. See also note 38 above.

49. One of Fontaine's four servants. Fontaine may have been paying the gunsmith for boarding Morriset and teaching him a trade or he may have been hiring him to the gunsmith on these terms. See also note 70 below.

50. The Long Bridge of Bideford (still in use today) spanned the River Torridge about three miles above its confluence with Bideford Bay. In Fontaine's day it had 24 arches, was 677 feet long, about 30 feet above low water, and nearly 10 feet wide. Watkins, *History of Bideford,* pp. 140–85; Charles Worthy, "A 'Second Essay towards a History of Bideford,' " Devonshire Assn. *Transactions,* 16 (1884):671-77; Alex-

ander G. Duncan, "The Long Bridge at Bideford," same, 34 (1902):223–64; F. E. Whiting, "Bideford Bridge," same, 80 (1948):127–38; Muriel Goaman, *Old Bideford and District* (Bristol, 1968), pp. 19–33.

51. On Feb. 9, 1715, Fontaine paid the controller of Bideford Port 4 shillings 10¼ pence duty for 200 pounds of bound books, 27 pounds wrought iron, 200 pounds old iron, and a parcel of paper valued at £2 (Bideford Port Books, E 190, 988/11 PRO). Oxford University since the 1630s had had a monopoly of the printing of Bibles and prayerbooks, though sometimes it had licensed the Stationers' Company in London to do such printing. Thus the Bibles and prayerbooks printed by Mr. Binauld in Dublin could have been regarded as contraband and subject to seizure. Charles Edward Mallet, *A History of the University of Oxford,* 3 vols. (New York, 1924, and London, 1927), 1:327–28; 2:311, 431–32.

52. Christopher Bedford (d. 1723) was the Church of England minister at St. Mary's in Bideford from 1700. He also served Doulton in Devon. "Incumbents of Devon Parishes," Exeter Cathedral Library, Bishop's Palace, courtesy of Mrs. Audrey M. Erskine, archivist; Watkins, *History of Bideford,* p. 89; Devonshire Assn., *Calendars of Wills and Administrations . . . Devon and Cornwall,* 13 parts (Plymouth, 1908–14), pt. 1: 24; W. H. Rogers, "Notes on Bideford" (Bideford copy), 3:50.

Fontaine seems to have made a mistake on the date of this entry. From 1662 to 1859 the execution of Charles I (Jan. 30, 1649) was observed in the calendar of the Church of England. Especially with the date falling on Sunday in 1715, it is unlikely that the observance would have taken place on Jan. 31. John R. H. Moorman, *A History of the Church of England* (New York, 1967), p. 241.

53. William Bartlet was, perhaps, the leading Presbyterian minister at Bideford, but Fontaine may not yet have met him. (See note 68 below). Other dissenters were Jacob Bayley, pastor of the Great Meeting (founded 1698) and Nathaniel Cocke (d. 1760), who moved from Chumleigh to Bideford in 1710. Fontaine was probably right in his estimate of the strength of Presbyterianism in 1715, though it declined in popularity during the remainder of the century. Watkins, *History of Bideford,* p. 138; W. H. Rogers, "Notes on Bideford" (Bideford copy), 2:117; 3:60–69; A. A. Brockett, "Nonconformity in Devon in the Eighteenth Century," Devonshire Assn. *Transactions,* 90 (1958): 31–59.

54. Dr. Louis Mauzy (Fontaine sometimes spells it Mosey, Mose, Moss, or Mosse) was probably the son of the Rev. Dr. Louis Mauzy, a friend of John's father. He came with his family from France on the same boat, was minister of the Huguenot congregation that met at St. Anne's Chapel in the enclosure of Barnstaple parish church, and baptized John's oldest brother James there in 1686. He was said to be still active in 1720, but John's companion does not seem to conduct services (see Journal entries, Feb. 6, 13, 20) and may have been a physician. Inkerman Rogers, *The Huguenots in Devonshire* (Barnstaple, 1942), pp. 16–17, 19, 23; J. F. Chanter, "The Parish Clerks of Barnstaple, 1500–1900," Devonshire Assn. *Transactions,* 36 (1904):410–12; James Fontaine, *Autobiography,* pp. 118, 134.

55. In 1699 Bideford sent 28 ships with 146 boats to Newfoundland, Barnstaple furnished seven ships, and Appledore one. London had 71 ships in the trade, and Exeter and Topsham together 34 with 70 boats. Watkins, *History of Bideford,* pp. 59–61; I. Rogers, *Bideford Ships,* pp. 11–12; I. Rogers, *Concise History of Bideford,* pp. 21–24; Stephens, "West-Country Ports and Newfoundland Fisheries," Devonshire Assn. *Transactions,* 88 (1956):90–101.

For Fontaine's interest in the fisheries, see note 35 above.

56. Charles Davie, a merchant and shipbuilder, was the mayor (elected on Sept. 21, 1714), and he served again in 1723 and 1732. W. H. Rogers, "Notes on Bideford" (Bideford copy), 2:5–6, 3:3, 102. The certificate probably related the loss or spoilage of some of the goods Fontaine was carrying on Arnaud's account and may have enabled him to collect insurance or to prorate the loss among other merchants.

57. Dr. William Barbor (d. 1718) had been a leading merchant of Barnstaple but was probably living at Chittlehampton (his will was signed there) about seven miles southeast of Barnstaple. I. Rogers, *Devonshire Huguenots*, p. 18; *Barnstaple Records* (reprint), J. R. Chanter and Thomas Wainwright, eds., 2 vols. (Barnstaple, 1900), 2:181; *Barnstaple Parish Register of Baptisms, Marriages, and Burials, 1538–1812*, Thomas Wainwright, ed. (Exeter, 1903), p. 116; Devonshire Assn., "Index of Wills and Administrations . . . Proved in the Court of Archdeaconry of Barnstaple, 1563-1858 . . . Destroyed by Enemy Action in 1942" (typescript), John J. Breckerlegge, ed., 5 vols. (1952), 1:71.

58. This entry contains errors. Maurice Bond, clerk of the records, House of Lords, London, kindly pointed out that the election took place on Feb. 3 (not Feb. 7 as Fontaine has it) and that John Rolle and Sir Arthur Chichester (not Squire Barlow) were elected. E. L. C. Mullins, secretary to the Editorial Board, History of Parliament Trust, London, then generously examined the manuscript precept and return in the Public Record Office and confirmed Mr. Bond's conclusion. See also Daphne Drake, "Members of Parliament for Barnstaple, 1689-1832," Devonshire Assn. *Transactions*, 73 (1941): 181–83; Romney Sedgwick, *The House of Commons, 1715-1754*, 2 vols. (London, 1970), 1:225, 548; 2:391.

59. That is, Mr. Smith promised to hurry the repairs on the "Dove."

60. Jacob Mounier (1696–1743) was only nineteen at this time, but Fontaine obviously thought highly of his ability and integrity. I. Rogers, *Devonshire Huguenots*, p. 20; *Barnstaple Parish Register*, p. 136; Gribble, *Memorials of Barnstaple*, p. 530.

61. Mr. Coulter was probably the son or other relative of Dr. David Coultre or Coulter (d. 1706), a minister of the French congregation in Barnstaple. I. Rogers, *Devonshire Huguenots*, p. 19; *Barnstaple Parish Register*, p. 106.

62. George Buck (1672–1743) seems to have traded more heavily with Virginia and Maryland than did his brother John (1665–1719). The Buck family came to Bideford from Ireland in the seventeenth century and was prominent in trade, shipbuilding, and the Bridge Trust. George was mayor six times, John four times, and George's son John (1703–1745) thrice. George was justice of the peace for 24 years and was married to Sarah Stucley (1677–1742), daughter of the prominent and wealthy nonconformist, Lewis Stucley. Watkins, *History of Bideford*, pp. 62–66, 87, 226; I. Rogers, *Bideford Ships*, pp. 13–14, 23; I. Rogers, *Concise History*, pp. 21–24; W. H. Rogers, "Notes on Bideford" (Bideford copy), 1:5–6; 3:101-3; J .R. Powell, "Notes on Devonshire & Cornwall Parishes" (Ms.), 27 vols. (ca. 1870–1900), Exeter City Record Office, 5:102, 6:682; 12:133–35; Barnet Morris Index, Exeter Public Library.

63. George Strange engaged in the Irish and Leghorn trade and was mayor of Bideford, 1695, 1704, and 1713. W. H. Rogers, "Notes on Bideford" (Bideford copy), 2:5; 3:105.

64. William Pawley (d. 1728) had several leases from the Bridge Trustees, and his daughter Judith (1711-1739) was married to George Buck's son John (see note 62 above). Pawley had con-

nections with the Potomac River area in Virginia for on May 15, 1717, William Kelly and he gave letters of attorney to Capt. Edward Collins, John Harris, Daniel McCarty, Col. Peter Presley, and Capt. George Eskridge (see notes 77, 81, 294 below). Bideford Bridge Trust Leases, nos. 3, 63, 68; Powell, "Devonshire and Cornwall Parishes" (Ms.), 12:133–35; William White, *History, Gazeteer, and Directory of Devonshire* (Sheffield, 1850), p. 760; *VMHB*, 23 (1918):308.

65. William Peard (d. ca. 1716), a Congregational or Independent minister, was the son of Oliver Peard (1636–1696), a Puritan divine. William served at Appledore in 1699 as a candidate for ordination and then at Bideford, for a time with John Hamner (1642–1707). He was ordained in 1705. Courtesy of the Rev. Kenneth Twinn, secretary and librarian, Dr. Williams Library, London. See also Arnold Gwynne Matthews, *Calamy Revised: Being a Revision of Edmund Calamy's Account of the Ministers and Others Ejected and Silenced, 1660–62* (Oxford, 1934), pp. 246–47, 384; Miss Wickham, "Early Nonconformity in Bideford," *Devonshire Assn. Transactions*, 34 (1902):415–16. John Fontaine's father may have tutored young Peard at Barnstaple or at Taunton. James Fontaine, *Autobiography*, pp. 122–35, 142–44, 157.

66. The Long Bridge at Barnstaple over the Taw River, still used today, was built about 1300. Bruce W. Oliver, "The Long Bridge at Barnstaple," *Devonshire Assn. Transactions*, 70 (1938): 193–97; 78 (1941):177–91; Ward, Locke & Co., *Guide to Bideford*, pp. 1–12.

67. By 1727–28 Barnstaple had outstripped Bideford in manufacturing wool. About 100 combers were processing two tons of wool each week, most of it imported from Ireland. The weavers produced Barnstaple stuffs (similar to merinos), flannels, plushes, and everlastings. Almost every poor family had a loom. Gribble, *Memorials of Barnstaple*, pp. 524–44, 601–2; Hoskins, *Devon*, p. 328; I. Rogers, *Concise History*, p. 23.

68. Probably William Bartlet (1678–1720), the leading Presbyterian minister of Bideford. No Berkeley appears in Bideford records, and Miss Maury may have transcribed the name incorrectly from the original Journal. Bartlet was the son and grandson of Independent ministers, attended Edinburgh University but did not take a degree, and came to the Great Meeting at Bideford in 1702, at first as co-pastor with Jacob Bayley. Defoe found him "not only a learned Man and Master of good Reading, but a most acceptable Gentlemanly Person, and one, who . . . had not only good Learning and good Sense, but abundance of good Manners, and good Humour, nothing Soure, Cynical, or Morose in him, and in a Word, a very valuable Man." Watkins, *History of Bideford*, pp. 133–37; Matthews, *Calamy Revised*, p. 32; Defoe, *Tour Thro' Great Britain*, 1:260–61; Hoskins, *Devon*, p. 238; W. H. Rogers, "Notes on Bideford" (Bideford copy), 3:68–69.

69. Anne Hutchinson Mauzy was the daughter of Edward Hutchinson (1632–1699) and Anne Batty. There was no one named Hugh Hutchinson prominent in Boston mercantile and church affairs of the time, and none of Anne's true uncles lived there. The eighteenth century was careless about relationships, however, and she had three cousins in Boston—Col. Elisha Hutchinson (1641–1717) and his two sons, Thomas (1675–1739), the father of Gov. Thomas Hutchinson, and Edward (1678–1752). Elisha was retired by 1715, but both Thomas and Edward were active merchants and respected church members. Thomas Hutchinson, *The Diaries and Letters of His Excellency* . . . , Peter Orlando Hutchinson, ed., 2 vols. (London, 1883), 2:446–47, 457–58; *New England Historical and Genealogical Register*, 1 (1894):299–310.

70. Probably Morriset, the servant referred to in note 49 above. He could have worked with the gunsmith on the wooden stocks of guns and have been interested in coopering.

71. See note 35 above.

72. Probably the sailors' or Fontaine's corruption of "corposant," also called St. Elmo's fire or the corona discharge. During stormy weather a bluish glow appears on the extremities of church steeples, ships' masts or spars, or aircraft wings, often accompanied by a crackling or fizzing noise. It is caused by discharges of atmospheric or static electricity. Sailors regarded St. Elmo as their patron and the fire as a sign of his protection. Corposant comes from the Italian or Portuguese *corpo santo* meaning "body of a saint." McGraw-Hill *Encyclopedia of Science and Technology,* (rev. edn., 1966), s.v. "Corposant" and "St. Elmo's Fire."

73 A few geographers and practical sailors including North American whalers knew something of the limits of the Gulf Stream and how to avoid it sailing towards America and use it going the other way. But in general the English ship captains ignored the current as Benjamin Franklin found in 1769 when as postmaster general he tried to speed up the packet service. Henry Chapin and F. G. Walton Smith, *Ocean River* (New York, 1952), pp. 109–12; Lloyd A. Brown, "The River in the Ocean," *Essays Honoring Lawrence C. Wroth* (Portland, Me., 1951), pp. 69–84.

74. Fontaine is describing a crossstaff or forestaff with three transversaries or vanes for use in various bands of latitude. For its use in sighting the sun, see note 42 above.

75. Cape Henry bounds the mouth of Chesapeake Bay on the south, and Cape Charles on the north. Walter Hoxton, *This Mapp of the Bay of Chesepeack* . . . ([London,] 1735), Colonial Williamsburg photostat of British Museum copy; Joshua Fry and Peter Jefferson, *A Map of the Inhabited Part of Virginia . . . 1751* (London, [1754]) in University of Virginia, *The Fry and Jefferson Map of Virginia and Maryland* . . . , 2nd edition (Charlottesville, 1966); Leonard Leland, "Map of the Chesapeake Bay Country during the Eighteenth Century . . ." (1939), a modern original painting based on sound historical research hanging in Earl Gregg Swem Library, College of William and Mary.

76. The Horse Shoe is a well-known shoal in Chesapeake Bay off Old Point Comfort between the James and York rivers and the Wolf Trap, a small shoal southeast of Gwynn's Island. In 1691 H. M. S. *Wolfe* was aground three months on the latter shoal; hence the name. Hoxton, *Chesapeake Bay,* 1735; Middleton, *Tobacco Coast,* pp. 314–15, 317.

77. Daniel McCarty (1679?–1724), lawyer and planter, was collector of customs for the South Potomac District. He was a member of the quorum of Westmoreland County, burgess at various times, 1706-23, and speaker, 1715–18. The "Dove" was probably anchored between the Yeocomico and Nomini rivers but the Naval Office Returns for the district are missing, 1707–25. McCarty is referred to in the Audit Office Enrolment Books, PRO AO 15/25, 1713–1715, p. 174; AO 15/94, 1718–1728, pp. 381, 421, Colonial Williamsburg (microfilm), courtesy Harold B. Gill. See also *Tyler's Magazine,* 4 (1922–23):199; *VMHB,* 2 (1894–95):2; 8 (1900–01):248; 14 (1906–07):409, *WMQ* (2), 2 (1922):119–28; Hoxton, *Chesapeake Bay,* 1735; Fry and Jefferson, *Virginia,* 1751.

78. Each passenger who was a native of England or Wales paid an import tax of 6d. per head; Fontaine and his four servants would thus pay 2s. 6d. His merchandise must account for the remainder. Beverley, *History,* pp. 247, 250.

79. Probably St. Stephen's Church, because Mrs. Hewes (see next note)

lived in that parish, of which her late husband had been a vestryman. The Rev. John Span was minister at St. Stephen's, 1712–22. Edward Lewis Goodwin, *The Colonial Church in Virginia* (Milwaukee, 1927), pp. 308, 335.

80. Mrs. Mary Hewes (d. 1721) was the widow of Joseph Hewes (d. 1713). She had had previous husbands named Johnson and Ball; by the second she had a daughter Mary, who was to become George Washington's mother. *VMHB*, 8 (1900–01):283–87; *WMQ* (1), 21 (1912–13):104–06.

81. Capt. George Eskridge (d. 1735), lawyer and planter, was tobacco agent of Northumberland County, coroner, member of the quorum, and burgess for Westmoreland County. He lived at "Sandy Point" just west of Yeocomico River and the county line between Northumberland and Westmoreland. He was the guardian of Mary Ball before her marriage to Augustine Washington, and their renowned son George was probably named for Eskridge. *Tyler's Mag.*, 4 (1922–23):190; *VMHB*, 2 (1894–95):10, 14; 7 (1899–1900); 434–36; 22 (1913–14):307–9; 37 (1928–29):128; *WMQ* (1), 21 (1912):104–6.

82. The Coan River flows into the Potomac about five or six miles east of the Yeocomico. Hoxton, *Chesapeake Bay*, 1735.

83. Fontaine seems to have reversed his entries for June 1 and June 3. The shallop would have come to Wicomico ("Wiocomico") before reaching New Point Comfort. Miss Maury must have noticed the error, for in the printed version of the Journal she sensibly corrects it. John Fontaine, *Journal*, p. 262.

84. Alexander Spotswood (1676–1740) was lieutenant governor of Virginia, 1710–22. Spotswood, *Official Letters;* Leonidas Dodson, *Alexander Spotswood, Governor of Colonial Virginia, 1710–1722* (Philadelphia, 1932); *D. A. B.*, s.v. "Spotswood, Alexander."

85. A "Jo. Irvin" signed a memorial of the Virginia Indian Company favorable to Governor Spotswood, Williamsburg, Apr. 23, 1716. John Holloway and Edmund, Michael Kearny's brother (see notes 216, 218 below), were other signers. Irvin may have been related to Henry Irwin (Irvin), prominent Hampton merchant, whom Spotswood appointed naval officer in place of John Holloway, June 12, 1716, and county clerk in 1720. A Jonathan Erwin (Irwin) was a lieutenant in the 9th Regiment, 1709–14, in Ireland. Courtesy of Maj. W. G. Cripps and Lt. Col. A. Joanny, regimental secretaries, Norfolk Regiment Association, Norwich. *Cal. State Paps., Am. and West Indies, 1716–1717*, no. 146; *Executive Journals of the Council of Virginia* (Richmond, 1928), 3:428; *WMQ* (1), 9 (1900–1901):124.

86. Probably John Clayton (1694–1774), the botanist, who was educated in England, perhaps at Eton and Cambridge, and arrived in Virginia about 1715. He became clerk of the Gloucester County Court in 1720, a position he held for 53 years. Edmund Berkeley and Dorothy Smith Berkeley. *John Clayton, Pioneer of American Botany* (Chapel Hill, 1963), pp. 11–24, 73, 169–70.

87. Maj. Philip Rootes (d. 1756) at this time seems to have been living on the south side of the Pamunkey River opposite West Point. Dr. Malcolm H. Harris of West Point, preeminent authority on the local history of King William, New Kent, and King and Queen counties, thinks he was residing east of Col. William Bassett's "Eltham" (see note 214 below) and that this area was known as "Rootes Meadow." Later he moved to "Rosewall" on the north bank of the Mattaponi River across from West Point. He was a vestryman of Stratton Major Parish and a justice of the peace in 1738–39 for King and Queen County. *VMHB*, 4 (1896–97):204, 207–8, 211; 14 (1906–7):240; *WMQ* (1), 7 (1898–

99):139; 12 (1903–4):270–71; Fry and Jefferson, *Virginia,* 1751.

88. Augustine Moore (1685–1743) had an 1800-acre estate "Chelsea" on the south side of Mattaponi River in the parish of St. John, King William County. He was a prosperous tobacco planter and merchant, vestryman, and justice of the peace. *Calendar of Virginia State Papers and Other Manuscripts Preserved in the State Capitol at Richmond, 1652–1869,* William R. Palmer et al., eds., 11 vols. (Richmond, 1875–93), 1: 215–16; Hening, 1:285–87; *VMHB,* 2 (1894–95):7; 25 (1917):431–37; *WMQ* (1), 19 (1910–11):177–84; Fry and Jefferson, *Virginia,* 1751. "Chelsea" still stands, and its owner Mrs. W. W. Richardson, hospitably showed me around. Some of the points on the route of Fontaine and Clayton are shown on the map described in note 173 below.

89. Elizabeth (Todd) Seaton, the widow of Henry Seaton, had become Augustine Moore's second wife by this date. Mary Gaze, his first wife, died in 1713. *VMHB,* 25 (1917):89, 91, 431–37.

90. John Baylor (d. ca. 1722–26) was a wealthy planter, merchant, and shipowner. His plantation "Mantua" and principal warehouses were on the north side of Mattaponi River east of Walkerton. He was a burgess from King and Queen County in 1718, belonged to the Indian Company, served on a grand jury that supported Governor Spotswood in 1719, and was his partner in the Massaponax land grant of 1720. *Virginia Historical Register . . .* William Maxwell, ed., 6 vols. (Richmond, 1848–53), 4:18; *VMHB,* 2 (1894–95):7; 4 (1896–97):350–52; 6 (1897–98):197–98; 25 (1917):91, 316–22; 13 (1924):6; *WMQ* (1), 5 (1896–97):138; Dodson, *Spotswood,* pp. 86, 229; Fry and Jefferson, *Virginia,* 1751.

91. This hut, unusual for Virginia, probably shows the influence of the white man. The natives of the area com-monly used a beehive-shaped hut with rounded roof or a larger house shaped like a loaf of bread. The supporting saplings had both ends placed in the ground and formed an arch at the top. The family occupying the hut could have been Mattapony, Chickahominy, or Pamunkey (all Algonquian speaking). Beverley, *History,* pp. 172–75, 232; John R. Swanton, *The Indians of the Southeastern United States,* Smithsonian [Institution] *Miscellaneous Collections,* 82 (1931):no. 12, 32; Frederick Webb Hodge, ed., *Handbook of American Indians North of Mexico,* Smithsonian Inst., Bur. Am. Ethn. *Bulletin,* 30 (1907–10), 2 vols., 1:259–60; 822; 2:197–99.

92. Robert Beverley, Jr. (ca. 1673–1722), the historian, lived on the upper waters of the Mattaponi at "Beverley Park," an estate of 6000 acres patented in 1699 by his father Maj. Robert Beverley (ca. 1641–1687). Editor's Introduction, Beverley, *History,* pp. xi-xxxv; Louis B. Wright, *The First Gentlemen of Virginia . . .* (San Marino, Calif., 1940), pp. 286–311; Fairfax Harrison, "Robert Beverley, the Historian of Virginia," *VMHB,* 36 (1928):333–44.

93. For more on Beverley's wine making, see Beverley, *History,* pp. 133–36; Jones, *Present State,* pp. 91, 140, 216.

94. The Rev. Lewis Latané (1672–1732) was rector at South Farnham Parish, Essex County. The son of Henry Latané, a Huguenot, he matriculated in 1691 at Queen's College, Oxford University, and was ordained deacon and priest in 1700. He brought his wife and child to Virginia that year with the Huguenots of the Manakin settlement. In 1716 his vestry tried to unseat him (supposedly because his French accent made him difficult to understand), but Governor Spotswood stoutly defended him and the attempt at removal failed. Fontaine later, on May 25, 1720, wrote Latané from Dublin that he was sending a young gentleman of French de-

scent named Dalliriens to Latané's care. Fontaine hoped he might be apprenticed to Robert Beverley to learn the merchant's trade. Lucy Temple Latané, *Parson Latané, 1672–1732* (Charlottesville, 1936), pp. 13–50, 78–79; Goodwin, *Colonial Church,* pp. 286, 325; Perry, *American Church,* 1:285–86, 357.

95. William Beverley (1698–1756), the only child of Robert Beverley, Jr., later served as county lieutenant of Orange and Augusta, in the House of Burgesses, and on the Council. He owned the great "Beverley Manor" in Augusta County of more than 18,000 acres and built "Blandfield" in Essex County. *VMHB,* 22 (1914):297–301; 36 (1928):27–35, 161–69.

96. A well-known landmark on the Rappahannock River just below the site of Port Royal. Hening, 4:252; *VMHB,* 30 (1922):333; Beverley, *History,* 1722 ed., p. 110.

97. Mrs. William Woodford lived on the Rappahannock at "Windsor," about ten miles below the falls. Her husband, a member of the quorum of Essex County in 1714, was apparently dead. *VMHB,* 2 (1894–95):4; 33 (1925):34. ,

98. The falls today lie about one mile upstream of Fredericksburg. U. S. Geological Survey, *Fredericksburg* (1943) quad.

99. About five miles below the falls as shown by Fry and Jefferson, *Virginia,* 1751.

100. John Henry Hager (1644–1737), the first pastor of a German Reformed congregation in America, was pastor at Oberfischbach near Siegen, 1703–11. He came to Virginia in 1714 with the twelve German families that settled Germanna. The congregation was constituted the Parish of St. George by the Assembly. Hager in 1721 moved to German Town in Fauquier County, where he continued as pastor until his death. *VMHB,* 12 (1904–5):75, 283; Scott, *Orange County,* pp. 77–86;

Slaughter, *St. Mark's Parish,* pp. 98–105; Willis Miller Kemper and Harry Linnwright, *Genealogy of the Kemper Family in the United States . . .* (Chicago, 1899), pp. 5–53; Willis Miller Kemper, *Genealogy of the Fishback Family . . .* (New York, 1914), pp. 27, 30–35, 40, 45–52.

101. Augustine Smith (d. 1726), who lived near the falls of Rappahannock River, was surveyor of Essex County, a justice of the new Spotsylvania County, 1722, and a large speculator in lands in the Rapidan area. *VMHB,* 3 (1895–96):36; 32 (1925):133–34; 36 (1928):229; *Cal. Va. State Paps.,* 1: 198, 214.

102. Richard Buckner (d. 1733), clerk of Essex County from 1703 to at least 1714, was also tobacco agent for the county and clerk of the House of Burgesses. His seat at "The Neck" on Rappahannock River became part of Caroline County in 1728. *Tyler's Mag.,* 2 (1920–21):272; *VMHB,* 2 (1894–95):2, 4; 20 (1912):203; 32 (1924): 49; *WMQ* (1), 6 (1897–98):196–98; *Cal. Va. State Paps.,* 1:112–13; Fry and Jefferson, *Virginia,* 1751.

103. Thomas Walker lived on the north side of the Mattaponi River, probably at Walkerton. In 1707 he was a captain in the militia and in 1714 a member of the quorum for King and Queen County. His son Dr. Thomas Walker (1715–1794) was an early explorer of Kentucky. *VMHB,* 2 (1894–95):357–58; *Cal. Va. State Paps.,* 1: 114; *D.A.B.,* s.v. "Walker, Thomas"; Fry and Jefferson, *Virginia,* 1751.

104. Capt. Joshua Story represented King and Queen County in the House of Burgesses, 1692–96, but was replaced when he became sheriff. He was also a justice and a major of the militia. *VMHB,* 1 (1893–94):234; 3 (1895–96):425; 10 (1902–3):215; 14 (1906–7):125; 15 (1907–8):437–41.

105. For long a landmark in New Kent County on the south side of York River. As early as 1702 one could take

a ferry from there to West Point in King William County for 1s. for a man and 6d. for a horse, or from there across the York to King and Queen County for 1s. for a man and 10½d. for a horse. Hening, 2:473; 3:219, 471–72; 6:16; *WMQ* (1), 6 (1897–98):100, 231; 25 (1916–17):120; Fry and Jefferson, *Virginia,* 1751.

106. Stephen Forneau (d. ca. 1751) kept a tavern situated about halfway between Williamsburg and West Point at what is now Toano. It was probably succeeded by Chiswell's Ordinary. Several references to it in the Williamsburg *Virginia Gazette* include Jan. 26, 1738/39 (Parks); Mar. 28, 1751 (Hunter). See also *The Vestry Book of Blisland (Blissland) Parish, New Kent and James City Counties,* C. G. Chamberlayne, ed. (Richmond, 1935), pp. 26, 36, 37, 55, 159, 235. Chiswell's is shown on Fry and Jefferson, *Virginia,* 1755 and subsequent editions.

107. Governor Spotswood kept accounts of his travel on public service. On May 7, 1714, he journeyed to Germanna to settle the group of Germans. He estimated the round trip at 322 miles but may have examined several sites before choosing the final one. Alexander Spotswood, "Journal of . . . Travels and Expeditions undertaken for the Public Service of Virginia, 1711–1717," *WMQ* (2), 3 (1923):40–45.

108. Fort Christanna was situated on the south side of the Meherrin River. Its site is about one-quarter mile east of the monument erected by the Colonial Dames of Virginia at Fort Hill in Brunswick County on Route 686 southwest of Lawrenceville, the county seat. Governor Spotswood made a treaty with the Saponi, Stenkenocks, and Tutelo at Williamsburg on Feb. 27, 1713/14 by which they agreed to live on a six-mile-square tract on the Meherrin protected by the fort and twelve rangers and an officer. That spring Spotswood laid out five large log houses as bastions connected by a curtain of wooden palisades

and earth and with a great gun of about 1400 pounds at each house. The fort contained a trading post of the Virginia Indian Company which had a monopoly of the Indian trade for twenty years. It was ultimately to maintain the garrison of the fort and a school for Indian children. Spotswood took a large land grant to help support the school and paid £50 from his own pocket to Charles Griffin as teacher. In 1716 Spotswood was reported building a house for himself worth £500-600 sterling and hoping to attract other settlers.

Some of the members of the Council of Virginia were already engaged in the Indian trade, and with the help of British merchants who disliked the monopolistic aspect of the arrangement, they managed to secure the disallowance of the Indian Company Act in 1717 by the English authorities in London. Spotswood then tried without success to persuade the Assembly to assume the cost of the fort. He argued that the frontiers were being protected economically and that the Indians had never been so peaceful. Mr. Griffin was instructing and catechising 78 Indian children including 11 hostages from the southern tribes.

But Spotswood's efforts were in vain. Mr. Griffin moved to the College of William and Mary in 1718 to teach Indian lads at the Brafferton school, built and supported by the chemist Robert Boyle's foundation. Spotswood abandoned his house and allowed his land grant to lapse. Iroquois raiders in 1719 ravaged the cornfields of the Christanna Indians and lay in ambush before the gate of the fort. Still, Spotswood's treaty with the Iroquois at Albany in 1722 was largely effective, and it was really the white man's encroachments, rum, and diseases that ruined the Indians. They abandoned Christanna about 1740.

*Cal. State Paps., Am. and W. I., 1714–1715,* nos. 188, 320, 449; *1716–1717,* nos. 146, 243, 452; *1717–1718,* no. 699; *1719–1720,* nos. 357, 535i; *1724–1725,* no. 210; Jones, *Present State,* pp. 12, 59, 162–63, 167.

109. There was no courthouse at Jamestown, though Fontaine may have seen the ruins of the statehouse that burned in 1698. Jones, *Present State,* p. 66; Edward M. Riley and Charles E. Hatch, Jr., *James Towne in the Words of Contemporaries* (Washington, D. C., 1955), pp. 31-34.

110. Jamestown was not an island when Fontaine visited there, but part of the peninsula washed out at the time of the Revolution. Same, p. 34.

111. This ferry was probably named for John Simmons (d. 1738) of Surry County and was situated on Nottoway River below the present Carey's Bridge (on Route 653 southwest of Sebrell in Southampton County) near where the stream called Buckhorne Swamp flows into the Nottoway from the south. Simmons in 1710 petitioned Governor Spotswood to permit him to build a mill at Buckhorne Swamp within the six-mile-square tract granted the Nottoway Indians. The Indians had agreed to the mill, and apparently the petition was granted. In 1734 Simmons's mill-pond was drained to recover the body of a missing man said to have been killed by Nottoway Indians. Bolton's Ferry over the Nottoway in 1748 landed on Simmons's property. He represented Surry County in the House of Burgesses, 1710-14, 1720-22, and purchased much land from the Nottoways and also around Fort Christanna. *Cal. Va. State Paps.,* 1:147–48; Hening, 4:363, 460; 6:19; Virginia (colony) Council, *Executive Journals,* H. R. McIlwaine, ed., 4 vols. (Richmond, 1928), 3:526; 4:39, 72–73, 245, 283, 331, 333; *VMHB,* 33 (1925):19, 42–43, 295; Elizabeth Timberlake Davis, comp., *Wills and Administrations of Surry County, Virginia* (n. p., 1955), pp. 84, 151; Lewis R. Binford, "An Ethnohistory of the Nottoway, Meherrin, and Weanock Indians of Southern Virginia," *Ethno-*

*history,* 14 (1967):176–78; U. S. Geol. Sur., *Sebrell* (1957) quad.

112. This house may have been the residence of Capt. Robert Hicks or Hix (ca. 1658–1740), then probably commanding the rangers at Fort Christanna. The house was situated at Hicks Ford on the Meherrin River about 15 miles east of the fort and today part of Emporia, Va. Douglas Summers (Mrs. Henry D.) Brown and Eleanor Little (Mrs. Ennis E.) Eanes of Emporia have carefully analyzed Hick's will of Mar. 6, 1738/39 (proved Feb. 7, 1739/40) and other land transfers to identify natural features and neighboring grants and thus prove that Hicks lived in the Hicks Ford vicinity. Still, the home could have belonged to one of Hick's older sons—Robert (d. 1737) or David (d. 1735). They were both Indian traders, and it is often impossible to separate clearly the two Roberts. Brunswick County Will Book No. 2 (1739–85) pp. 3–5, Va. State Lib.; Mrs. Brown to the editor, June 19, 1970; Douglas Summers Brown, ed., *Historical and Biographical Sketches of Greensville County, Virginia, 1650–1967* (Emporia, Va., 1968), pp. 17–18, 28. See also notes 113 and 166 below.

113. Ann Maury incorrectly changed "Herrin" to "Herring" in the published *Journal,* whereas it seems to be short for "Meherrin." There was a Meherrin (today Great) Creek that ran into the Meherrin River east of Fort Christanna but about 11 miles west of Hicks Ford (today Emporia). Mrs. Brown, however, has found two later deeds of Hicks property in the Hicks Ford area that refer to a Meherrin Branch there. Interpreting this stream as Fontaine's Herrin Creek, the trip of Apr. 14, 1716 with its description of the savannas along the river becomes more intelligible. John Fontaine, *Journal,* p. 271; *The Prose Works of William Byrd . . . ,* Louis B. Wright, ed. (Cambridge, Mass., 1966), pp. 147, 316, 382-83; Robert Hicks to Stephen Hicks, deed, June 11, 1764,

Brunswick County Deed Book, 7:749, also, 9:640. Va. State Lib. Mrs. Gay M. Curtin, formerly of the Colonial Williamsburg Research Department has helped locate and interpret maps of the region. See also note 112 above.

114. Charles Griffin had charge of the Indian School at Fort Christanna from 1716 to 1718. Born in England, he came from the West Indies to Pasquetank Precinct, North Carolina, in 1706. As Anglican lay reader and clerk he won over even the Quakers of the neighborhood, who sent their children to his school, though he conducted prayers twice daily and required his pupils to make the proper Anglican responses. He moved to Chowan Precinct in 1708 but was accused of committing fornication and joining a Quaker faction. Spotswood brought him to Christanna, and the Rev. Hugh Jones, who visited his school in 1717, reported that "These children can all read, say their catechisms and prayers tolerably well. . . . The Indians so loved and adored him that I have seen them hug him and lift him up in their arms, and fain would have chosen him a King of the Sapony nation." William Byrd described Griffin as "a man of good family, who by the innocence of his life and the sweetness of his temper was perfectly well qualified for that undertaking. Besides, he had so much the secret of mixing pleasure with instruction that he had not a scholar who did not love him affectionately." Still, one of his students named Charles Griffin was charged later with stealing a hog and setting the woods on fire, and Byrd finally concluded that "all the pains he had taken among the infidels had no other effect but to make them somewhat cleanlier than other Indians." Griffin was master of the Indian School at the College of William and Mary as late as 1724. William L. Saunders, ed., *The Colonial Records of North Carolina*, 10 vols. (Raleigh, 1886–90), 1:684, 689, 714, 721; Goodwin, *Colonial Church*, pp. 275, 342;

Cal. State Paps., Am. and W. I., 1716–1717, no. 452i; 1717–1718, no. 59; Jones, *Present State*, pp. 12, 59, 167; Byrd, *Prose Works*, pp. 220–21; Perry, *American Church*, 1:196–97, 306.

115. Sometimes all the Fort Christanna Indians were called Saponi, but at the Albany Conference with the Five Nations in 1722, Governor Spotswood said there were five tribes at Christanna —the Saponi, Occaneechi, Stuckanox (or Stegaraki), Meipontski, and Tutelo —and that they numbered about 300. They were of the Eastern Siouan language family. The Five Nations and other Iroquoian speakers were their deadly enemies. N. Y. Col. Docs., 5: 673; James Mooney, *The Siouan Tribes of the East*, Smithsonian Inst., Bur. of Am. Ethn. *Bulletin* 22 (1894):21–22, 26, 37, 42–50; David I. Bushnell, *Five Monacan Towns in Virginia, 1607*, *Smithsonian Miscellaneous Collections*, 82(1931), no. 12:1–38; Frank G. Speck, "Siouan Tribes of the Carolinas as Known from Catawba, Tutelo, and Documentary Sources," *American Anthropologist*, n.s., 37 (1935):201–25; John R. Swanton, "Siouan Tribes and the Ohio Valley," same, 45 (1943):49–66; Swanton, *Indians of Southeastern U. S.*, pp. 178–79, 200–201; Hans Wolff, "Comparative Siouan," *International Journal of American Linguistics*, 16 (1950):64–65; John R. Swanton, *The Indian Tribes of North America*, Smithsonian Inst., Bur. of Am. Ethn. *Bulletin*, 145 (1952):71–74; William C. Sturtevant, "Siouan Languages in the East," *Am. Anthrop.*, n.s., 60 (1958): 738–43; Wallace L. Chafe, "Another Look at Siouan and Iroquoian," same, 66 (1964):852–61.

116. Probably the Seneca or Oneida, two of the Five Nations of the Iroquois. In 1701 when Lawson visited the Saponi in North Carolina, they had captured five Sinnagers or Jennitos. Gallatin thought them Seneca or Oneida. John Lawson, *A New Voyage to Carolina . . .* (London, 1709), Hugh Tal-

mage Leffler, ed. (Chapel Hill, 1967), p. 33; Horatio Hale, "The Tutelo Tribe and Language," American Philosophical Society *Proceedings,* 21, no. 114 (1883):3.

117. Miss Maury probably omitted this vocabulary from the printed version of the Journal because she thought it too detailed and specialized, but possibly because her Victorian sensibilities were offended by the sexual connotations of several of the phrases. See also Introduction, p. 12. For a careful historical analysis of the vocabulary, see Edward P. Alexander, "An Indian Vocabulary from Fort Christanna, 1716," *VMHB,* 79 (1971):303–13. The editor is deeply grateful to several experts on American and Virginia Indians for advice and suggestions for the treatment of this vocabulary: Prof. Ben C. McCary, College of William and Mary; Dr. William G. Sturtevant and Dr. Ives Goddard, Museum of Natural History, Smithsonian Institution; Dr. C. G. Holland, University of Virginia; Col. Howard A. Mac-Cord, Sr., archaeologist, Virginia State Library; Dr. Christian F. Feest, Museum for Folk Art, Vienna, Austria; and Philip L. Barbour, Newtown, Conn.

118. Clearly Siouan: Omaha-Ponca, Osage, and Kansa all—*mi* (Wolff); Hidatsa—*midi* (Wolff; Matthews, 236); Tutelo—*mie, min,* or *mi* (Hale). Algonquian words are: Powhatan — *keshowghe* (Smith) or *keshowse* (Strachey); Delaware — *gischuch* (Brinton, 43:21). These notes do not include all the words found in the various Indian vocabularies but only enough similar and dissimilar to Fontaine's version to show the reason for assigning it to a language group or groups. Wolff, "Comparative Siouan," 16 (1950):61–66, 113–21, 168–78; 17 (1951):197–204; Washington Matthews, *Ethnography and Philology of the Hidatsa Indians,* U. S. Geological and Geographical Survey *Miscellaneous Publications,* no. 7 (1877); Hale, "Tutelo Tribe," 36–45; Captain John Smith, *The General His-*

*torie of Virginia* . . . (London, 1624) in John Smith, *Travels and Works,* Edwin Arber, ed., 2 vols. (Edinburgh, 1910), 1:82–84; William Strachey, *The Historie of Travel in Virginia Britania* (London, 1612), Louis B. Wright and Virginia Freund, eds., Hakluyt Society *Works* (2), 103 (1953):174-207; Daniel G. Brinton and Rev. Albert Seqaqkind, eds., *A Lenâpé-English Dictionary* . . . (Philadelphia, 1888).

119. Probably Siouan. "Come" is: Biloxi—*hu;* Ofo—*kiukna;* Osage—*gio;* Dakota—*u* (Wolff); Hidatsa—*hue* or *ate* (Matthews); Tutelo—*yahua, howa,* or *hi* (Hale). Delaware is *petscholtin* (Brinton, 115:3).

120. Probably Siouan for "stay" or "sit": proto-Siouan—*nak;* Dakota—*lyotaka* (Wolff), *yanka,* or *nanka* (Hale); Mandan—*kinkanak;* Biloxi—*naki;* Ofo — *noki;* Winnebago — *manak* (all Wolff); Hidatsa—*naka, daka* (Hale), *amaki,* or *kiamaki* (Matthews); Tutelo —*mahanaka* (Wolff, Hale) or *nanka* (Hale). Delaware is *nipawin* (Brinton, 97: 18).

121. Analyzing the words for "horse" (*chunkete*) and "head" (*posse*) makes this phrase appear probable Siouan. Horse: Biloxi—*cuki;* Ofo—*acuki;* Osage—*suke;* Tutelo—*cuk* (all Wolff), *tut-tsongide* (Frachtenberg), or *tsungide* (Sapir). Head: Omaha-Ponca, Osage, Biloxi, Dakota, and Chiwere all —*pa;* Quapaw—*pahi;* Mandan—*paah* (all Wolff); Woccon—*posse* (Lawson); Tutelo—*pasuye* (Hale) or *pasui* (Hale, Wolff). In Delaware: horse— *nenajunges;* head—*wil* (Brinton, 93: 25; 158:18). There conceivably may have been a hill or other natural or man-made feature in the area known as "the horse head." William B. Hill, director of Roanoke River Museum, Prestwould Foundation, near Clarksville, thinks that "the horse head" refers to a landmark known as "the horseford" (and later as Horseford Mills) on Meherrin River, where the traders forded on horseback. Leo J. Frachten-

berg, "Contributions to a Tutelo Vocabulary," *Am. Anthrop.*, n.s., 25 (1913): 477-79; Edward Sapir, "A Tutelo Vocabulary," same, 295-97; Lawson, *New Voyage*, 233-39.

122. Probably neither Algonquian nor Siouan: Delaware — *chans*, older brother; *chesimus*, younger brother; *nimat*, my brother, friendly salutation (Brinton, 27:5, 16; 97:9); Biloxi— some words for brother end in *noqti* (Riggs); Tutelo—*niwagenumpai* or *iginumbai* (Hale). Stephen Return Riggs, *Daktota Grammar, Texts, and Ethnography*, James Owen Dorsey, ed., U. S. Geographical and Geological Survey of the Rocky Mountain Region *Contributions to North American Ethnology*, 9 (1893) :xviii-xix.

123. Probably neither Algonquian nor Siouan: Powhatan—*husque* (Strachey); Delaware—*gintsch, juke*, or *metschimi* (Brinton, 45:24; 51:13; 83:12). The closest resemblance is Hidatsa— *itekoahi* or *itekoahidak* (Hale).

124. This phrase is definitely Siouan. They use the same word, here *mihu*, for "woman" and "wife": Dakota—*mitawin* (Riggs) or *wiya;* Ofo—*iya;* Mandan—*mih;* Hidatsa and Chiwere—*wia* (all Wolff); proto-Siouan — *wihah;* proto-Siouan-Iroquoian — *wiho* (Chafe, 857); Tutelo—*mihani* (Hale) or *mihai* (Wolff). Carolina Algonquian is *crenepo* (Smith) and Powhatan, *noungasse* (Strachey). Chafe, "Another Look," 852-61.

125. Conceivably Siouan: Hidatsa— *mapoksa* (Matthews) or *mapokca*. Tutelo is *wageni* (both Hale). Powhatan for "adder" is *keihtascooc* (Strachey) and Delaware, *achgook* (Brinton, 11: 11).

126. Probably Siouan: Hidatsa— *midulia* or *bidulia* (Matthews); Dakota —*mahzah* (Gallatin) or *mazakan;* Tutelo—*minkte* (both Hale). Powhatan is *pawcussack* (Smith), *paccusac-on,* or *pokosack* (Strachey). Delaware is *paiachkhikan* (Brinton, 106:8). Albert Gallatin, *A Synopsis of the Indian Tribes of North America,* American Antiquarian Society *Transactions and Collections,* 2 (1836).

127. The few words in known vocabularies do not come close to this one. Siouan: Assinboin—*tauhan* (Gallatin, 374); Hidatsa—*midatsapi* or *hidatsapi* (Matthews). Algonquian: Ojibwa—*makate* ("black") for "powder" (Dr. C. G. Holland, University of Virginia); Delaware—*punk* for "gunpowder" (Brinton, 120:21).

128. Probably Siouan and close to *mikta*—"gun." Siouan for "ball" or "shot": Dakota—*tapa* (Hale, Wolff); Hidatsa—*maotopi* (Hale) or *wau-topi;* Biloxi—*nitapi, tut-tapi,* or *nitwa;* Osage —*tabe* (all Wolff); Tutelo—*tapi* (Hale, Wolff). Tuscarora (Iroquoian) is *uttaque* (Lawson). Delaware is *allunsinutey* (Brinton, 18:21), which Dr. C. G. Holland, University of Virginia, points out should be *allunsmutey*.

129. Probably Siouan, for "leggings" is *hunska* (Feest). Delaware for "stocking" or "legging" is *gagun* (Brinton, 36:21).

130. This word could not be identified. Hidatsa is *itadsi* or *masiitadsi* (Matthews, 231), and Delaware *chessagutakan* means "leather breeches" (Brinton, 27:17).

131. Possibly Algonquian, for Powhatan "apron" is *pagwotawun* and "girdle," *bagwanchy basson* (Feest). Hidatsa —*ituhi* or *matse ituhi* (Matthews, 219); Delaware—*schackhokquiwan* (Brinton, 126:8).

132. Again, possibly Algonquian.

133. Possibly Siouan, for *neto* seems to be "brain," "head," or sometimes "hair." Thus, Dakota — *natu* (Hale, Wolff); Hidatsa—*ana* (Hale); Biloxi— *nato;* Ofo—*natu;* Chiwere—*natolusla;* Winnebago—*nasu* or *nack* (all Wolff); Tutelo — *natonwe, natoi,* or *nantoi* (Hale, Wolff). Delaware for "hair" is *meichheken* or *milach* (Brinton, 84:11; 85:2). Dr. Feest thinks the "f" in *dufas* is a copying error.

134. The *pa* in the first word seems to be Siouan for "head." See note 121 above. Dakota for "hat" is *wapaha* and Hidatsa, *apoka* (Hale). Powhatan is close with *pattihquapisson* or *puttaiqua pisson* (Strachey) and Woccon—*intome posswa* (Lawson). Thus, this may be both Siouan and Algonquian.

135. Obviously the Algonquian word for moccasin: Powhatan — *mockasin* (Smith), *mawacasun*, or *mawhcasun* (Strachey); *makasoon* for several Algonquian tribes (Gallatin); Delaware—*machtschipak* or *machsin* (Brinton, 71: 6).

136. Probably Siouan: Osage—*hobe;* Dakota, Hidatsa—*hapa;* Mandan—*hupa* (all Wolff); Tutelo—*angohlei, agore,* or *agode* (Hale). The fact that the two words for "shoes" are used in the area strengthens the probability that the vocabulary is a composite or trade language.

137. This word does not appear in a Siouan vocabulary. Powhatan is *roycoy-hook* or *roykayhook* (Strachey) and Delaware, *gunammochk* (Brinton, 45: 23).

138. This word might be Siouan, for Biloxi is *pade* (Feest); Powhatan is *monacooke* (Smith), *monowhauk, monowhaake,* or *monohacan* (Strachey).

139. Probably Siouan. See notes 126, 128 above.

140. Probably Siouan. See previous note.

141. Probably Siouan: Omaha Ponca, Dakota, Mandan—all *mini* (Wolff); Hidatsa — *midi* or *mini* (Matthews, Hale); Tutelo—*mani* (Hale, Wolff) or *meni* (Sapir). The Delaware *mbi* (Brinton, 76:15) is far away.

142. Nothing near this sentence appears in either Algonquian or Siouan word lists.

143. Dr. Feest thinks this Algonquin from its inflexion. "Kiss": Powhatan—*tsepaantamen* (Strachey); Delaware—*moskdonamen* or *sissama* (Brinton, 87: 6); Hidatsa—*ikidatsope* or *kidatsope* (Hale).

144. May have been used by both Siouan and Algonquian speakers. Hidatsa—*e* (Hale) or *hao* (Matthews); Dakota—*han* or *ho;* Tutelo—*aha, ahan,* or *awaga* (all Hale). Delaware is *bischi, biesch, bischik, egohan, gohan,* or *kehella* (Brinton, 26:7, 8; 30:7; 45:2; 52:11).

145. Again, Dr. Feest thinks the inflexion Algonquian, and Powhatan *nepaun* means "he sleeps." The words from 143 to 146 may have sexual connotations.

146. Possibly Siouan: in Dakota, *ikce* means "for nothing" or "freely" (Riggs, 193). In Delaware, *ajema* is "be so good, please" (Brinton, 15:12).

147. Probably Algonquian: Powhatan—*matah* or *tah* (Strachey); Delaware—*makhta* (Gallatin), *matta,* or *mattage* (Brinton, 75:8, 9). Siouan: Dakota—*hiya;* Hidatsa—*desa* or *nesa;* Tutelo—*yahan* or *ihao* (all Hale).

148. Possibly Siouan, for the Dakota use *wiki* as a prefix for "woman" with several verbs (Riggs, 576). "Queen" in Powhatan is *wiroansqua* (Strachey).

149. Nothing is close to this sentence. In Delaware "to save" is *wtakolsin* or *wulaton* (Brinton, 169:6; 172:4).

150. Possibly Algonquian, for Strachey gives *kenah* as Powhatan for "I thank you." Tutelo—*bilahuk, bilahenk,* or *biwa* (Frachtenberg, Sapir).

151. Nothing makes sense here. In Powhatan, "welcome" is *wingapo, chama,* or *netah.*

152. Used by both Algonquian and Siouan speakers; Algonquian: Powhatan—*necut* (Smith, Strachey); Nansemond—*nikatwin;* modern Pamunkey—*nekkut* (both Mooney); Mohegan, Pequot, Narraganset, Natick—all *negut* or *nequit* (Prince and Speck); Delaware —*ngutti, ngutelli,* or *nukti* (Brinton, 95:16, 17; 101:7); Siouan: Hidatsa—*nuetsa;* Tutelo—*nonc, nons, nosah,* or *nonsa* (all Hale). James Mooney, "The Powhatan Confederacy, Past and Present," *Am. Anthrop.,* n.s., 9 (1907): 129–52; J. Dyneley Prince and Frank

G. Speck, "Glossary of the Mohegan-Pequot Language," same, n.s., 6 (1904): 18–45.

153. Closest to Iroquoian, though some Algonquians may have used. Iroquoian: Mohawk—*tekkehnih;* Onondaga —*tekini;* Seneca—*ticknee;* Oneida—*teghia;* Nottoway—*dekanee* (all Gallatin, 358). Algonquian: Micmac—*tapo* (Philip L. Barbour, Newtown, Conn.); Powhatan—*ningh* or *ninge* (Smith, Strachey); Mohegan-Pequot—*neese* (Prince and Speck); Delaware—*nischa* (Brinton, 97:21). Siouan: Biloxi—*nopa;* Ofo—*nupa* (Wolff); Tutelo—*nomp* or *nomba* (Hale).

154. Probably Algonquian: Powhatan—*nuss* (Smith), *nousough, nussaugh,* or *nus* (Strachey); Micmac—*nes* (Philip L. Barbour, Newtown, Conn.); Narraganset and Natick—*nish* (Prince and Speck); Pamlico—*nish-wonner* (Lawson); Delaware—*nacha* (Brinton, 88:2). But Siouan is not far from it: Biloxi—*nani;* Ofo—*tani* (Wolff); Tutelo —*nan, nani, lani,* or *na* (Hale).

155. Could be Algonquian or Siouan: Powhatan—*yowgh* or *yeough* (Smith, Strachey); Penobscot—*yau* (Gallatin, 370); Pamlico—*yau-oonner* (Lawson); Mohegan-Pequot—*yow, yoh,* or *yah* (Prince and Speck); Delaware—*newo* (Brinton, 94:26); Chiwere—*towe;* Winnebago—*jop* (Wolff); Tutelo—*top, topa, topai,* or *toba* (Hale).

156. Almost certain Algonquian: Powhatan—*paranske* or *porance* (Smith, Strachey); Delaware—*palenach* (Brinton, 107:5). It is far from Tutelo—*kasa, kise, kisan, kisahi,* or *kisahani* (Hale).

157. Like "two," closest to Iroquoian: Mohawk—*yahyook;* Onondaga—*achiak;* Oneida—*yahiac* (Gallatin, 359); Tuscarora—*houeyac* (Lawson). Algonquian: Powhatan—*comotinch* or *camatinge* (Smith, Strachey); Mohegan-Pequot—*cuddusk. qutta,* or *nequattash* (Prince and Speck); Delaware—*guttasch* (Brinton, 46:22); but notice Pamlico—*whoyeoc* (Lawson). Siouan:

Tutelo—*agus, akasp,* or *akaspei* (Hale).

158. Probably Algonquian: Powhatan — *topawoss* (Smith); Mohican — *tupouwous;* Long Island Algonquian—*tumpawa;* Pamlico—*topposh* (Gallatin, 360, 375); Delaware—*nischasch* (Brinton, 97:23). Tutelo is *sagom, sagomei, sagomi,* or *sagomiq* (Hale). Dr. Feest thinks the word should end in "ous" instead of "ons," and the next word the same.

159. Possibly Algonquian if the "m" in *massons* is a mistake for "n" as Philip L. Barbour, Newtown, Conn., thinks. Algonquian: Powhatan—*nusswash* (Smith), *nuscawes,* or *nuschawes* (Strachey); Pamlico — *nauhaushshoo* (Barbour); Delaware—*chaasch* (Brinton, 26:20). Siouan: Dakota—*cadoghan;* Hidatsa—*nopapi;* Tutelo—*palan, palani, palali,* or *palaniq* (all Hale).

160. Probably Algonquian: Powhatan—*kekatawgh* (Smith) or *kykeytawe* (Strachey); Delaware — *peschgonk* (Brinton, 113:22). Tutelo has some forms not too dissimilar—*tsaen, tca, sa, san, ksank, ksahka, ksakai,* or *kasankai* (Hale).

161. Probably Algonquian: Algonquin of Canada—*mit asswois* (Gallatin, 368); Potawatomi — *metatso* (same, 375); Cree—*mitaht* (Philip L. Barbour, Newtown, Conn.); Delaware—*metellen* or *tellen* (Brinton, 83:3; 140:4). Tutelo is *putck, putsk, potsk, butck, putskai,* or *patskani* (Hale).

162. The combining system could be Siouan or Algonquian: Biloxi—prefix *ohi* as separate syllable (Riggs, xxviii); Tutelo—*age, agi* or *aki*; and Delaware—*ate* (Feest) in the same manner.

163. Possibly Algonquian: Micmac—*tabonickta* (Gallatin, 362) or *tapoisgag* (Philip L. Barbour, Newton, Conn.); Dr. Feest points out that "two" and "ten' are *tak* (Algonquian) and *apoke* (Powhatan—Strachey) or *apooesku* (Smith); Iroquoian: Wyandot—*tendeitawaughsa;* Mohawk—*toowashum;* Onondaga — *twasshe;* Seneca — *tawashah* (Gallatin), 362). Tutelo is two words

—*putska nomba, putcka, nomba,* or *putska nomba* (Hale).

164. The land patents in the Virginia State Library contain no record of this grant. None of the Fontaine children in Virginia settled on this tract. James Fontaine and Matthew Maury lived on the King William County plantation (note 289 below). Peter Fontaine became rector of Westover Church (note 290 below), and Francis of Yorkhampton Parish as well as teacher of oriental languages at the College of William and Mary (Introduction, note 45 above). Perhaps John Fontaine followed Spotswood's example and allowed his grant on the Meherrin River to lapse. *Cal. State Paps., Am. and W.I., 1724–1725,* no. 210i.

165. The Meherrin actually flows into Albemarle Sound instead of Currituck Sound.

166. Capt. Robert Hicks (ca. 1658–1740), prominent Indian trader, probably commanded the twelve rangers at Fort Christanna. He later accompanied Governor Spotswood to Albany in 1722 to make a treaty with the Iroquois. In 1728 for a few days he joined the commissioners from Virginia and North Carolina running the boundary line. William Byrd II admired his cheerful energy and "his disdaining to be thought the worse for threescore and ten. Beauty never appeared better in old age, with a ruddy complexion and hair as white as snow." One evening the old captain entertained the expedition "with one of his trading songs which he quavered out most melodiously." Brown, *Greensville County,* pp. 16–30; *Cal. Va. State Paps.,* 1:155–56; *N. Y. Col. Docs.,* 5:674, 676, 677; *Va. Exec. Counc. Jls.,* 3:357–58; 4:15; Nell Marian Nugent, comp., *Abstracts of Virginia Land Patent Books,* 3 vols. (Richmond, ca. 1960, Xerox copy), Virginia State Library, no. 10: 589; no. 12:674; no. 14:794; Byrd, *Prose Works,* pp. 96–100; *WMQ* (1), 11 (1902–3):130–31; Perry, *American Church,* 1:123–24; Dodson, *Spotswood,*

pp. 104, 105, 107, 108. See also note 112 above.

167. See note 91 above.

168. The Meherrin were Iroquoian speaking and enemies of the Saponi and other Eastern Siouan tribes. Swanton, *Southeastern Indians,* p. 149; Binford, "Ethnohistory of Nottoway et al.," pp. 103–218.

169. See note 108 above.

170. They probably laid out this avenue for the governor's proposed new house. See note 108 above.

171. The Nottoway, an Iroquoian-speaking tribe, were neighbors of the Meherrin. As late as 1825 they were living on a reservation in Southampton County and were ruled by a queen. Swanton, *Southeastern Indians,* pp. 163–64, 412, 439, 741–42; Binford, "Ethnohistory of Nottoway, et al.," pp. 103–218.

172. Spotswood estimated the distance for this trip at 200 miles. *WMQ* (2), 3 (1923):40–45. Fontaine's estimate of 160 miles seems on the low side, for a direct line on a modern map from Williamsburg to Emporia and on to Fort Hill is about 90 miles one way. U. S. Geol. Sur., *State of Virginia* (1957).

173. See note 105 above. The Virginia State Library has a helpful map showing the route of Fontaine and Spotswood going and coming between Williamsburg and Germanna. By W. L. P., 1948, no. 755/1716/1948, Colonial Williamsburg (photostat).

174. See note 88 above.

175. See note 92 above.

176. See note 97 above.

177. See note 101 above.

178. For Fontaine's description of Germanna on his previous journey, see Journal entries, Nov. 20–21, 1715, above.

179. Governor Spotswood in May 1714 settled 40 Germans at Germanna. He had for long hoped to establish an iron industry in Virginia, and these

Germans were skilled miners and iron-workers from the Sieg Valley (later Westphalia). Since the Board of Trade frowned on colonial manufacturing, Spotswood told them he was placing the Germans on the northern frontier to guard against Indian attack just as he was setting up Fort Christanna for that purpose in the south. He also hinted that the mine near Germanna might yield silver instead of iron. After Spotswood was removed as governor, he returned to England to marry a young wife "said to be wonderfull pritty but no money." In 1730 he settled his family at Germanna, where he had acquired an estate of 85,000 acres. He established a promising iron business near there. *Cal. State Paps., Am. and W. I., 1717–1718*, no. 800; *1722–1723*, no. 529; *1724–1725*, no. 210; Fairfax Harrison, *Landmarks of Old Prince William; a Study in the Origins of Northern Virginia*, 2 vols. (Richmond, 1924), 1: 207–21; "News out of London in 1725," Virginia Historical Society *Occasional Bulletin*, no. 11 (Oct. 1965):5-6; Lester J. Cappon, ed.. *Iron Works at Tuball: Terms and Conditions for Their Lease as Stated by Alexander Spotswood* . . . [July 20, 1739] (Charlottesville, 1945).

180. Fontaine's friend, Capt. Robert Hicks, could have been one of these officers. See note 166 above.

181. See p. 14 and note 19 to Introduction, above.

182. Fontaine seems to have been suffering another attack of malaria. See note 11 above.

183. Cinchona bark contains the alkaloid quinine, the specific for malaria. The Jesuits knew it in Peru in 1630 and introduced it into Europe soon afterwards as Jesuits' bark, Peruvian bark, or simply the bark. In eighteenth-century Virginia, it was considered the sovereign remedy for the seasoning sickness (almost certainly malaria) experienced by newcomers and characterized by ague and fever. The bark was prescribed against many other disorders, known and unknown, and was tried against yellow fever. Wyndham B. Blanton, M.D., *Medicine in Virginia in the Eighteenth Century* (Richmond, 1941), pp. 50, 66, 139, 185.

184. All authorities agree that Expedition Run is the present Russell Run on the south side of the Rapidan, shown both on Fry and Jefferson, *Virginia*, 1751, and U. S. Geol. Sur., *Mine Run* (1943) quad. Slaughter, *St. Mark's Parish*, pp. 83–96; Scott, "Knights Route," 145–53; Church, "Tidewater to Shenandoah," pp. 19–25; Carpenter, "Spotswood Route," pp. 405–12. See also Introduction, pp. 13–19.

185. On May 30, 1718, Beverley secured an entry for 10,000 acres "on the branches of the River Rapidanne." This tract was the land east of the Robinson (Robertson) that Fontaine reported him interested in (see Journal entry, Sept. 9, 1716), though he did not secure a patent and Spotwood later acquired it. Randolph W. Church, the Virginia state librarian, has tried to determine the identity of members of the expedition by studying the land grants of the Rapidan area and generously shared his findings with the editor. Harry Beverley, Robert's cousin, was not in Virginia at the time of the expedition but was one of the eight patentees of the Octuna (Octonia or Octona) grant of July 20, 1722. It lay along the south side of the Rapidan near Swift Run and the Blue Ridge. Robert Beverley in 1719 obtained 4000 acres in Essex County on the south side of the Rapidan. Harrison, "Beverley," p. 340; Octuna Patent, 1729, and James Taylor's Survey Map, 1721, Virginia Historical Society; *Abst. Va. Pat. Bks.*, no. 10:619; no. 13:762. See also note 92 above.

186. See notes 101 above and 190 below.

187. Again the authorities agree that the travelers crossed Mine River (today Mine Run) and camped on Mountain Run considerably south of the Rapidan.

U. S. Geol. Sur., *Mine Run* (1943) and *Unionville* (1943) quads.; Slaughter, *St. Mark's Parish,* p. 73; Scott, "Knights Route," pp. 145–53; Church, "Tidewater to Shenandoah," pp. 22–23; Carpenter, "Spotswood Route," pp. 408–9.

188. This camp was named for William Todd (ca. 1685–1736-40), a member of the quorum in King and Queen County in 1714. On Dec. 23, 1720, Todd, John Bataille, and John Taliafero petitioned for 20,000 acres in Spotsylvania County in the Rapidan area, adjoining a tract of John Baylor and James Taylor above the Mountain Run as well as the Octuna tract. James Taylor surveyed the 20,000 acres and was admitted to a one-fourth share. A bitter lawsuit followed, Todd maintaining that Taylor had taken some 2000 acres at his expense. Todd also had another grant south of the Rapidan in 1726. *VMHB,* 2 (1894–95):7; 3 (1895–96):80; 25 (1917):89–91, 221–22, 302–4; 33 (1925):297, 392; 34 (1926):206; *Cal. Va. State Paps.,* 1:200; Hening, 4: 238–39; *WMQ* (1), 22 (1913–14):54, 58; *Abst. Va. Pat. Bks.,* no. 12:705.

189. The expedition had been considerably south of the Rapidan but in about five miles came out on the river again and crossed it, probably at Summerville Ford. It then recrossed the river east of the present town of Rapidan. Carpenter shows the camp on the south side of the Rapidan (in better accord with the Journal), and Church has it north of the river; both place the camp west of the town of Rapidan. U. S. Geol. Sur., *Unionville* (1943) and *Rapidan* (1961) quads.; Slaughter, *St. Mark's Parish,* p. 72; Church, "Tidewater to Shenandoah," pp. 22–23; Carpenter, "Spotswood Route," pp. 408–9.

190. This camp seems to have been named for Augustine Smith, who went home from the expedition with a fever on Aug. 30. Miss Maury's manuscript copy of the Journal clearly reads "O Smith's Camp," but she must have meant "A Smith's." For Smith, see note 101 above.

191. This camp probably was named for Christopher Robinson (1681–1727) who lived on Rappahannock River near Urbanna in Middlesex County. He was naval officer, justice of the peace, and sheriff, as well as burgess from 1704 to at least 1714. His stepmother and wife were both widows of Beverleys. Christopher's uncle, John Robinson, was ambassador to Sweden, first plenipotentiary to the Congress of Utrecht, 1712, and bishop of London. He left his Yorkshire estate "Hewick," worth about £425 sterling yearly, to Christopher. The camp conceivably could have been named for Christopher's brother John (1683–1749) of Essex County who later lived in Spotsylvania. He was a member of the House of Burgesses in 1714 and of the Council after 1720. His first wife was a Beverley. Thus both brothers were friends of Spotswood, connected with the Beverley family, and interested in Rapidan lands as grantees under the Octuna patent of 1722. Fontaine refers to "Dr. Robinson" and "Mr. Robinson," obviously the same person. Neither Christopher nor John was customarily called "Dr.," though their uncle, the bishop, was. *Cal. Va. State Paps.,* 1:88, 105–6, 167–68; *VMHB,* 2 (1894–95):2, 8; 3 (1895–96):3–4; 10 (1902–3): 381; 16 (1908):216–17; 22 (1924): 127; Octuna Patent, 1729, Va. Hist. Soc.

192. The two explanations of the route of the expedition now begin to diverge widely. Church and the traditionalists think it followed the south fork (the Rapidan), while Carpenter argues that it turned north and went along the Robinson (Robertson). Blind Run is not found on modern maps. Slaughter places Robinson's Camp on Big Run considerably west of modern Liberty Mills and not far from the Thornton or South Prong (today South River) of the Rapidan. Church puts it on Blue Run that enters the Rapidan from the south to the northeast of

Liberty Mills. There is a hill to the south that could meet Fontaine's description. Carpenter thinks the camp was south of the Robinson (Robertson) near Lillard Ford northeast of the town of Madison. The Geological Survey map shows no named stream at that point. U. S. Geol. Sur., *Rapidan* (1961) and *Gordonsville* (1961) quads.; Slaughter, *St. Mark's Parish*, p. 73; Church, "Tidewater to Shenandoah," pp. 22–23; Carpenter, "Spotswood Route," pp. 408–9.

193. This day's journey is most puzzling. Whether the Rapidan or the Robinson (Robertson) is the proper route, there seems no good reason for crossing it, and there is no mention of recrossing, though the camp would seem to be on the south side of either river. Also neither river appears as narrow as Fontaine's description implies. Slaughter has the expedition cross the South Prong and the Conway River and camp along the latter's east bank at the foot of the Blue Ridge. Church thinks they camped near Dawsonville where White Run enters the Rapidan from the south. Carpenter argues that the camp was on White Oak Run south of the Robinson (Robertson). He admits, however, that White Oak Run was known as Island Run as late as 1726. U. S. Geol. Sur., *Rapidan* (1961), *Gordonsville* (1961), and *Madison* (1930) quads.; Slaughter, *St. Mark's Parish*, p. 73; Church, "Tidewater to Shenandoah," pp. 22–23; Carpenter, "Spotswood Route," pp. 407, 408–9.

194. James Taylor (1674–1729), for whom this camp was named, lived in Drysdale Parish, King and Queen County. He was the great-great-grandfather of two Presidents—James Madison and Zachary Taylor. As surveyor of King and Queen and later Spotsylvania, he ran the bounds of Spotsylvania, Hanover, and Orange counties. He was a justice of the peace and member of the House of Burgesses, 1704–14. He surveyed the Octuna tract on the Rapidan (see note 185 above), acquired an interest in William Todd's adjoining grant (see note 188 above), had a grant of 8500 acres in 1722 on the Rapidan near the mouth of the Robinson (Robertson), with John Baylor possessed a tract above Mountain Run, and in 1729 secured another 10,000 acres adjoining the Octuna tract. *Cal. Va. State Paps.*, 1:198, 200; Hening, 4:514; *VMHB*, 9 (1901–2):311; 25 (1917):66–67; 30 (1922):387; 32 (1924):2, 16–17, 121, 375; 33 (1925): 22–23; 34 (1926):203–4, 206, 269; 35 (1927):350–51; *Abst. Va. Pat. Bks.*, no. 11:641.

195. Slaughter has the expedition go south along the edge of the Blue Ridge recrossing the Conway and the Thornton or South Prong and camping southwest of the present Stanardsville at the edge of Price's Mountain. Church places the camp in about the same area but has them reach it by traveling west along the South River (Thornton or South Prong) and then turning south to Blue Run. Blue Run is a tributary of the North Fork of the Rivanna which runs into the James and thus would meet Fontaine's description of "the head almost of James River." Carpenter puts the camp near the junction of Robinson (Robertson) River and Quaker Run, about one mile above the present Criglersville. He argues that Fontaine mistook the Rapidan for the James. Swift Run and the Rapidan are less than 15 miles apart in that area. U. S. Geol. Sur., *Madison* (1930) and *Stanardsville* (1964) quads.; Slaughter, *St. Mark's Parish*, p. 73; Church, "Tidewater to Shenandoah," pp. 22–23; Carpenter, "Spotswood Expedition," pp. 408–10.

196. This camp was named for William Robertson (d. 1739), clerk of the Council and General Assembly, 1702–38. A lawyer, he served as clerk and later trustee of the College of William and Mary, receiver of quitrents, clerk of James City County, and naval officer and then collector of York River. He lived at Williamsburg, and was a vestryman

of Bruton Parish, an early director in laying out Williamsburg, and an alderman under the charter of 1722. He was a heavy plunger in western lands and in 1720 with Cole Diggs and Peter Beverley patented 12,000 acres on the Rapidan beginning at the mouth of the Robinson (Robertson) River. He might have been with Spotswood and Fontaine on the journey to Germanna but does not seem to have returned with them. *Va. Coun. Exec. Jls.*, 2:220, 223, 237; 3:78, 127, 512, 538; 4:180, 442; *Abst. Va. Pat. Bks.*, no. 11:641; *Cal. Va. State Paps.*, 1:209, 219; *VMHB*, 3 (1894–95):180; 8 (1900–01):143–44; *WMQ* (1), 10 (1901–2):73, 74, 85; *Va. Hist. Reg.*, 3 (1850):196.

197. Again, Fontaine says it was the James River, "where a man may jump over it." Slaughter thinks they went over Bridger's Mountain to the east side of Swift Run Gap. Church traces the route along Blue Run west and then to Swift Run. The small mountain could have been Powell's Mountain. Carpenter says the expedition went southwest along Quaker Run and over Chapman's Mountain to the Rapidan and that the camp was on that stream just east of President Hoover's Camp. U. S. Geol. Sur., *Madison* (1930), *Stanardsville* (1964), and *Fletcher* (1965) quads.; Slaughter, *St. Mark's Parish*, p. 73; Church, "Tidewater to Shenandoah," pp. 22–23; Carpenter, "Spotswood Route," pp. 408–10.

198. Robert Brooke (d. 1744), for whom this camp was named, lived at "Farmer's Hall" on Rappahannock River in Essex County between Port Royal and Tappahannock. He was deputy clerk of the county, 1700, justice of peace, 1727, and county surveyor. He laid out many tracts in the Rapidan area, and in 1737 —as surveyor for the commissioners who settled the dispute between Lord Fairfax and the colony about the Northern Neck—he made a much-imitated map of the Potomac east from the mouth of the Shenandoah. He owned about 200,000 acres, and his patents in

Spotsylvania County included 331 acres in the fork of the Rappahannock (1731), 10,000 acres adjoining the Octuna tract (1732), and 951 acres adjoining Mountain Run (1732). His grandson Robert was governor of Virginia, 1794–96, and another grandson Judge Francis Taliafero Brooke in 1841 said he had seen the small golden horseshoe set with garnets given his grandfather by Governor Spotswood. W. W. Corcoran, the Washington financier, also asserted he had seen it. Robert Brooke, "A Plan of Potomack River . . . 1737," Enoch Pratt Free Library, Baltimore (Colonial Williamsburg photostat); *Cal. Va. State Paps.*, 1:214, 229, 230, 240–41; *Absts. Va. Pat. Bks.*, no. 14:813, 815, 827; *VMHB*, 9 (1901–2):315, 436–38; 11 (1903–4):93; 12 (1904–5):106–7; 14 (1906–7):28, 326, 327; 15 (1907–8): 104; 19 (1911):320; *WMQ* (1), 11 (1902–3):211–12; (2), 4 (1924):2–3, 12–13; Davis, *Chronicler of Cavaliers*, pp. 250–52.

199. For the full discussion of the crossing at the summit, see Introduction, pp. 16–18 above. U. S. Geol. Sur., *Fletcher* (1965) and *Swift Run Gap* (1965) quads.

200. There is great disagreement about the location of this camp on the east bank of the South Fork of Shenandoah River. Fontaine said the expedition went four and one-half miles to the top of the mountain, found the western descent too steep and returned to the top to take a blazed trail to the bottom (this maneuver took two and one-half miles), and then went seven miles to the river. Slaughter and Scott placed the camp near Elkton, Kemper and Church, near Shenandoah, and Carpenter, near Alma. The first location is only about five and one-half miles from the mountains, but the last two meet the test of distance. Church thinks the group descended slightly north and east of Swift Run and followed Elk Run and Dry Run to a spot between Boone's Creek and Naked River south of the

town of Shenandoah. Carpenter maintains they took Tanner's Ridge to Hawksbill Creek about two miles south of Stanley and then reached the river near Alma. U. S. Geol. Sur., *Swift Run Gap* (1965), *Elkton East* (1965), *Elkton West* (1965), *Big Meadows* (1965), and *Mt. Jackson* (1942) quads.; Slaughter, *St. Mark's Parish,* p. 73; Scott, "Knights Route," pp. 145–53; Kemper, "Spotswood Expedition," pp. 123–24; Church, "Tidewater to Shenandoah," pp. 22–23; Carpenter, "Spotswood Route," pp. 408 10.

201. This is the Shenandoah River, first named by the Iroquois Indians who often raided the Shenandoah Valley. *VMHB,* 29 (1921):414.

202. According to the traditional Swift Run Gap route, Mount George is today Hightop Mountain (3587 feet) and Mount Spotswood, Saddleback Mountain (3200 feet). The Milam's Gap adherents would make Mount George today Fork Mountain (3670 feet) and Mount Spotswood, Doubletop Mountain (3455 feet). U. S. Geol. Sur., *Swift Run Gap* (1965) and *Fletcher* (1965) quads.; Church, "From Tidewater to Shenandoah," pp. 22–23; Carpenter, "Spotswood Route," pp. 408–9.

203. This camp was named for Capt. Jeremiah Clowder, though on the way west it was called Colonel Robertson's or Hospital Camp (see note 196 above). Notice that Fontaine gives the distance coming back as 16 miles, while going out it was 18 miles (4 miles on Sept. 4 and 14 miles on Sept. 5). The difference is probably accounted for by the false start down the western descent on Sept. 5. Captain Clowder commanded a company of horse in King and Queen County, 1707, and was a member of the quorum there, 1714, and sheriff, 1716. In 1726 he was a justice of Spotsylvania County and the next year a charter trustee and director of the new town of Fredericksburg. He was one of the eight grantees of the Octuna tract, 1722 (see note 185 above). *Cal. Va.*

*State Paps.,* 1:113–114; *VMHB,* 2 (1894–95):7; 17 (1909):155; 48 (1950):150; Hening, 4:234–38.

204. Notice that Fontaine first says they made 27 miles this day and then finally 20 miles. If the latter figure is correct (and it seems to be) they could have camped at or near what was Robinson's Camp on the way out. It was 20 miles from there to Robertson's or Hospital Camp going (see Journal entries, Sept. 2–3). Church places Mason's and Robinson's camps at the same place. Carpenter for some unexplained reason has the expedition swing south after White Oak Run and camp on a branch of the Robinson (Robertson) River called Dark Run about two miles from the present town of Madison. Church, "Tidewater to Shenandoah," pp. 22–23; Carpenter, "Spotswood Route," pp. 408–9, 411. George Mason (1690–1735) for whom the camp was probably named, was sheriff of Stafford County and a member of the quorum there in 1714. In 1718 he was elected to the House of Burgesses where he was still serving in 1726. Four years earlier he was county clerk. In 1719 he was on a General Court grand jury that sent the king an address praising Spotswood's administration. He does not seem to have invested in land about the Rapidan. Mason's son George (1725–1792) was author of the Virginia Declaration of Rights of 1776. *Va. Hist. Reg.,* 4 (1851):18, 66, 74; *VMHB,* 2 (1894–95):13; 4 (1896–97):350, 352; 18 (1910):447; *WMQ* (1), 3 (1894–95):223; 10 (1901–2):141.

205. Slaughter puts this camp on the north bank of the Rapidan just west of Summerville's Ford, while Church places it on the south bank opposite the ford. Carpenter argues that since this is the only time Fontaine mentions the Rapidan, he had been following the northern or Robinson (Robertson) branch before. For Beverley's interest in the land near there, see note 185 above. Slaughter, *St. Mark's Parish,* p. 73; Church. "From

Tidewater to Shenandoah," pp. 22–23; Carpenter, "Spotswood Route," p. 411.

206. Capt. Christopher Smith (d. ca. 1740) was probably the one for whom this camp was named. A lieutenant in the rangers in King William County, 1712, and surveyor of New Kent County, 1716, he was paid £100 the next year for taking a message to Governor Hunter in New York and then attending an Indian council at Albany. He owned land in King William, King and Queen, Hanover, and Spotsylvania counties. Two of his tracts lay south of the Rapidan—400 acres on the East North East River (1730) and 1000 acres on the North Anna (1728). *Cal. Va. State Paps.,* 1:233; *Abst. Va. Pat. Bks.,* no. 13:749; *Tyler's Mag.,* 4 (1922–23):150; *VMHB,* 4 (1896–97): 175, 372, 374; 32 (1924):74, 154; 35 (1927):411; *WMQ* (1), 21 (1912–13):249; (2), 3 (1923):45. Some have thought that Capt. Charles Smith, Augustine's brother, might have been the one for whom the camp was named, but he had died in 1714. Same (1), 9 (1900–01):42–44.

207. Since Mason lived at Mason's Neck on Potomac River, his route home was different from those of the other gentlemen. Leland, "Map of the Chesapeake Bay Country."

208. Augustine Smith and George Mason had already gone home. Robert Beverley, Jr., William Todd, James Taylor, and Capt. Christopher Smith all lived in King William and King and Queen counties so that they might have ridden together. Robert Brooke who resided on the Rappahannock could have gone part way with them. William Robertson of Williamsburg did not accompany the governor and Fontaine. Christopher Robinson, who lived near Urbanna, and Jeremiah Clowder of King and Queen County could have ridden together part way.

209. The church of St. Mary's Parish in Essex County had the Rev. Owen Jones as minister, 1702–ca. 1724. At that time or later it was known as the Old Mount Church and was situated west of Port Royal at what is now Rappahannock Academy Post Office. Goodwin, *Colonial Church,* p. 323; Marshall Wingfield, *A History of Caroline County, Virginia* (Richmond, 1924), pp. 12, 293–94.

210. See note 102 above.

211. See note 90 above.

212. John Monro, Jr. (d. ca. 1723) was minister of St John's Church from 1695 until his death. He was an ancestor of President James Monroe. Goodwin, *Colonial Church,* pp. 294, 331, 334.

213. Charles West (d. ca. 1734) lived on a 4000-acre plantation situated between the Mattaponi and Pamunkey rivers near the town of Delaware commonly called West Point. Dr. Malcolm H. Harris of West Point kindly showed the editor the remains of the pier where Colonel Bassett called for Governor Spotswood and Fontaine on the north bank of the Pamunkey. Hening, 7:488–90; *Va. Counc. Exec. Jls.,* 3:326–27; *VMHB,* 8 (1900–01):385.

214. Col. William Bassett (1670–1723), who lived at "Eltham" in New Kent County on the south bank of the Pamunkey, was Governor Spotswood's close friend. His father William (d. 1670) had served in the English army, and the son took an active part in the militia, was captain and major in New Kent County, became lieutenant colonel when he raised his own troop of horse, and finally commanded the militia for both New Kent and King William counties. He was also justice of the peace, sheriff, and one of the visitors and governors of the College of William and Mary. He was in the House of Burgesses, 1695–1702, and then took his seat on the Council. In 1720 with Gawin Corbin he took up 15,000 acres on the South Branch that flowed out of the North Fork of the Rappahannock in Spotsylvania County. *Va. Counc. Exec. Jls.,* 1:444, 446; 2:32, 274; 3:151, 420, 538; *VMHB,* 1 (1893–94):369, 375;

4 (1896–97):161–62, 174; 7 (1899–1900):399–400; 23 (1915):359–60.

215. Spotswood estimated the total distance at 445 miles. *WMQ* (2), 3 (1923):40–45. Since Fontaine put the round trip from Williamsburg to Germanna at 292 miles (see Journal entry, Nov. 26, 1715, above), the round trip from Germanna to the Shenandoah was 146 miles—74 miles going and 72 returning (see Introduction, note 34 above).

216. John Holloway (1671–1739) practiced law in Virginia for about 30 years. He was an attorney in the Marshalsea Court in London and served in the army in Ireland before coming to Maryland and then Virginia about 1700. He was justice for Elizabeth City and King and Queen counties, naval officer for the lower James River, judge of the Court of Vice Admiralty, and burgess from King and Queen, 1710–14. Later he was a vestryman of Bruton Parish, first mayor of Williamsburg under the royal charter of 1722, speaker of the House of Burgesses, 1720–34, and treasurer of the colony, 1723–34. Fontaine, by this time, had purchased a plantation in King William County (see note 289 below) and doubtless left the deed and other legal papers with Holloway. The hazards of travel made it mandatory for the prudent man to take such precautions. *Va. Historical Reg.,* 1 (1848):119–22; Hening, 4:index; *VMHB,* 2 (1894–95):2, 4, 7; 32 (1924):137; *WMQ* (1), 3 (1894–95):174–76; 10 (1901–2):85, 175.

217. See note 85 above.

218. Michael Kearny (1669–1741) and his brother Edmund, a merchant, were living in Hampton by 1712. Michael and another brother Philip came from Ireland to Philadelphia about 1703. Edmund was a member of the Virginia Indian Company, and patented land with Michael in North Carolina, where Edmund moved. Michael was married to Sarah (ca. 1695 or 1697–1736), daughter of Col. Lewis Morris

of Morrisania (see note 231 below). Family records place the marriage in 1715, but their first child was not born until 1717. By 1719 they had moved to Perth Amboy, where Colonel Morris was president of the Council of New Jersey. He had his son-in-law appointed treasurer of the province, secretary, surrogate, clerk of the Assembly, and clerk of the Court of Common Pleas. *WMQ* (2), 4 (1924):184–85; New Jersey (state), *Documents Relating to the Colonial History of New Jersey,* Frederick William Ricord et al., eds., 19 vols. (Trenton, 1880–1914), *Archives of the State of New Jersey* (first series), 5:142–51, 155; 12:6–12; 14:135–36; 15:69, 124; William A. Whitehead, *Contributions to the Early History of Perth Amboy . . .* (New York, 1856), pp. 90–92, 239; Dodson, *Spotswood,* p. 86; Elizabeth Morris Lefferts, *Descendants of Lewis Morris of Morrisania* (New York, 1893) charts A, C; Saunders, *N. C. Col. Recs.,* 2:18, 122, 425; Historical Society of Pennsylvania: Leach Collection, 60:33; 129:479–501; 158:1; Hildeburn Mss., 1:44; Rogers Collection, 28:419–26.

219. Old Point Comfort marks the division between Hampton Roads and Chesapeake Bay. Fry and Jefferson, *Virginia,* 1751.

220. The ferry crossed the Narrows of New York Bay between Staten and Long islands. The Staten Island landing was near the present Federal Quarantine Station at Rosebank. Good maps of about 1730 and 1734 appear in I. N. Phelps Stokes, *The Iconography of Manhattan Island, 1498–1909 . . .,* 6 vols. (New York, 1915–28), 1:plates 27A, 29. See also Francis F. Wayland, "John Fontaine's Visits to Staten Island in 1716," *Staten Island Historian,* 13 (Jan.–Mar. 1952):1–2.

221. The ferry at the village of New Utrecht was probably run by Hendrick Hendricks. In 1717 he and Isaac Hansen secured a patent from the New York Council to operate a ferry between

Hendrickson's Landing on Long Island and Hanson's Landing on Staten Island. In 1719 the Council upheld the right of the brothers Peter and Jacques Cortelyou to operate the ferry and mentioned that Hendrick Hendricks was their brother-in-law. New York Secretary of State, *Calendar of Historical Manuscripts . . .,* E. B. O'Callaghan, ed., 2 vols. (Albany, 1866), 2:374, 445, 446; New York Secretary of State, *Calendar of . . . Land Papers . . .* (Albany, 1864), p. 122; Stokes, *Iconography,* 1: plates 27A, 29; 4:974 (Mar. 27, 1717).

222. Brooklyn was served by the Long Island ferry over the East River with three stops on the Manhattan side. Same. 1: plates 27A, 29; 3:942; 6:22 (Sept. 29, 1707).

223. There were so many Schuylers in New York during this period that it has not been possible to identify the landlady of Fontaine and Kearny.

224. Andrew Freneau (André Fresneau) (d. 1725), merchant, became a freeman of New York, Aug. 22, 1710. He left a considerable estate, and his will mentions his nephew Andrew Fresneau of Ireland. *Burghers of New Amsterdam and Freemen of New York, 1675–1866* in New-York Historical Society *Collections* (1885), p. 90; *Abstracts of New York Wills,* II, in N. Y. Hist. Soc. *Collections* (1893), pp. 65, 81, 318–19.

225. Probably the New Coffee House, later the Exchange Coffee House, situated on the northeast corner of Broad and Water streets fronting on East River. Stokes, *Iconography,* 3:978; 4: 466 (Sept. 22, 1709).

226. Robert Hunter (d. 1734), like Spotswood, was a Scot and had fought under Marlborough. Appointed lieutenant governor of Virginia in 1707, he was captured by a privateer on his voyage there and taken to France as prisoner. Later exchanged, he served as captain general and governor in chief of New York and New Jersey, 1709–19— efficient, popular, and successful. After

a period in England, he was governor of Jamaica, 1727–34. *D.A.B.,* s.v. "Hunter, Robert."

227. The fort's name was changed from Anne to George on news of the latter's accession, Oct. 1714. Stokes, *Iconography,* 1:190; 3:944.

228. In 1713, 100 soldiers arrived from London to recruit the four companies stationed at New York. Stokes, *Iconography,* 4:479 (Oct. 15, 1713).

229. Dr. John Johnstone (1662– 1732) became mayor in October 1714 and served for five years. He was also in the Assembly, 1709–10, and on the Council, 1716–22. He was superseded when he had removed to New Jersey. New York (city), *Common Council Minutes, 1675–1776,* 8 vols. (New York, 1905), 3:73–213. *N. Y. Col. Docs..* 5:34, 201, 207, 437, 471, 541, 649, 697; *N. J. Archives* (1), 4:119; 11:299; Whitehead, *Perth Amboy,* pp. 68–75; Edgar A. Werner, *Civil List and Constitutional History of the Colony and State of New York* (Albany, 1889), p. 364.

230. Probably an error for Colonel DeLancey. See note 246 below.

231. Lewis Morris (1671–1746), lord of the manor of Morrisania situated just north of Harlem River, had a somewhat stormy political career. He was a close friend of Governor Hunter and named a son for him. Hunter appointed Morris chief justice of the Supreme Court of New York in 1715. He served as governor of New Jersey, 1738–46, and held much land in both provinces. *D.A.B.,* s.v. "Morris, Lewis"; William Smith, *The History of the Late Province of New York . . .,* 2 vols., in N. Y. Hist. Soc. *Collections* (1826, 1829), 1:179–83; Lefferts, *Morris Descendants,* chart A; Stokes, *Iconography,* 1: plates 27A, 29, 50; 4:386 (Dec. 9, 1694); 6: plate 86.

232. The East River. Same, 1: plates 27A, 29, 50.

233. The Harlem River, probably by Morrisania Ferry. Otto Hufeland, *West-*

chester County during the American
Revolution . . . (White Plains, 1926),
p. 102 (map).

234. John Hamilton (d. 1747) was
the son of Andrew Hamilton (d.
1703), governor of New Jersey and deputy
postmaster general of America. John
became postmaster general, was appointed to the Council of New Jersey in 1713
by Hunter, and was later governor. *D.A.B.,*
s. v. "Hamilton, John"; *Cal. N.Y. Hist.
Mss.,* 2:412, 580; *N.J. Archives* (1),
4:183–84; Whitehead, *Perth Amboy,*
pp. 168–70; Stokes, *Iconography.* 4:471
(June 1, 1711), 482 (Dec. 6, 1714);
*N. Y. Col. Docs.,* 4:200; 5:361.

235. Henry Lane (d. 1744), well-
known merchant, was the son of Sir
Thomas Lane, prominent in the affairs
of West Jersey and a former lord mayor
of London. Henry came to New York
in 1710 and became a member of the
Council in 1733. New York (colony),
*Journal of the Legislative Council . . .,*
2 vols. (Albany, 1861), 1:626–845;
*N. J. Archives* (1), 3:38; 5:323; *N.
Y. Col. Docs.,* 5:980; 6:261; *N.Y. Abstract of Wills,* 4:8; Berthold Fernow,
ed., *Calendar of Wills* [in New York],
*1626–1836* (New York, 1896), no.
1024; Stokes, *Iconography,* 4:527 (Feb.
11, 1731); Werner, *N. Y. Civil List,*
p. 364.

236. Trinity Church, chartered in
1697, occupied the same site on Broad-
way as the present Trinity. The Church
of England was supported by a tax on
freeholders but was not so strongly
established as in the southern colonies.
Stokes, *Iconography,* 1:183–84, 244,
plate 25 (described, pp. 239–51).

237. The French Church (L'Eglise
du St. Esprit) that Fontaine saw was
built in 1704 on the north side of Pine
Street east of Nassau. Same, 1:179, 187,
245, plate 25; 3:932; 4:444 (Apr. 16,
1703).

238. The South Dutch Church on
Garden Street (Exchange Place) was
built in 1692. Same, 1:244, plate 25;
3:936.

239. The New York Assembly met
in the City Hall (begun in 1699) at
the head of Broad Street, the site today
of the Sub-Treasury Building, main-
tained as a national historical monument by the National Park Service.
Same, 1:244, plate 25; 3:973.

240. The Dutch and those of Dutch
descent still outnumbered either the
French or English. William Smith in
1708 said the inhabitants consisted "of
Dutch Calvinists upon the plan of the
church of Holland; French refugees, on
the Geneva model; a few English epis-
copalians; and a still smaller number of
English and Irish presbyterians." Smith,
*History,* 1:160–61.

241. Col. Richard Ingoldsby or In-
goldesby (d. 1719), after service as a
field officer in Holland and Ireland,
came to New York in 1691 as commander of the troops there. He took a
leading part against Jacob Leisler, and
when Lt. Gov. Henry Slaughter died in
July, Ingoldsby became commander-in-
chief until Lt. Gov. Benjamin Fletcher
arrived in 1692. Ingoldsby was com-
missioned lieutenant governor of New
York and New Jersey, Nov. 1702, under
Lord Cornbury and was acting governor
in 1709 after Lord Lovelace's death. He
was not closely related to Lt. Gen. Ingoldsby, the Fontaines' friend (note 2
above). *N. Y. Col. Docs.,* 3:757, 810,
845–46; 4:431, 716, 719, 1002, 1162;
5:80, 82, 508; *Cal. N. Y. Hist. Mss.,*
2:201, 234, 235, 238, 269, 363, 405;
*N. Y. Abstracts of Wills,* 2:200; Smith,
*History,* 1:105-08, 170; Stokes, *Iconography,* 4:361 (Jan. 25, 1691).

242. The Exchange, established by
Gov. Francis Lovelace, 1670. Same, 1:
244–45, plate 25; 3:924.

243. The name of Fooks is not found
in the records of the Holy Trinity or
Merchants Guild of Dublin. The French
refugees frequently avoided joining craft
guilds. Nor is Fooks on the 1724 list of
merchants—in and out of the guild—
agreeing not to accept William Woods's
halfpence and farthings (see note 37

above). A John Fooks was a godfather at the baptism of John Cossé in Dublin, June 24. 1723. "Dublin Holy Trinity or Merchants Guild, Charters and Documents, 1438–1824," (Ms. transcripts for J. T. Gilbert) 2 vols., 1867, Dublin Public Library; Thomas Hume's *Dublin Courant,* Aug. 22, 1724; Hug. Soc. London, *The French Conformed Churches of St. Patrick and St. Mary, Dublin, Registers,* J. J. Digges La Touche, ed. (Dublin, 1893), p. 43.

244. "James Maxwell, Merchant," became a freeman of New York City, Nov. 25, 1712. *N. Y. Burghers and Freemen,* p. 91.

245. L'Eglise du St. Esprit. James Laberie had been its minister since 1709, and the Council of New York voted him a yearly salary of £20 from the provincial revenue. Stokes, *Iconography,* 4:467 (Dec. 13, 1709). See note 237 above.

246. Stephen DeLancey (1663–1741), a native of Caen in Normandy, came to New York in 1686 and was soon its wealthiest, best-known merchant. He was married in 1700 to Anne, daughter of the prosperous and powerful Col. Stephanus Van Cortlandt. DeLancey served on the Common Council and in the Assembly and was an elder of the French Church. His eldest son James became lieutenant governor of New York. See also note 230 above. *N. Y. Burghers and Freemen,* p. 53; *N. Y. Abstracts of Wills,* 2:186, 202, 238, 288–89; 3:336–37; *N. Y. Common Counc. Mins.,* 1:214; 236; 3:44, 50; *N. Y. Col. Docs.,* 5:769; Smith, *History,* 1:179; Margharita Arlina Hamm. *Famous Families of New York* . . . , 2 vols. (New York, 1901), 1:91–92.

247. Thomas Byerly (d. 1722) was collector and receiver general of the province of New York, proprietor of the Jerseys, and member of the Councils of New York and New Jersey. He came to New York as collector in 1702 and quarreled violently with his prede-cessors in that post and with Governor Cornbury. *Cal. N. Y. Hist. Mss.,* 2:314, 332, 349, 412. 459, 471; *N. Y. Col. Docs.,* 4:1066; 5:205, 296, 458, 698, 777; *N. Y. Burghers and Freemen,* pp. 86, 457; Stokes, *Iconography,* 4:446 (July 30, 1703); Werner, *N. Y. Civil List,* pp. 180, 364.

248. Maurice Birchfield, surveyor general of the customs, came to New York with Governor Hunter about 1710. He quarreled with the merchants and suspended Thomas Byerly (see preceding note). Governor Hunter complained of his actions to the Commissioners of Customs in 1711. *N. Y. Col. Docs.,* 5: 229–37. 264–65; *Cal. N. Y. Hist. Mss.,* 2:375, 377, 378, 380.

249. Obviously there was a ferry between New York and Perth Amboy at this time. For a later notice of it, see Stokes, *Iconography,* 4:556 (Apr. 3, 1738). The continuing contrary wind made Fontaine and Kearny decide to return as they had come.

250. Capt. Lancaster Symes (d. 1729), a well-known New York merchant, came there with his nephew, Maj. Richard Ingoldsby (see note 241 above) in 1691. He served in the garrisons of Albany and New York, was an army contractor, and became a large landowner. A ship captain for a time, he was often called on to audit the accounts of men-of-war in New York harbor. The Common Council leased him a pier and slips but canceled the lease when Symes did not keep up the repairs. He was vestryman of Trinity Church. *Cal. N. Y. Hist. Mss.,* 2:229, 248, 318, 346, 350, 354. 365, 371; *N. Y. Burghers and Freemen,* p. 76; *N. Y. Common Coun. Mins.,* 2:250, 443; 3:38–39, 83, 85; *N. Y. Col. Docs.,* 3:767; 4:128. 528, 1135; 5:110, 532, 759, 875, 876; *Cal. N. Y. Land Paps.,* pp. 64, 81, 84, 89, 94, 95, 97.

251. See note 221 above.

252. Probably a part of the West Bank shown on a map of the harbor

of 1734. Stokes. *Iconography,* 1: plate 29.

253. Alexander Stuart kept tavern at Stony Brook between New Dorp and Oakwood on what is now Amboy Road. Wayland, "Fontaine on Staten Island," p. 2.

254. Col. Thomas Farmer owned the ferry situated at the southwest end of what is now Amboy Road. He was collector of the customs at Bentley, Staten Island, but in 1711 moved to Perth Amboy, where he became a judge of the Supreme Court and member of the Council. *N. J. Archives* (1), 4:123; Whitehead, *Perth Amboy,* pp. 92–93; Wayland, "Fontaine on Staten Island," p. 2; *N. Y. Col. Docs..* 5:201, 207, 231; 6:24, 36.

255. Governor Hunter served both New York and New Jersey. His house on a knoll south of where St. Peter's Church was to be built, had a fine view of the harbor. Whitehead, *Perth Amboy,* pp. 90n., 153.

256. Perth Amboy was connected with Staten Island by a ferry across Arthur Kill and with southern New Jersey by another ferry over the Raritan River. Same, pp. 57 (map), 270–72.

257. Probably the old church that had been built in 1695 near the Raritan ferry and was serviced by Church of England missionaries. In 1718 Governor Hunter chartered an Anglican congregation, which erected St. Peter's Church, 1719–31. Same. pp. 209, 223.

258. Probably John Johnston, Jr. (1691–1732), son of the mayor of New York (see note 229 above). The son dropped the final "e" from his last name. He may have been judge of the Court of Common Pleas in New York, 1712–20. Governor Hunter had him appointed to the Council of New Jersey in 1718. *N. Y. Abstracts of Wills.* 2: 97, 216; *Cal. N. Y. Hist. Mss.,* 2:367; *N. J. Archives* (1), 4:363; 5:197; 14: 111–12, 135; 30:270; Whitehead, *Perth Amboy,* pp. 72, 239.

259. May Bickly or Bickley (d.

1724) served as recorder of New York City and as attorney general of the province, 1705, 1709–12. He held land in New York and New Jersey. *Cal. N. Y. Hist. Mss.,* 2:354, 370, 483, 485, 488; *N. Y. Abstracts of Wills,* 2: 272–73; *N. Y. Burghers and Freemen,* pp. 88, 454. 462, 472; *N. Y. Common Counc. Mins.,* 2:367; 3:294, 328, 341; *N. Y. Col. Docs.,* 4:1186; 5:341, 357; *N. Y. Cal. of Wills,* no. 54; Werner, *N. Y. Civil List,* p. 177.

260. Probably John Ballinger (ca. 1690–1722), sometimes Bellange or Ballengee, a Burlington tanner whose father was a Huguenot. Courtesy of Mrs. Rebecca B. Colesar, reference librarian, New Jersey State Library, Trenton. *N. J. Archives* (1), 22:25, 210, 283; William Wade Hinshaw, *Encyclopedia of Quaker Genealogy,* 7 vols. (Ann Arbor, 1936–62), 2:195; George DeCou, *Moorestown and Her Neighbors . . .* (Philadelphia, 1929), p. 120; Huguenot Society of New Jersey, *Huguenot Ancestors . . . ,* 3rd ed. (Bloomfield, N.J., 1915), p. 5; Thomas Shourds, *History and Genealogy of Fenwick's Colony* (Bridgeton, N.J., 1876), pp. 218–19.

261. The Delaware River.

262. Samuel Pérés, a Huguenot from France by way of London, was an early settler of Philadelphia. He made an inventory of the estate of the goldsmith Peter Dubac in 1683 and was a member of the Anglican congregation of Christ Church. *Pennsylvania Magazine of History and Biography,* 57 (1933): 245; 80 (1956):174, 196; Charles P. Keith, *Chronicles of Pennsylvania . . . ,* 2 vols. (Philadelphia, 1917), 1:333; Register of Wills, 1732, no. 276, Will Book "E," p. 208, Philadelphia City Hall.

263. The Lower Ferry crossed the Schuylkill River. Lewis Evans, *Pensilvania, New-Jersey, New York, and the Three Delaware Counties,* 1749; Lewis Evans, *Middle British Colonies . . . ,* 1755; Nicholas Scull, *Pennsylvania,*

1759; Reading Howell, *Map of . . . Pennsylvania,* 1792, *Pennsylvania Archives . . .* 9 series, 120 vols. (Philadelphia, 1852–56; Harrisburg, 1874–95) 3rd series, Appendix, vols. 1–10.

264. The exact location of Harlem is now unknown. Its site is probably a part of the present Chester, Pa. Lewis Evans in 1749 showed the road from Philadelphia running 7 miles to Derby and then 9 miles to Chester on the Delaware, thus equalling Fontaine's estimate of 16 miles distance from Philadelphia to Harlem. Evans, *Pensilvania,* etc., 1749. For Chester, see Writers' Program, Work Projects Administration, *Pennsylvania: A Guide to the Keystone State* (New York, 1940), pp. 202–8.

265. Over Brandywine and Christina creeks near Wilmington. Same sources as note 263.

266. Miss Maury's printed version of the Journal (page 302) contains the words here set in brackets and varies slightly in wording for the remainder of the entry for that day. She may have left out a line in her transcription of the original manuscript and amended the printed copy but forgot to change her manuscript transcription. For another variation in wording between manuscript and printed copies, see note 297 below.

267. Bohemia Landing lay in Cecil County, Md., near the junction of the Great and Little Bohemia rivers a few miles from the navigable waters of Appoquinimink Creek and only a short distance west of the Delaware line. In 1659 Augustine Herrman (ca. 1605–1686), a Czech from Bohemia, came to Maryland and named both the river and his Bohemia Manor. He made the first accurate map of Maryland and Virginia. George Johnston, *History of Cecil County, Maryland . . .* (Elkton, 1881), p. 196; Writers' Program, Work Projects Administration, *Maryland: A Guide to the Old Line State* (New York, 1940),

pp. 362–63; *D.A.B.,* s.v. "Herrman, Augustine."

268. Lewis Evans, *Pensilvania,* etc., 1749 shows a "Petersons" about four or five miles from the Bohemia River, apparently in Delaware and about 20 miles from Dover. The probate records in the Delaware Public Archives, Dover, contain a will of Charles Patterson, innkeeper, made in 1750. He resided in the Middletown-Odessa area of Delaware opposite Bohemia Manor. Courtesy of Leon de Valinger, Jr., Delaware state archivist, who has also checked the other Delaware references. "Peterson's" and "Patterson's" were probably the same inn.

269. Maryland effectively controlled the Three Lower Counties of Delaware at this period so that it is natural that Fontaine should think he was in Maryland from late on Nov. 17 into the morning of Nov. 23. The route can be followed on William Barker's map, *Delaware from the Best of Authorities* (Philadelphia, [1795]), which appears in William Guthrie, *The Grand Atlas for Guthrie's Geography* (Philadelphia, 1795).

270. The courthouse was at Dover, today the seat of Kent County, Del. See next note.

271. Philip Kearny's plantation lay in Kent County, Del., on the St. Jones River about two miles south of Dover in the neighborhood of the modern towns of Lebanon and Camden. On Aug. 24, 1718, Philip Kearny, merchant, of Philadelphia, and Michael Kearny, merchant, of Rappahannock River, Virginia, divided a 3200-acre tract between them. They had purchased the land jointly, Oct. 24, 1709, from Thomas England and others. Philip accepted the "Great Geneva" portion as his share. It contained only 600 acres but was apparently the developed part. Kent County Deeds, liber N-1, fols. 95ff., Del. Public Archives, Dover. See also *WMQ* (2), 4 (1924): 185; Evans, *Middle British Colonies,*

1755; Writers' Program, Work Projects Administration, *Delaware: A Guide to the First State* (New York, 1938), pp. 176–84, 352–53.

272. Sutton's would have been situated in the present Redden State Forest and the "poor man's house" about one mile below Georgetown, both in Sussex County. See also W.P.A. *Del. Guide,* pp. 379–85.

273. Probably should be spelled "Dukes's" since there was a Dukes family in this area. The house would have been on the road toward Millsboro in Sussex County. See also W.P.A. *Del. Guide,* pp. 385–87.

274. They probably crossed Indian River or Creek near the site of present-day Millsboro, Sussex County. Evans, *Middle British Colonies,* 1755; W.P.A. *Del. Guide,* pp. 385–87.

275. Leon de Valinger, Jr., Delaware state archivist, thinks this house was near Dagsboro, Sussex County, and there is a Pepper Creek in that area. Harold R. Manakee, director of the Maryland Historical Society, Baltimore, kindly sent the editor an index to certain records in the Maryland Hall of Records, that Dr. Edward M. Riley, director of research, Colonial Williamsburg, examined. This same procedure was followed for notes 276 and 278 below. William Pepper may have been the travelers' host. He had five land patents surveyed in Sussex County—"Pepper's Chance," 1713; "Safety," 1713; "Folley," 1713; "Luck," 1714; and "Pepper's Delight," 1714. They contained a total of 700 acres in the Indian River region. Patent Book, P. L. 46, no. 4, 323–24; Somerset and Dorcester County Rent Roll, no. 5, fols. 260, 264, 268–69.

276. They left Sussex County, Del., in eight or ten miles and entered Somerset County, Md. Thomas Mumford of Somerset County left property to six sons, including James, the eldest, by will probated May 17, 1728. James also served on the grand jury panel, March 1718. Somerset County Wills (1726–

30), fols. 452–55; Somerset County, Judicial Records (1718), p. 2, Md. Hall of Records.

277. Snow Hill in 1715 was situated in Somerset County, Md. Evans, *Middle British Colonies,* 1755; W.P.A. *Md. Guide,* pp. 443–45.

278. Probably still in Somerset County, Md. John Pope (d. 1721) owned a 300-acre patent called "Weaver's Choice" on the south side of the Pocomoke in the woods near Mattapony Landing. Somerset and Dorcester Counties Rent Roll, no. 5, fol. 154; Somerset County Deeds (1727–1731), p. 103; Wills, 16, fol. 430, Somerset (1721), Md. Hall of Records.

279. James Kempe (d. 1722), a leading businessman of Accomack County, Va., served as county attorney, surveyor, and tobacco agent. He was a friend of the Rev. Francis Makemie (ca. 1658–1708), Presbyterian clergyman, and wed his widow (née Naomi Anderson) in 1709. Naomi owned a tract on Crooked (later Holden's) Creek in the northwestern part of the county near the town of Sandford. The inventory of Kempe's estate indicates that he operated a tavern; the location would have been convenient for travelers crossing Chesapeake Bay. Stratton Nottingham, comp., *Wills and Administrations: Accomack County, Virginia, 1663–1800* (Onancock, 1931), pp. 30, 37, 45, 54; I. Marshall Page, *The Life Story of Rev. Francis Mackemie* (Grand Rapids, Mich., 1938), pp. 124, 189, 191, 223–26, 231–52; *VMHB,* 2 (1893–94):3; Ralph T. Whitelaw, *Virginia's Eastern Shore: A History of Northampton and Accomack Counties,* 2 vols. (Richmond, 1951), 2:819, 1266, 1282. John A. Upshur of Accomac, Va., has verified much of this account.

280. John Sandford owned property next to that on which Kempe's tavern was probably located. Sandford's tract was on Crooked (Holden's) Creek near its outlet on Pocomoke Sound in the Chesapeake and about one mile east of

the present town of Sandford. Nottingham, *Accomack County Wills,* p. 44; Whitelaw, *Eastern Shore,* 2:1274, 1281–82, 1293; John A. Upshur, Accomac, Va.

281. There may have been an Egg Island in the vicinity of Watts's Island, though none appears on early charts or maps. It is rather unlikely that the heavily laden shallop would have been driven nearly 60 miles south and west to the Egg Island near Back River (south of the York River) and then nearly 40 miles north again to Watts's Shoal. Hoxton, *Chesapeake Bay,* 1735; Fry and Jefferson, *Virginia,* 1751; Hening, 6:492–93; Whitelaw, *Eastern Shore,* 2:973, 975.

282. Joseph Bird is on the Accomack County tax lists, 1692–1695. Stratton Nottingham, comp., *Accomack Tithables (Tax Lists), 1663–1695* (Onancock, 1931), pp. 52, 55, 57, 60.

283. Windmill Point is on the north side of the Rappahannock and Stingray Point on the south side. Then Stove (Store) Point is on the north of the Piankatank and Cherry Point, a part of Gwynn's Island, on the south. Fry and Jefferson, *Virginia,* 1751; U.S. Geol. Sur., *Deltaville* (1964) quad.

284. Queens Creek does not empty into the Piankatank River but lies just south of it and enters Hills Bay west of Gwynn's Island. U.S. Geol. Sur., *Mathews* (1965) quad.

285. Col. Armistead Churchill (1707–63) lived at "Bushy Park" in Middlesex County on the lower Rappahannock. His father's will listed 61 Negroes at "the quarter," "hill neck," "green branch," and "the freshes quarter." The son was justice of the peace, colonel of the militia, and collector for Rappahannock River. *WMQ* (1), 7 (1898–99): 186–88; 8 (1899–1900):47–49; Fry and Jefferson, *Virginia,* 1751; Leland, "Map of the Chesapeake Country"; U. S. Geol. Sur., *Deltaville* (1964) quad.

286. There were two ferries over the Piankatank at this time. Bailey's was only about six or seven miles from Churchill's, and Turk's was seven miles further upstream. Thus it is more likely that the travelers crossed at Bailey's. It was probably in the area of the present Ferry Creek or Twigg Bridge. Hening, 3:220, 472; Fry and Jefferson, *Virginia,* 1751; U. S. Geol. Sur., *Wilton* (1964) quad.

287. Mr. J. J. Nicolson, member of the Colonial Williamsburg presentation staff and keen student of Gloucester County history, helped identify this river. It was probably North End (today Burke) Mill Stream that entered North River about where Midlothian Plantation was situated. The land thereabouts belonged to Iveson, and the stream could have been referred to as Iveson's River. It was only one mile away from the main Gloucester road. This explanation fits with the travelers' use of Bailey's Ferry and also with their making about 25 miles from the ferry to Gloucester Point in 5 hours. Fry and Jefferson, *Virginia,* 1751; U. S. Geol. Sur., *Ware Neck* (1965) quad.

288. Edward Powers (d. 1719) ran an ordinary next to the courthouse in Yorktown. He was married in 1714 to Elizabeth, widow of another tavernkeeper, Humphrey Moody. Powers obtained his first tavern license, Mar. 21, 1714/15. The inventory of his estate listed 15 beds, decanters, punch bowls, and quantities of liquor. Edward M. Riley, "The Ordinaries of Colonial Yorktown," *WMQ* (2), 23 (1943): 13–15.

289. Fontaine probably purchased a plantation between Sept. 17 (his return from the Blue Ridge) and Oct. 14, 1716 (his departure for New York; see note 216 above), though he could have bought it between Apr. 22 (his return from Christanna) and Aug. 20, 1716 (his leaving for the Blue Ridge). Several fires have destroyed the early records of King William County, and none exists for this year.

The plantation was on the north side

of the Pamunkey near Philip Williams's Ferry (Journal entry, April 29, 1718). Matthew Maury purchased a portion of this plantation (James Fontaine, *Autobiography,* p. 240), and his son James in 1742 wrote that his father lived on Hickory Hill in King William County on Pamunkey River (James Maury, "Places of Abode and Genealogies of the Fontaines in Virginia," June 24, 1742, Colonial Williamsburg). In 1755 Maury's widow was living there "among the headsprings of Jack's Creek which empties into the Pamunkey, on the north side" (Fontaine Family, *Letters, p.* 379). Dr. Malcolm H. Harris of West Point thinks the plantation lay along Nectawance (today Harrison's) Creek, which falls into the Pamunkey just below Williams's Ferry, and that it was north of "Elsing Green," the Dandridge plantation (Fry and Jefferson, *Virginia,* 1751). The Maury house may constitute the upper story of "Green Hill," a present home of the Hill family.

Fontaine and his brother James and family for a time stayed with Capt. Richard Littlepage on the south side of the Pamunkey (see note 295 below). On Apr. 25, 1701, he was granted 2367 acres in King William County in Pamunkey Neck near the courthouse (Littlepage and Henry Fox also gave land for the courthouse), and on Nov. 2, 1702, he sold John Williams 155 acres on Jack's Creek. Fontaine might well have purchased the plantation from Littlepage. *Abst. Va. Pat. Bks.,* no. 9: 365; Elizabeth Hawes Ryland, "Abstracts of King William County Record Books," (typescript), 5 vols. (n. p., n. d.), 1:5–6, Va. State Lib.; Elizabeth Hawes Ryland, comp., *King William County, Virginia, from Old Newspapers and Files* (Richmond, 1955), pp. 3, 101.

290. Peter Fontaine (1691–1759) was born at Taunton. In 1713 Capt. Boulay, a Huguenot half-pay cavalry officer, told James Fontaine that he had long admired his sons and proposed that his granddaughter Elizabeth Fourreau marry one of them. She moved into the Fontaine household, and she and Peter were married, Mar. 29, 1714. The next year the captain died, leaving Peter £1000. He received his B.A. degree at Trinity College and was licensed as a minister to Virginia, Mar. 12, 1715. Upon his arrival there with his wife that October, he preached at Weyanoke, Martin's Brandon, Wallingford, and Jamestown. In 1720 he became the minister of the parish of Westover, 30 by 12 miles in extent with about 230 families and three churches—Westover, Weyanoke, and Wallingford. He was chaplain to Col. William Byrd's commission that surveyed the North Carolina-Virginia boundary, 1728–29. When Elizabeth Fourreau Fontaine died, he married Sarah Wade. He had two children by the first marriage and six by the second. James Fontaine, *Autobiography,* pp. 234, 237–38; Fontaine Family, *Letters,* pp. 333–55; Peter Fontaine's will, June 30, 1757, Colonial Williamsburg; Perry, *American Church,* 1:270–72; Goodwin, *Colonial Church in Va.,* pp. 269–70, 323, 329, 336, 337; *VMHB,* 32 (1924):228, 254; 36 (1928): 115; 37 (1929):248.

291. Error for Weyanoke Parish. See preceding note.

292. Capt. Joseph and Capt. Samuel Harwood of Charles City County married sisters, Agnes and Temperance, daughters of Capt. Thomas Cocke. Both men were justices. Samuel was a burgess, 1712–14, and Joseph, 1715. It is impossible to tell which Captain Harwood Fontaine refers to. *Va. House of Burg. Jls., 1712–14,* vii; *1715,* viii; *1720–22,* x; *1723–26,* xi; *Cal. Va. State Paps.,* 1:142. 196; *VMHB,* 2 (1894–95):184; 4 (1896–97):90; 31 (1923):315.

293. This cryptic entry, so unlike anything else in the Journal, was omitted by Miss Maury.

294. James Fontaine (1686–1746), John's eldest brother, was born at

Barnstaple and baptized by the Rev. Louis Mauzy. In 1694 when the family was moving to Cork, his father sent him and his brother Aaron (1688–1699) to Amsterdam to stay with a relative, possibly the Rev. Peter Forestier, at one time minister of a church at Balk. The boys returned two years later to Cork and James later was his father's chief assistant at Bear Haven. After the French privateer ruined the Fontaines' fortified house in 1708, James continued to live in County Cork, perhaps at Bear Haven. He became a justice of the peace in 1710 and John spent three months with him in 1714. He married Lucretia Desjarrie in Cork and brought his wife, their oldest child Elizabeth, and his mother-in-law to Virginia in 1717. He lived on the plantation John had purchased in King William County and served as a member of the quorum, 1726, and as sheriff, 1730–32. He had six children by his first marriage; about 1737 or 1738 he married Elizabeth Harcum, by whom he had three children. He was then living in Northumberland County, for a time with Col. Peter Presley on the Potomac. He died in October 1745 leaving considerable property, and he may have been serving as a collector of taxes paid in tobacco. James Fontaine, *Autobiography,* pp. 134, 167–68, 177–79, 182, 211, 224, 228, 230, 240; Fontaine Family, *Letters,* pp. 325–26; James Maury, "Fontaine Genealogies," June 24, 1742, Colonial Williamsburg; Cork Hist. and Archaeol. Soc. *Journal,* 3 (1897):47, 62; Brock, *Huguenot Emigration* p. 121; *VMHB,* 35 (1927): 405, 415; 37 (1929):125; *WMQ* (1), 21 (1912–13):96; Beverley Fleet, comp., *Northumberland County Record of Births, 1661–1810* [n. p., 1939], p. 49; James F. Lewis and J. Motley Booker, comps., *Northumberland County Wills and Administrations, 1750–1770* (n. p., 1964), p. 101; Northumberland County Record Book, 1743–1749, pp. 191–92, 262a, Va. State Lib. For Peter Forestier, see Hug. Soc. Lon-

don *Proceedings,* 12 (1917–23):456. See also note 35 above.

295. Capt. Richard Littlepage (d. 1718) of St. Peter's Parish, New Kent County, was vestryman, churchwarden, justice of the peace, and tobacco agent. He had large land holdings in both New Kent and King William counties. Horace Edwin Hayden, *Virginia Genealogies . . .* (Wilkes-Barre, 1891), pp. 397–98; St. Peter's Parish, New Kent . . . , *Vestry Book and Register, 1684–1786,* C. G. Chamberlayne, ed. (Richmond, 1937), pp. 166, 434–35; *Cal. Va. State Paps.,* 1:150–51; *VMHB,* 2 (1894–95):9; 12 (1904–5):366, 367; 31 (1923):222; 32 (1924):69; *WMQ* (1), 6 (1896–97):79; Ryland, *King William County,* p. 3. See note 289 above.

296. Probably John Sutton who with Michael Jennings received a patent in King William County, 1716. Another patent in that county to Sutton and Henry Yarborough is mentioned in a deed of 1722. Sutton in 1728 was a member of the quorum of the newly created Caroline County. *VMHB,* 17 (1909):154; 20 (1912):202; 25 (1917): 176; 32(1925):14, 35.

297. Miss Maury's printed version (p. 307) contains these extra words. See also note 266 above.

298. Matthew Maury (d. 1752), whose Huguenot family came from Castle Mauron, Gascony, after two years in Dublin was married there to Mary Ann Fontaine (1690–1756), Oct. 20, 1716. After this exploratory trip to Virginia, he returned to Dublin for his wife and son James (1718–1769), with whom he sailed for Virginia, Sept. 1719. He settled at "Hickory Hill" on a portion of the plantation John had acquired. He was a justice of King William County. 1732, 1744, and sheriff, 1739. James Fontaine, *Autobiography,* pp. 157, 240; James Maury, "Fontaine Genealogies," June 24, 1742, Colonial Williamsburg; Fontaine Family, *Letters,* pp. 329–31, 346; Hug. Soc. London,

*Registers, Lucy Lane and Peter Street Churches, Dublin,* p. 54; *Va. Counc. Exec. Jls.,* 4:267, 439; 5:150.

299. See note 81 above.

300. See note 90 above.

301. Probably James Bridgforth, who in 1704 owned 355 acres in King and Queen County. *VMHB,* 32 (1924): 145.

302. Bowler's Ferry was a well-known landmark on the south side of Rappahannock River with a tobacco warehouse and tavern. It belonged first to Thomas Bowler (d. 1679), who was appointed to the Council in 1670. Hening, 3:220, 472, 473; 4:267 *WMQ* (1), 6 (1897–98):30 Fry and Jefferson, *Virginia,* 1751; Leland, "Map of the Chesapeake Country."

303. Fontaine probably stayed at Naylor's Hole on the north side of the Rappahannock in Richmond County, but the plantation belonged to William Fauntleroy (1684–1757). Hening, 4: 267; *VMHB,* 21 (1913):108; 32 (1924):128–29; Fry and Jefferson, *Virginia,* 1751; Leland, "Map of the Chesapeake Country."

304. Captain Littlepage had died, Mar. 20, 1717/18 but his widow, Mrs. Frances Littlepage (1678–1732), was in charge of the plantation. St. Peter's Parish, *Vestry Book,* 434–35; *WMQ* (1), 5 (1896–97):79.

305. Philip Williams's Ferry, based on the north side of Pamunkey River in King William County, connected with Robert Peasley's (later Chamberlayne's) on the south side of the river in New Kent County. Hening, 3:219, 471; 4: 267; 5:16; *VMHB,* 31 (1923):343; 32 (1924):74; *WMQ* (2), 6 (1926): 74; Leland, "Map of the Chesapeake Country."

306. The Naval Office returns for York River are missing for these years, so that Captain Brunnequil cannot be identified.

307. See note 224 above.

308. John Arnaud may have consigned the ship to Fontaine. See Journal entry, July 23, 1719.

309. Aston's Quay was—and is—on the south side of the River Liffey about one-half mile from St. Stephen's Green. Warburton. *Dublin,* 2: frontispiece map.

INDEX

# Index

# Index

# Index

Fontaine, Anne Elizabeth Boursiquot (Mrs. James or Jacques; John's mother), 4, 6-9, 29, 129-32; portrait, 5

Fontaine, Barbara Terrell (Mrs. Aaron), 130

Fontaine, Daniel, 24, 131

Fontaine, David, 24, 29, 130

Fontaine, Elizabeth, *see* Barret

Fontaine, Elizabeth, *see* Mills

Fontaine, Elizabeth, *see* Torin

Fontaine, Elizabeth Fourreau (Mrs. Peter), 130

Fontaine, Elizabeth Harcum (Mrs. James), 129

Fontaine, Elizabeth Whiting Thruston (Mrs. Aaron), 130

Fontaine, Elizabeth Winston (Mrs. Peter), 130

Fontaine, E. Smith (Mrs. George David), 131

Fontaine, Frances Elizabeth, 32

Fontaine, Frances Elizabeth Sheppard (Mrs. James), 131

Fontaine, Francis (John's brother), 7, 8, 21, 26, 29, 131

Fontaine, Francis (John's brother Francis's son), 131

Fontaine, George David, 131

Fontaine, James or Jacques (John's father): 44, 60, 64; childhood and education, 4-5; flees France to Barnstaple, 6; marriage, 6-7; at Bridgewater and Taunton, 7; at Cork, 7; at Bear Haven, 3-4; 7-8; children, 7, 8-9, 29, 129-32; academy in Dublin, 8; Autobiography, 31-32; death, 8; portrait, 5

Fontaine, James (John's brother), 7, 19, 21, 26, 29, 44, 123, 125, 129

Fontaine, James (John's brother James's son), 26, 129

Fontaine, James (John's son), 24, 29, 130

Fontaine, James (John's son David's son), 131

Fontaine, James (John's son William's son), 131

Fontaine, James Maury, 132

Fontaine, Jane, 129

Fontaine, John (Journalist): birth, 7; childhood, 2-3; army service, 9, 37-43; studies navigation, 10, 44; journeys, to Virginia, 10-11, 46-59, 67-80; visits north Devonshire, 10, 60-66; to Germanna, 11-12, 83-89; to Fort Christanna, 12-13, 90-100; ot Blue Ridge, 13-19, 101-9; to New York, 19-21, 110-22; plantation in King William County, 19, 122-26; watchmaking in London, 21-24; marriage, 24; children, 24-27, 29, 130-131; silkweaver, 24; retires to Wales, 24-31; death, 24; journal, 31-34; portrait, *frontispiece.*

Fontaine, John (John's son), 24, 27, 29, 130

Fontaine, John (John's brother Francis's son), 131

Fontaine, John (John's brother James's son), 129

Fontaine, James (John's brother James's son James's son), 27, 129

Fontaine, John (John's son David's son), 131

Fontaine, John (John's son John's illegitimate son), 27, 130

Fontaine, John (John's son William's son), 131

Fontaine, Joseph, 130

Fontaine, Judith Babar, *see* Moody

Fontaine, Levenah, 129

Fontaine, Lucretia, 129

Fontaine, Lucretia Desjarrie (Mrs. James), 129

Fontaine, Lucretia Lemoine (Mrs. James), 29, 130

Fontaine, Margaret, *see* David

Fontaine, Margaret Howell (Mrs. William), 29, 131

Fontaine, Mary (John's daughter), 24, 131

Fontaine, Mary (John's brother Francis's daughter), 131

Fontaine, Mary Ann (John's brother James's daughter), 129

Fontaine, Mary Ann (John's sister), *see* Maury

Fontaine, Mary Anne, *see* Winston

# Index

# Index

*THE JOURNAL OF JOHN FONTAINE*
*was composed and printed by*
*Monumental Printing Company of Baltimore, Maryland,*
*and bound by Kingsport Press of Kingsport, Tennessee.*
*The book is set in Linotype Garamond and printed on*
*Warren's Publishers Eggshell. It was designed*
*by Richard J. Stinely, who also drew the maps.*